The Money Connection:

Where And How To Apply For Business Loans And Venture Capital

By Lawrence Flanagan

Published by The Oasis Press
Grants Pass, Oregon

040195

Published by The Oasis Press
Grants Pass, Oregon
Published by The Oasis Press®
300 North Valley Drive
Grants Pass, OR 97526

040195

Please direct any comments, questions, or suggestions regarding this book to:

The Oasis Press/PSI Research
300 North Valley Drive
Grants Pass, OR 97526
(503) 479-9464
(800) 228-2275

The Oasis Press is a Registered Trademark of Publishing Services, Inc., an Oregon corporation doing business as PSI Research.

ISBN: 1-55571-351-3 (paperback)
       1-55571-352-1 (3-ring binder)

Printed in the United States of America
Second edition 10 9 8 7 6 5 4 3 2 1

 Printed on recycled paper when available.

Acknowledgments

A special thank you to the U.S. Small Business Administration, the Farmers Home Administration, U.S. Department of Agriculture, and the many other generous contributors who provided the vital information and assistance needed to make this book possible.

Dedication

To Lindi

About The Author

Lawrence Flanagan's background spans over 35 years in business management and he has worn virtually all of the hats in the corporate world. A few years ago, he elected to pursue his hobby as a writer, but continues to enjoy helping entrepreneurs grow their businesses as a consultant in the Minneapolis/St. Paul metropolitan area. His specialties include reorganization, financial counseling and the development of marketing strategies for his clients.

He is also the author of *What Every Executive Should Know About Preparing and Using A Cash Flow Forecast*, published by Dartnell; has recently completed an informative book entitled *Raising Capital: How to Write a Financing Proposal*, published by The Oasis Press. He also writes for a number of business magazines and has finished a new book, to be published in 1995, which he hopes will help small companies compete more effectively in today's markets.

His other hobbies include fishing, botanical farming and minerals prospecting, and he is working on his first novel. He and his wife, Lindi, have four children and four grandchildren.

Table of Contents

Appendices

Introduction

This book is intended to assist the entrepreneur and small business owner with the problem of finding money to finance a new enterprise or expand an existing one.

Section I consists of six chapters. Chapter 1 offers tips on selecting the business organizational form that will work for you; Chapter 2 explains how to prepare a financing proposal; Chapter 3 gives a brief description of the business loan and investment sources in your state; Chapter 4 lists a multitude of federal loan and quasi-federal and private loan and investment programs; Chapter 5 discusses private investors and what they expect; and Chapter 6 suggests alternative sources of help.

Section II consists of nine appendices. The appendices list hundreds of current loan, venture capital and business assistance sources as described in **Section I**. To aid the reader, and when known, I have included details about their lending/investment preferences. Because these companies and institutions frequently modify their financing policies, change management and move to new locations, I cannot guarantee 100 percent accuracy regarding the information presented. Since projects and proposals for financing vary considerably, no assurance can be given that requests for loans or venture capital will be successful. Also included in the appendices is a glossary of commonly used financial terms.

As an entrepreneur who has participated in the startup of several companies and the expansion of others, I hope you will find this book helpful in your search for business financing. Unlike a few years ago, there are a large number of new funding sources on the scene today. Not only has the federal government expanded its role in assisting small businesses, but so have the states and hundreds of local communities. Many are offering millions of dollars in loans and other incentives to businesses that will create or retain jobs.

Finding the necessary capital to finance a business still requires a good business plan or proposal, a personal commitment and perseverance. It could happen quickly or it may take months to make the right financial connection. The fact is there are many business owners operating successful companies today who were turned down several times before they eventually received the financing they needed. Certainly it wasn't an easy task, but the vast majority will tell you it was worth every minute they invested in the quest.

Users of the information presented in this book should be aware that all businesses and their operations are regulated by the statutes and laws of their respective communities, states and the federal government. Therefore, it is advisable to seek legal and accounting advice before engaging in any business operation. This book is not intended to replace the professional assistance you will need from time to time.

The Money Connection is updated annually to ensure the information it provides is the most current available. This edition alone includes over 1,000 changes and updates. Readers are invited to contact the publisher for new edition release dates and prices.

Recently, I completed a new book that offers considerable detail about writing a business financing proposal and it presents six complete plans for you to use as a guide in preparing your own. It's called *Raising Capital: How To Write A Financing Proposal*. To order your copy, write to The Oasis Press, 300 North Valley Drive, Grants Pass, Oregon 97526, or call (800) 228-2275.

I would like to take this opportunity to thank the thousands of entrepreneurs and business managers who have utilized *The Money Connection* over the past three years and sincerely hope you have found the financing you needed.

My continuing goal is to increase the number of prospective financing sources presented in each new edition and to keep you informed about the latest business financing methods and opportunities as they develop in the future.

Wishing you every success in your endeavors, I remain,

Lawrence Flanagan

Chapter 1
Selecting The Business Organizational Form That Will Work For You

If you are starting a new business, one of your first decisions will be to select the type of organizational form that best meets your personal and business needs. Here are some of the more popular options to consider:

Sole Proprietorship

This form of business is owned and controlled by one individual. He or she receives the profits, assumes the losses from the business and is personally responsible for the debts and obligations of the enterprise. Income and expenses are reported in the individual's personal tax returns and profits are taxed at his or her individual income tax rates.

The sole proprietorship is the simplest and least expensive way to organize a business. The owner registers the business name, secures the necessary licenses to operate, applies for a federal tax identification number and begins operations.

General Partnership

A general partnership is a business organization owned by one or more persons who agree to form a partnership. Generally, the partners share equally in the ownership and the management responsibilities. They also are equally liable for all debts and other obligations of the business. The distribution of profits or losses, management duties and other issues are normally defined in a written partnership agreement. A general partnership is not a taxable entity, but income and expenses are reported on federal and state *information tax returns* filed by the partnership. Partners are taxed on their individual share of the partnership's profits (less expenses) and at their individual income tax rates.

A general partnership is relatively easy and inexpensive to form. Although legally not required, a written agreement is recommended and one should consult legal counsel before entering into such an agreement.

Limited Partnership

A limited partnership involves at least one general partner and one limited partner. The limited partner's share of the partnership's liability exposure is no more than his or her equity investment. The general partner has the right and responsibility to manage the business and is liable for all other debts and obligations because the limited partner(s) give up the right to participate in and to manage the affairs of the business. A limited partnership must be formed in compliance with statutory requirements, including tax and securities laws, and it is more expensive and complex to organize than a general partnership. It should not be entered into without legal representation.

Corporation

A corporation can be owned by one or more shareholders, is a separate legal entity in its own right and it must be organized in compliance with the statutory requirements of the state where it is incorporated. The shareholders elect a board of directors that control and manage the company through a president or chief executive officer which they appoint or hire. Since it is a separate legal entity, the corporation and not its shareholders is generally liable for all debts, contractual obligations, claims and lawsuits.

The corporation is also a separate taxable entity. It may be taxed under Subchapter C of the Internal Revenue Code (a C corporation), or Subchapter S of the Code (an S corporation). A C corporation reports its income and expenses using federal and state tax returns and its profits are taxed before any dividends can be distributed to the shareholders. They in turn must report these dividends on their individual income tax returns. The result is actually "double taxation" because a C corporation's profits are literally taxed twice.

If the shareholders of a company wish to organize their business as an S corporation, the corporation must meet the Sub S organizational laws of the state in which it is incorporated and it must file the appropriate notice with the Internal Revenue Service. However, some states do not recognize an S Corporation as a special taxing entity. Check your state laws before you elect S Corporation status. In this event, the income and expenses of the business pass directly to the shareholders in proportion to their percentage of ownership in the company. The profits, if any, are then taxed at their individual income tax rates. Usually, the S corporation is a closely held business where most of the shareholders actively participate in its management; although this is not a requirement for S status. Be sure to check with your state regarding the maximum number of shareholders it will allow to form an S corporation and thoroughly investigate and comply with the regulating laws that apply. Even though an S corporation can offer limited liability exposure to a company's shareholders and has certain tax advantages over the C, one should seek professional advice before deciding which form is the most appropriate for a particular business.

Other Forms Of Business Organizations

Other organizational forms include business trusts, professional corporations, not-for-profits and cooperative associations. Because they are all regulated by state and federal laws and involve legal, financial and accounting issues, organizing a business under any of these forms should not be attempted without legal and professional accounting guidance.

The best approach is to select the business organizational form that will serve the interests of the founders and the enterprise, and to keep it as uncomplicated as possible. Should future circumstances warrant, the organization's structure can usually be changed.

Chapter 2
How to Prepare A Financing Proposal To Secure Loans Or Equity Investment

Whether you intend to seek financing for a new business or expand an established one, it is essential to develop a business financing proposal. It should include: a history of the new or existing company; the financing needed; how the proceeds will be used and repaid (if a loan); details about the company's facilities and equipment; technology; products or services; production capabilities; markets; competition; sales strategies; management; employees; company goals; complete proforma financial projections for three years, plus financial statements and tax returns for the past three years — if the company has such a history.

Why A Business Plan Is Important

1. For any business seeking financing, most lenders and investors require a well thought out financing proposal which is usually a modified or condensed version of a company's current business plan. Although some components of a business plan cannot be included in a public stock offering prospectus (e.g., financial projections), it is not unusual for private investors or a bank to request the more detailed business plan and financial projections for review.

2. For any startup or existing company, whether financing is needed or not,

a current business plan will help keep the enterprise on track. One of the leading reasons why businesses fail is because their managers did not develop or follow a plan. When prepared each year, complete with monthly goals, a good business plan can serve as a valuable monitoring tool for all areas of a business.

The Components Of A Financing Proposal

Certainly there are many forms a proposal can take, but if one is searching for a loan or equity financing, it should include the following components:

A Summary

The summary should be brief (no more than 2 to 5 pages long) and provide:

- The name, address and telephone number of the business and contact person.
- The purpose for requesting the loan or investment and the amount required.
- A brief description of the company's history, facilities, equipment, products, services or project.
- A brief description of the company's markets, competition and sales strategies.
- A brief description of management's expertise and background.
- A brief description of how the funds requested, once received, will be used.

- A short paragraph about the company's goals.

The summary is nothing more than a condensed version of the more detailed financing proposal. Very often, it is mailed to a prospective lender or investor, along with a cover letter, to determine if there is an interest in the company or project. When submitted with a formal proposal, the summary is intended to give the reader a quick overview and encourage a thorough reading of the proposal, prospectus or circular itself.

The Company

This opening section of the proposal should fully describe the historical development of the company. Include its formal name; date of formation; legal structure (sole proprietorship, partnership or corporation); significant changes in ownership; business industry; its products or services (or those planned); acquisitions and subsidiaries (if any) and the dates when they occurred. Include your investment and percentage of ownership plus that of others and each owners role in the formation and operation of the company. If you are seeking financing for a non-operating business in the development stage, give as many of the above details as possible and fully explain the investment you or others intend to contribute to the enterprise.

Products and Services

In this section, provide information about the company's products or services or those it proposes to offer. Include inventories in stock or to be purchased; their costs; current or estimated production costs; selling prices and briefly present a sales forecast for the next three years. When possible, list some of your suppliers and any credit terms they may offer. A good way to approach this subject is to present all of the information you would want to know about the products or services of a company if it was asking you for money.

Use of Proceeds

When financing is needed to fund a new business or a project, use this section to describe how the money will be used (product development, inventories, equipment, marketing, working capital, etc.), complete with cost figures for each line item. Be sure the funds requested are adequate to finance the business startup or expansion planned. If you are requesting a loan, explain the repayment schedule desired and refer the reader to the Cash Flow Projections to demonstrate how the loan will be repaid, with interest, in context with the company's other operating expenses. This is important because all lenders want to know when and how they are going to be repaid.

Marketing

This important section must provide the details concerning your marketing, advertising and sales plans — complete with projected sales and annual expenses for each product or service to be offered. Include any marketing research and analysis data that will support your sales projections. Describe who your competitors are and explain how the company will be able to compete favorably in the marketplace. One of the major reasons for turning down a financing request is because the proposal submitted did not include a *viable* sales and marketing plan. Be honest and reasonable in your forecasts and forget about smoke and mirrors because just about everyone in the business of providing loans and venture capital will instantly recognize a *wild-eyed projection* when they see it.

Management

In this section, discuss the company's management, their individual job responsibilities, employment histories and education. Resumes may be submitted with your proposal, but they should be limited to one page or less for each manager. Include each manager's current or projected salary for at least three years plus any other forms of intended compensation. Fully describe any additions in management you are planning for the near future and the compensation to be paid.

Ownership

Furnish the names, addresses and business affiliations of all principal owners of the company's stock or those who have a equity interest in the business. Explain the degree to which these individuals are involved in the company's management. Also include the names and addresses of the board of directors (if incorporated), and the areas of their expertise. Describe the amount of stock (common or preferred shares) authorized (if incorporated), and the number of shares issued and outstanding. If the enterprise is in the development stage, present the details about the planned ownership and if you are seeking a loan, include a personal financial statement (assets less liabilities) for each individual who will own equity in the company.

Technology

Describe the technical aspects of your products or services and mention any patents or copyrights you or the company may own. Include any new technology you intend to develop in the near future and the associated costs for same. If you own the rights to or intend to purchase a unique technology, this is the section where the complete details should be disclosed.

Employees

List all employees of the business by job title and tabulate the projected wages and benefits to be paid for each individual over a three year period. Always indicate the total number of employees the company plans to employ for each year (both full-time and part-time), because a number of federal and state loan programs use this information to determine the total loan amount they can provide. In some cases, this loan limit is $10,000 to $15,000 per job created or retained.

Equipment

Provide a brief description of the company's offices, building, warehouse, store or other facilities; the type of construction (wood frame, concrete or steel); size of the space in square feet; mortgage or lease and utility costs, and describe any equipment now owned or that you intend to purchase. If new facilities and equipment are required, describe the company's needs fully together with the costs for same.

Supporting Reference Information

In this section, list the names, addresses and telephone numbers of your business and personal banker, business credit references, legal counsel, accountant and auditor (if you have one). By furnishing this information up front, you will speed up the financing decision you are waiting for.

Business Financials

When seeking a business loan or private venture capital, your plan must include proforma (projected) financial statements for up to three years into the future. The statements normally required are a: Balance Sheet; Profit and Loss Statement; Sales Forecast; Inventory Schedule and a Cash Flow Forecast for each year of operation. If your company has a operating history, submit the above proformas together with your business financial statements (audited or unaudited) for the previous three years and copies of the company's tax returns. Some lenders and private investors may also want to see your personal tax returns for the same period and a copy of your current business plan.

Keep It Brief and Informative

You may wish to include other items with your proposal such as drawings, photographs of the facilities, equipment, products, etc., but when possible,

attempt to keep the total document length to 50 pages or less. One way to view this *short proposal* philosophy is to imagine a desk piled high with 100 deals or more, and your job was to read and evaluate each one! It is only human nature to select the *thin ones* first.

If your proposal is easy to read, realistic, factual and contains the information required by a lender or investor, it does not have to be a *book* to gain a favorable response. Although some may argue the point, my advice is to keep it brief unless the project is exceptionally large and warrants the detail.

The other exception would be if you are asked to submit a copy of your business plan with the proposal. In this event, the business plan (usually a separate document), should include considerably more detail about how and when you expect to attain your business goals together with the same financial information provided in the proposal.

Additional Tips

Consider double spacing the text for easy reading (however, the financial projections are not double spaced). Number each page and include a table of contents for quick reference to the individual sections.

Make several copies of your proposal for submission to prospective lenders or venture capital companies and keep the original in a safe place. Fancy covers or jackets are not required. It's what the reader finds between the covers that counts! Always enclose a cover letter with each proposal you mail and use first class postage to ensure safe and prompt delivery.

Response Time

It usually takes from two to three weeks to get an answer to a loan/investment inquiry letter and up to six weeks when a complete proposal is submitted. If you don't hear from the prospective source within that time frame, it's OK to call and politely inquire about the status of your request. *No News* is not necessarily *Bad News*. It could mean they are seriously considering your proposal!

Incidentally, there is nothing wrong with mailing an inquiry letter or the proposal to several prospects at one time. Some states do limit the number of private placement prospectuses one can mail in a calendar year when they offer a company's shares of stock in exchange for funds, but this requirement does not apply to loan or investment inquiries when you are simply trying to determine if there is an interest in your company or a project that needs financing.

If you are searching for a loan, but will consider an equity investment, be sure to state this in your inquiry letter and your proposal. A lender may decide not to give you a loan, but might know of someone else who is looking for an investment opportunity. If you mention that you are willing to entertain all options to properly finance your business, you could receive a referral to another source. Remember, you have to ask for referrals to get them!

Unsure About Your Plan Writing Ability?

Developing a good financing proposal does require advance planning, some accounting knowledge, patience and writing ability, but most entrepreneurs do prepare their own. Check with your local bookstore or library to discover what books they have available on the subject. My recent book, *Raising Capital: How To Write A Financing Proposal*, does offer a step-by-step guide and examples that can help you.

Another excellent source of information is *The Successful Business Plan*, by Rhonda Abrams, and available from The Oasis Press. *The Successful Business Plan* also contains many helpful hints about raising venture capital as well as help in writing your business plan.

Should you still have doubts about your talent to draft a good presentation, contact a business consultant or accountant in your community who specializes in preparing business financing proposals. Ask for samples of his or her work, and if you like what you see, negotiate a reasonable fee for the service. It could be money well spent!

Chapter 3
Where To Find Business Loans And Equity Investors

There are two traditional ways to finance a business. One is debt financing which is borrowed funds that must be repaid from the earnings of a company. The other is equity financing which is capital contributed by the founder(s) and/or investors and does not have to be repaid. Equity investors do expect to receive a *reasonable return* on their investment, but this return can be in the form of dividends based on their percentage of ownership or through the appreciated value of a business and its accumulated assets.

Borrowed Money

It is not unusual to experience difficulty when attempting to borrow money for a startup retail or service type of business. Generally, these enterprises need financing for working capital, fixtures or inventories and most bankers do not view these forms of collateral as sufficient to back a loan. The reason is that inventories and fixtures are not easy to sell should a business fail and they must often be sold at *fire sale prices* far below their original cost. Therefore, most retail and service startup companies seek their financing from equity investors. Once a retail or service business has established a good track record, most banks will then consider a loan request or make a revolving line of credit available.

The great majority of bankers prefer to lend money for the purchase of fixed assets such as land, buildings and capital equipment because they are a more salable form of collateral should a borrower default. This policy may seem unfair, especially with the rash of bank and savings and loan failures recently, but it still makes good sense.

It is also true that in order to obtain a loan to start a business, the owner(s) must be willing to contribute between 10 and 50 percent of the funds needed. Your equity investment can be in the form of cash, a building, marketable real estate or securities, equipment or other assets of value. The actual percentage of equity one must pledge or invest depends on:

- The proposed business or project
- The industry involved
- Personal financial net worth and other resources
- The borrower's credit history
- The intended use of the funds requested
- The lender's loan policy

Personal Loan Sources

Many new businesses are initially financed with personal funds committed by the entrepreneur. These sources might include:

- Personal savings

- A personal signature loan or a loan collateralized by certain assets
- A second mortgage on a home, farm or other real estate
- Cash values in a whole life insurance policy
- Cash values in a profit sharing or pension plan
- Credit cards
- Loans from friends, relatives or associates

Business Loan Sources

Lenders who will consider making business loans if you and/or others also invest in the enterprise include:

- Savings and Commercial Banks
- Credit Unions
- Savings and Loan Companies
- Finance Companies
- Federal, State and Local Government/Community Loan Programs
- Small Business Investment Companies (SBICs)
- Specialized Small Business Investment Companies (SSBICs)
- Venture Capital Companies
- Private or Corporate Lenders
- Foundations that provide "seed money" for the development of a nonprofit organization

Venture Capital Sources

If you need a equity investment from others to finance a new business or to expand an existing one, these sources should be considered:

- Small Business Investment Companies (SBICs)

- Specialized Small Business Investment Companies (SSBICs)
- Private or Corporate Investors
- Venture Capital Companies
- The Public or Private Sale of Stock
- Friends, Relatives and Associates

Keep in mind that an equity investment from others (depending on the amount of their financial commitment), might involve giving up a large percentage of ownership because of the risk you are asking them to assume. The up-side of the equation is: you get the opportunity to own a part of a new business that may not have seen the light of day without outside equity participation. The down-side is: once you have investors in your company, whether they are actively involved or not, the relationship revolves on how well the business performs. It can be an enjoyable experience or a very unpleasant one if the business should fall on hard times.

What Venture Capitalists Are Looking For

Typically, equity investors are searching for startup and expansion stage companies that offer a unique product; a potentially large market; a competitive advantage and a management team that will deliver. They are also looking for a return on their investment within three to seven years and very often are more interested in firms that can eventually be taken public or sold to a larger company to maximize their investment.

While you may agree or disagree with their motives for investing in your business, it is important to know and understand exactly what *their* objectives are before accepting *their* money.

When Searching For Business Financing

When applying for a business loan or equity investment, always offer a copy of your financing proposal and submit any business and personal financial information that may be requested. Some lenders/investors may not require an extensive plan or proposal to make a financing decision, but having one available will demonstrate your management capabilities and that you have given careful thought to the enterprise.

If you elect to *shop* for a prospective lender or investor using inquiry letters, you might wish to enclose a copy of the proposal "summary." Be sure to mention in your letter that a complete proposal is available for review. Sometimes, a short, informative inquiry will receive prompt attention, while a lengthy proposal may be set aside to be *read later*. Also ask the prospective sources about their current financing policies; their industry preferences and what information they require to make a decision.

Expect Rejection

Just about everyone who has ever started a business has experienced loan or investor rejection. Don't take it personally! Remember that the policies of all lenders and investors are different and change periodically. Perhaps they are already committed to other firms in their portfolios or prefer to assist specific industries where they have a certain expertise. Some may be willing to lend or invest money in businesses throughout the nation while others prefer to work with local enterprises.

Although rejection of a proposal or application is not a morale builder, it shouldn't be taken as a personal affront to one's character, sincerity or capabilities. The best way to get rejection out of your mind is to move immediately on to the next prospective source.

As most entrepreneurs know, the road to success is not always a smooth one! It takes time, energy and perseverance to locate the right financing. Your search may involve contacting many sources and in some cases, it could mean revising or improving your proposal to secure the funding needed. Yes, it can entail a lot of hard work and even disappointments along the way, but then so does any other worthwhile endeavor that offers a great potential reward. In retrospect, and because I have experienced the lesson at least a dozen times in my lifetime, I can honestly say that the *reward* one is striving to achieve usually far out-distances the *effort* one has to make in order to realize it.

Other Financing Sources To Consider

The next two chapters provide new information concerning federal and state loan programs; quasi federal and private loan/investment companies and venture capital sources. After reading about them, you will be able to decide which ones might best serve your business situation. Once your financing proposal has been written, you will be ready to begin your search.

In the Appendices of this book, hundreds of sources have been listed which offer various forms of financing. All of these institutions, organizations and companies are actively engaged in either providing loan guarantees, making business loans or investing capital. All will give your proposal a fair hearing and several provide a wide range of business services that are free or available at modest cost. A few telephone calls or letters can lead to a world of assistance should you need it.

Chapter 4
Federal Loans And Quasi-Federal/ Private Loan And Investment Programs

There are a number of federally supported programs that regularly make loans available to both existing and startup businesses based on a number of qualifying factors and requirements. Some of these programs have expanded their services; some have changed their lending policies; and a few are brand new business financing innovations.

If you previously rejected the idea of borrowing money through a federally guaranteed or supported program because of the assumed red tape involved, you might want to rethink the possibility. The paperwork isn't any more demanding than one would expect to secure other types of financing and many of these programs offer some excellent opportunities that were not available a few years ago. Here are the more popular ones and their services:

U. S. Small Business Administration (SBA)

The vast majority of new and existing small businesses are eligible for SBA financial assistance if they do not dominate their field; are independently owned and can prove they have been unable to obtain a bank loan or other private financing without the SBA's assistance.

Although the SBA does make a limited number of direct loans, it normally provides a *guarantee* to a private lender who in turn makes a loan to the borrower. Guaranteed loans carry a maximum of $750,000 and the SBA can guarantee up to 90 percent of a loan, depending on the amount requested. Maturity may be up to 25 years although the average size of a guaranteed business loan is $175,000 with an average maturity of about eight years.

The SBA's Basic Program Includes:
A. Regular business loans
B. Special loan programs that offer:
   1. Small general contractor loans
   2. A seasonal line of credit guarantee
   3. Energy loans
   4. Handicapped assistance loans
   5. Export revolving lines of credit
   6. International trade loans
   7. Disaster assistance
   8. Physical disaster loans
   9. Economic injury disaster loans
   10. Pollution control financing
   11. Assistance to veterans
   12. Assistance to women
   13. Business development programs
   14. Small Business Microloan Program
C. Certified Lenders Program
D. Certified Development Companies (CDCs)
E. Surety Bonds
F. Small Business Investment Companies (SBICs)
G. Specialized Small Business Investment Companies (SSBICs)

As you can see, there are a number of SBA programs and services, and I will briefly outline them in this chapter. You can also request a free *Directory of Business Development Programs* by contacting your local SBA office, or calling the Small Business Administration's Answer Desk at 1-800-827-5722. Their directory has over 100 business publications available for a nominal fee and these materials are designed to answer your questions about how to start, operate and manage a business and where to get SBA financing and assistance.

You can also call The Oasis Press at 1-800-228-2275 to obtain information on its *Starting and Operating a Business* book series (available for each state and the District of Columbia), or numerous other books and software for small business owners.

The SBA's Basic Eligibility Requirements

Depending on the type of business seeking SBA financing, certain standards will determine eligibility as follows:

Manufacturing: The total number of employees may range up to 1,500 but the actual number is based on the industry in which the business is engaged in.

Wholesale: Up to 100 employees are permitted.

Service Companies: Maximum annual sales can range from $3.5 to $14.5 million, depending on the industry.

Retail Companies: Maximum annual sales can range from $3.5 to $13.5 million, depending on the industry.

General Construction: Maximum annual sales can range from $9.5 to $17.0 million, depending on the industry.

Special Trade Construction: Average annual sales receipts cannot exceed $7 million.

Agriculture: Annual sales receipts cannot exceed $500,000 to $3.5 million, depending on the industry.

Ineligible Businesses

The Small Business Act does exclude some forms of businesses from receiving loans. These include: not-for-profit organizations except sheltered workshops; newspapers; magazines; movie theaters, radio and television stations; theatrical productions; dinner theaters; book publishers; film, record or tape distributors; businesses involved in the creation, origination, expression or distribution of ideas, values, thoughts or opinions; manufacturers, importers, exporters, retailers or distributors of communications such as greeting cards, books, sheet music, pictures, posters, films, tapes, broadcasts or other performances and recordings of musical programs.

Those firms engaged as commercial printers, or those producing advertising and promotional materials for others or who provide motion pictures, video tapes, sound recording facilities or technical services WITHOUT editorial or artistic contribution, and general merchandisers that **sell** magazines, books, etc., ARE ELIGIBLE.

Other excluded businesses include those engaged in floor planning, gambling, speculation of any kind, and illegal activities. Applications from incarcerated persons or persons on probation or parole for serious offenses will not be accepted.

To determine if your business or proposed enterprise is eligible, contact the nearest SBA office listed in **Appendix A** or your local banker. If it isn't included in the above listing, it will probably qualify.

Other SBA Guaranteed Loan Requirements

Before the SBA will guarantee a loan through a lender, the applicant must demonstrate that:

- The business will be able to repay its current debts in addition to the new loan requested.

- There is a reasonable amount of equity invested in the business or collateral that the borrower can pledge for the loan. Generally, a new business applicant should have between 20 and 30 percent of the required equity investment to start a new business. The ACTUAL percentage is determined by the lender and the SBA. For existing businesses, the SBA considers a number of credit factors and the company's history before reaching a decision, which is essentially the same policy of any other lender.

- The company's past track record has been good and/or its financial projections are realistic and supportable.

- The company's management has the expertise to adequately conduct the operations of the business.

The fastest way to determine whether or not a SBA guaranteed loan is a viable option for your financing needs is to call your banker for an appointment. After all, you have to be turned down by a bank before you can qualify for SBA assistance anyway. Maybe your bank won't give you a loan directly, but if they say "no", ask if they would be interested in participating in a SBA guaranteed loan. If the answer is "yes", give the bank all of the information it requests. They will help you complete the loan application and then forward it to the SBA for approval. The entire process can take just a few days or several weeks depending on how well your business plan and the application have been prepared.

Low Documentation Program

The SBA is now offering a new loan program that makes small business financing faster and easier. Called "LowDoc" for low documentation, entrepreneurs starting a new business and established firms can apply for an SBA guaranteed loan up to $100,000 by completing a simplified one-page document. Personal financial statements are required and a participating lender may require additional information. Tax returns for the past three years must accompany requests above $50,000.

LowDoc loans (offering an SBA guarantee up to 90 percent) are made based on the applicant's character, credit history and experience. While a loan should be adequately secured, generally it will not be declined when inadequate collateral is the only unfavorable factor. Normally, business assets are pledged and occasionally personal assets. Personal loan guarantees of the principal borrower(s) are required.

According to the SBA, a LowDoc application can be processed in two or three days because more reliance is placed on the participating bank for underwriting and risk evaluation. To learn more about it, contact your local banker, the nearest Preferred or Certified Lending Institution listed in Appendix D or the nearest SBA office in your state listed in Appendix A.

Special SBA Lenders

An increasing number of lenders throughout the country serve in the SBA's Certified Lenders Program. Acting under SBA supervision, they review a client's financial information and process much of the necessary loan paperwork. This speeds up the loan process and frees the SBA's personnel for other small business assistance programs.

A very select group of lenders participate in the Preferred Lender Program. They handle all of the paperwork, processing and servicing. Although any lender can work with the SBA, you may wish to contact a Certified or Preferred institution directly. All of them understand small business problems, offer a wide range of excellent banking services and do make loans without SBA participation. A complete listing of the SBA's Certified and Preferred Lenders has been included in **Appendix D**.

Special SBA Loan Programs

In the general area of financial assistance, the SBA also offers several special loan programs:

Small General Contractor Loans

Designed to assist small construction firms with short term financing. Loan proceeds can be used to finance residential or commercial construction and rehabilitation of property for sale. Proceeds cannot be used for owning or operating real estate for investment purposes.

Seasonal Line of Credit Guarantee

Developed to provide short term financing for small firms having a seasonal loan requirement due to a seasonal increase in business activity.

Energy Loans

Available to firms engaged in manufacturing, selling, installing, servicing or developing specific energy saving measures.

Handicapped Assistance Loans

Available to physically handicapped small business owners and private non-profit organizations which employ handicapped persons and operate in their interest. For example: sheltered workshops.

Export Revolving Lines of Credit

Offers guarantees to provide short term financing for exporting firms having been in existence for one year or more and for the purpose of developing or penetrating foreign markets.

GreenLine Revolving Line of Credit

The SBA's new GreenLine offers the flexibility needed to finance the cyclical, recurring and short-term cash needs that so many businesses experience. Simply withdraw funds and repay as your cash cycle dictates, up to the approved amount of your GreenLine account. The SBA can guarantee up to $750,000 on such a loan or 75 percent of the actual amount provided by a participating lender.

International Trade Loans

Offers guarantees of up to $1 million for the acquisition, construction, renovation, modernization, improvement or expansion of production facilities or equipment to be used in the United States in the production of goods and services involved in international trade.

Disaster Assistance

When the President of the United States or the Administrator of the SBA declares a specific area to be a disaster area, two types of loans are offered:

1. Physical Disaster Loans are made to homeowners, renters, businesses (large and small), and non-profit organizations within the disaster area. Loan proceeds can be used to repair or replace damaged or destroyed homes, personal property and businesses.

2. Economic Injury Disaster Loans are made to small businesses which suffer substantial economic injury because of a disaster. Loan proceeds may be used for working capital and to pay financial obligations which the small business could have met had the disaster not occurred.

When a disaster is declared, the SBA establishes on-site offices with experienced personnel to help with loan information, processing and disbursement.

Pollution Control Financing

The SBA assists those small businesses needing long term financing for planning, design and installation of pollution control facilities or equipment. This financing is available through the loan guarantee program and offers a maximum of up to $1 million per small business with a 90 percent loan guarantee.

Assistance To Veterans

The SBA makes special efforts to help veterans get into business or expand existing veteran-owned small firms. The Agency, acting on its own or with the help of veterans organizations, sponsors special business training workshops for veterans.

In some areas of the country, the SBA sponsors special computer-based training and long term entrepreneurial programs for veterans. Each SBA office has a Veteran's Affairs Specialist to help give veterans special consideration with loans, training and/or procurement.

Helping Women Get Into Business

Since 1977, the SBA has had an ongoing women's business ownership program. In 1983, the Agency began organizing a series of business training seminars and workshops for women business owners and for women who want to start their own small firms. These programs offer a focus on business planning and development, credit and procurement. A woman-owned business is defined as a "business that is at least 51 percent owned by a woman, or women, who also control and operate it."

Business Development Programs

There are extensive and diversified business development programs. They include individual counseling, courses, conferences, workshops and a wide variety of publications. Counseling and training are not limited to small businesses that have a problem. They are also available to those considering starting a business and to managers of successful firms who wish to review their objectives and long range plans for expansion and diversification.

Counseling is provided through the Service Corps of Retired Executives (SCORE), Small Business Institutes (SBIs), Small Business Development Centers (SBDCs) and numerous professional associations. Realizing the importance of counseling, the SBA makes every attempt to match the need of a specific business with the expertise available.

SCORE is a 13,000 member volunteer program with over 800 locations. It helps small businesses solve their operating problems through one-on-one counseling and through a well developed system of workshops and training sessions. Another arm of SCORE is the Active Corps of Executives (ACE) which is staffed by actively employed business people. Since their addresses and telephone numbers change frequently, call 1-800-634-0245 or (202) 205-6762 for the nearest SCORE/ACE chapter in your area or write: Executive Director, SCORE, 409 Third Street SW, Washington DC 20024. You can also contact your nearest SBA office listed in **Appendix A** for this information.

The Small Business Innovation Research Program (SBIR)

The Small Business Innovation Research Program (SBIR) came into existence with the enactment of the Small Business Innovation Development Act of 1982. Under SBIR, agencies of the federal government with the largest research and development budgets are mandated by law to set aside funds each year for the competitive award of SBIR monies to qualified high technology small business firms.

The SBA was designated by the legislation as the federal agency having unilateral authority and responsibility for coordinating and monitoring the government-wide activities of the SBIR program, and it reports on the results annually to Congress.

In line with this responsibility, the SBA publishes the SBIR Pre-Solicitation Announcement (PSA) quarterly. The PSA contains pertinent information about the program and specific data on upcoming SBIR solicitations. Firms interested in learning more about the SBIR should contact their nearest SBA office.

The SBA's Microloan Program

If you are looking for a loan of $25,000 or less for your business, call the SBA office in your area and request details about the Microloan Program.

This recently established program allows non-profit intermediaries to make small loans of $25,000 or less to for-profit businesses that normally would have difficulty borrowing money because they lack sufficient collateral. It is aimed at helping entrepreneurs become self-sufficient by starting or expanding a small business enterprise. The non-profit organizations who sponsor these loans also receive assistance from the SBA to develop their small business management training programs.

A national listing of Microloan lenders can be found in **Appendix G.**

SBA Certified Development Companies (CDCs)

Business development loans are made to community development organizations called Certified Development Companies (CDCs) which are approved by the SBA for the purpose of encouraging economic growth in rural and urban areas. Many of these CDCs participate in three SBA loan programs called the *502, 503* and *504 Loan Programs.* Growth is measured primarily by job creation and retention. Loan proceeds are used by the development companies to assist small business enterprises with plant acquisitions, construction, conversion or expansion, including the purchase of machinery and equipment.

The 502 and 503 Loan Programs provide business loans up to $750,000 with terms up to 25 years. These loans carry a maximum SBA guarantee of 90 percent — depending on the actual loan amount — to participating lending institutions.

The 504 Loan Program links the SBA, a Certified Development Company and a Private Lender in a 10 to 20 year term business loan package. The SBA is authorized to provide up to 40 percent of the total package by issuing guaranteed debenture bonds sold in the capital market. A total financing package can be $2.5 million or more. Generally, 50 percent of the financing is provided by the lending institution, 40 percent by the SBA and 10 percent by the borrower.

Eligibility for a CDC loan requires that a business be a for-profit organization, partnership or proprietorship with a net worth not to exceed $6 million and net profits (after taxes) averaging less than $2 million during the previous 2 years. Ineligible applicants are the same as described for a regular SBA loan. Due to the number of lenders involved, and other requirements, the average size of any project is usually above $250,000 and would not normally exceed $1.25 million.

A listing of the Certified Development Companies (CDCs) is provided in **Appendix C.** The CDC listing is presented by SBA REGION because some offer their services to counties in adjoining states. Contact the nearest CDC that serves your county or community for complete information about their business loan and service programs. If you are planning to relocate your business, or wish to start one in a rural or urban area, contact the CDCs that serve the communities you are considering.

SBA Surety Bonds

Through its Surety Bond Guarantee Program, the SBA can help to make the bonding process accessible to small and emerging contractors, including minorities, who find bonding unavailable to them. The agency is authorized to guarantee to a qualified surety company up to 90 percent of the losses incurred under a prospective bid and payment of performance bonds issued to contractors on contracts valued up to $1.25 million. These contracts may be for construction, supplies, manufacturing or services provided by either a prime or subcontractor for government or non-government work. This program is administered through the 10 Regional Offices of the SBA (listed in **Appendix A**) with the participating surety companies and their agents throughout the United States.

Small Business Investment Companies (SBICs)

Money for *venture* or *risk* investments is often difficult for small businesses to obtain, but the SBA also licenses, regulates and provides financial assistance to privately owned and operated Small Business Investment Companies commonly called SBICs. Their main function is to make venture and risk investments by supplying equity capital and making unsecured loans, and loans not fully collateralized to small enterprises which meet their individual investment criteria. SBICs are privately owned, but obtain their financial leverage from the SBA. They are intended to be profit-making corporations, so many of them will not make loans or investments under $100,000.

SBICs finance small firms in two general ways — either by straight loans or by equity-type investments — which give the SBIC involved actual or potential ownership of a portion of the equity securities (shares of stock) in a small business.

The SBA also licenses a specialized type of SBIC solely to help small businesses and entrepreneurs considered to be socially or economically disadvantaged. This type of SBIC, formerly called a MESBIC or Minority Enterprise Small Business Investment Company, is now referred to as a SSBIC or a Specialized Small Business Investment Company.

A large number of SBICs are willing to consider loan and investment proposals from businesses located throughout the country. Others prefer to work with firms in their local communities or the states where they operate and many of them provide management assistance to the companies they finance.

As a general rule, companies are eligible for SBIC/SSBIC loans or investment if they have a net worth under $6 million dollars and after-tax earnings of less than $2 million annually during the past two years. Several SBICs will consider startups if the owners are willing to make a reasonable equity investment in the enterprise as well.

How To Present Your Case To A SBIC/SSBIC

You should prepare a report on a new or existing business that includes complete information about its operations, financial condition, key personnel, products, proposed new products or services, patent positions, market data, competitive position, distribution and sales methods together with financial projections.

Ideally, a complete financing proposal or business plan can speed up the process. There are no specific guidelines regarding the length of time it takes a

SBIC/SSBIC to investigate and close a transaction. Usually, an initial response, either positive or negative, is made quickly. On the other hand, the thorough study they must undertake before making a final decision could take several weeks.

Generally, SBICs are interested in generating capital gains, so they may want to purchase stock in a company, or advance funds through a note of debenture with conversion privileges or they may request the right to buy stock at a predetermined later date. Furthermore, SBICs often work together in making loans or investments in amounts larger than any of them could make separately. No SBIC should be ruled out as a possible source of financing whether you are searching for a loan or equity investment to begin or expand a business. For additional information about SBICs, please refer to **Chapter 5** where venture capital is discussed in greater detail.

An overview of how to seek SBIC financing and a complete listing of SBICs and SSBICs is provided in **Appendix E**, together with their individual investment policies, loan and/or investment limits, industry preferences and the areas of the country they serve.

U. S. Department of Agriculture/Farmers Home Administration (FmHA)

The FmHA offers a wide variety of loan guarantee programs that include:

- Farm Ownership and Operating Loans

- Farm Ownership and Operating Loans for the Socially Disadvantaged
- Buying Livestock and Equipment
- Home Loans
- Home and Building Improvement Loans
- Home Repair Loans and Grants
- A Farm Rental Assistance Program
- Converting Farms to Outdoor Recreation
- Rural Housing Site Loans
- Congregate Housing and Group Home Loans
- Rural Rental Housing Loans
- Community Facility Loans
- Youth Project Loans
- Refinancing Debt
- Soil and Water Loans
- Water and Waste Disposal Loans and Grants
- Business and Industrial (B&I) Loans
- Non-Farm Enterprise Loans

Since this book focuses on non-farming business activities, I will address the last two programs in detail — however, information about any of the others can be requested by contacting your local FmHA county supervisor or your state's FmHA office listed in **Appendix B**.

FmHA Business and Industrial (B&I) Loan Guarantees

Upgrading the economic environment to improve the quality of life in rural America makes a lot of sense, and the Farmers Home Administration's program of loan guarantees to further business and industrial development plays an important role toward accomplishing this mission.

FmHA Business and Industrial Loan Guarantees may be made in any area outside the boundary of a city of 50,000 or more and its immediate adjacent urbanized areas with a population density of no more than 100 persons per square mile. Priority is given to applications for projects in open country, rural communities, and towns of 25,000 and smaller.

Assistance from the FmHA is provided in the form of a loan guarantee whereby the agency contracts to reimburse the lender for losses up to a maximum of 90 percent of the principal and interest for guaranteed loans of $2 million or less, 80 percent for loans over $2 million but not over $5 million, and 70 percent for loans over $5 million.

Applications are considered without regard to race, color, religion, sex, national origin, age, disability, or marital status of the applicant or individuals represented by the applicant.

Priority is given to projects in areas of high unemployment, to projects which show a low amount of investment per job created or saved, and to projects that will employ members of displaced farm families. The following are the most frequently asked questions about FmHA B&I loans, and the answers.

Who May Borrow?

Any legal entity, including individuals, public and private organizations, and federally recognized Indian tribal groups, may borrow.

Are There Other Requirements?

Borrowers and lenders must comply with Federal requirements relating to equal employment opportunity, historic site preservation, flood and mud slide protection, environmental impact, the Clean Air and Water Act, the Architectural Barriers Act, and nondiscrimination.

What is the Maximum Loan Amount that Can Be Guaranteed?

Business and industrial loans are limited to a maximum of $10 million.

Where Can Loans Be Made?

Business and industrial loans can be guaranteed in the 50 United States, Puerto Rico, the Virgin Islands, Guam, American Samoa, and the Commonwealth of the Northern Marianas, except in cities of 50,000 or more and other adjacent urban or urbanizing areas. FmHA makes the "rural area" determination, and gives priority to applications for loans in open country, rural communities, and towns of 25,000 or less.

How Does FmHA Make a Guaranteed Loan?

A guaranteed loan can be made by contacting the FmHA county supervisor in the county where the proposed business or industrial project is or will be located. He or she will provide the advice on procedures, forms, and the requirements for making a pre-application or an application, or both. Applications and pre-applications, however, are processed by the FmHA state offices only.

Farmers Home Administration state offices are listed in **Appendix B** but are also listed in telephone directories under U.S. Government, U.S. Dept. of Agriculture. Locations of county offices may also be obtained by writing to FmHA, USDA, Washington, DC 20250.

How May Loan Funds Be Used?

The basic uses include developing or financing business or industry, increasing employment, and controlling or abating pollution. Within this framework, the funds may be used for, but are not limited to:

- Financing business and industrial construction, conversion, acquisition, and modernization;

- Financing the purchase and development of land, easements, equipment, facilities, machinery, supplies, or materials;

- Supplying working capital;

- Financing housing development sites;

- Financing processing and marketing facilities;

- Providing startup and working capital; and

- Controlling pollution.

What Purposes Are Ineligible?

Business and industrial funds may not be used for certain purposes, including:

- Any project likely to result in the transfer of business or employment from one area to another;

- Any project likely to cause production that exceeds demand;

- Any project involving transfer of ownership — unless this will keep a business from closing, prevent the

loss of jobs in an area, or provide more jobs;

- Paying a creditor more than the value of the collateral;

- Guarantee of lease payments;

- Payment of loan proceeds to owners, partners, shareholders, or others who retain any ownership in the business;

- Corporations and businesses that are not owned and controlled by U.S. citizens;

- Agricultural production;

- Charitable and educational institutions;

- Churches or church-sponsored organizations;

- Fraternal organizations;

- Hotels, motels, and tourist homes, and convention centers; and

- Tourist, recreation, and amusement facilities.

What Is the Guarantee?

The guarantee is a warrant to protect the lender, and may cover up to 90 percent of the principal advanced, including accrued interest.

The guaranteed fee is 1 percent of the loan amount multiplied by the percent of the guarantee. For example, if the loan was for $500,000 and the FmHA guarantee was 90 percent, the fee would be $4,500 — ($500,000 x 1% x 90% = $4,500). It is a one-time fee paid by the lender, who may pass it on to the borrower.

Is Collateral Required?

Yes, collateral is required. It must be of such nature that, when considered together with the integrity and ability of the project management, the soundness of the project, and the applicant's prospective earnings, repayment of the loan will be reasonably assured.

Must the Applicant Provide Equity?

Yes, the applicant(s) will be required to furnish sufficient cash or other assets to provide reasonable assurance of a successful project.

A minimum tangible balance sheet equity of 10 percent is required. Balance sheet equity of at least 20 to 25 percent will be required for new businesses, businesses without personal or corporate guarantees, and energy-related businesses.

What is the Repayment Schedule?

Loan maturity will not exceed:

- 30 years for land, buildings, and permanent fixtures;

- 15 years for machinery or equipment,, or the useful life of the machinery and equipment, whichever is less; or

- 7 years for working capital. Interest will be due at least annually after the loan is made.

What Will the Interest Rate Be?

For guaranteed loans, the interest rate may be either fixed or variable and will be determined between the lender and the borrower and is subject to FmHA review and approval.

NonFarm Enterprise Loans

The FmHA also makes business loans to family farmers and ranchers and gives technical and management assistance for the development and operation of nonfarm enterprises to supplement farm income. Each person applying for credit gets equal consideration without regard to race, color, religion, age, sex, disability, marital status, or national origin. Applicants of eligible veterans are given preference. Both veterans and nonveterans must meet the same requirements for a loan.

Enterprises for which loans can be made include:

- Repair shop
- Grocery Store
- Boarding Animals
- Sporting Goods Store
- Camping sites
- Restaurant
- Roadside Stand
- Service Station
- Welding Shop
- Cabinet Shop
- Beauty Shop
- Barber Shop
- Riding Stable
- Custom Services

The following are the most commonly asked questions about FmHA Nonfarm Enterprise Loans, and the answers.

Who May Borrow?

Individuals, partnerships, joint operations, cooperatives, and corporations directly engaged in farming and ranching on family-size operations may apply. A "family-size" farm is one that a family can operate and manage itself with a reasonable amount of hired labor.

To be eligible, applicants must:

- Be or intend to become the owner-operator of a not larger than family-size farm, or be a tenant on such a farm. If operating as a tenant, the applicant must have a satisfactory written lease for a sufficient period of time to provide a reasonable return on the nonfarm enterprise.

- Have the experience or training to assure reasonable prospects of success in the proposed nonfarm enterprise. However, the applicant need not have personally operated this type of enterprise.

- Possess the character (as relating to repayment ability), industry, and ability to carry out the nonfarm enterprise.

- Manage and operate the nonfarm enterprise.

- Be unable to obtain sufficient credit elsewhere at reasonable rates and terms.

- Be a citizen of the United States (or a legal resident alien), which includes Puerto Rico, the Virgin Islands, Guam, American Samoa, and the Commonwealth of the Northern Mariana Islands.

- Possess the legal capacity to incur the obligations of the loan.

Certain corporations, cooperatives, joint operations, and partnerships operating family-size farms are now eligible for nonfarm enterprise loans. Such entities must meet some of the same eligibility requirements as individual applicants.

In addition, if members of the entity are related by blood or marriage, at least one stockholder, shareholder, partner or joint operator must operate the family-size farm. In other entities, the members holding a majority interest and the entity itself must operate the farm. The entity must be authorized to operate a farm in which it is located.

Limited resource applicants who cannot repay loans at the standard interest rate also must meet the above requirements. In addition, they must have a low income and show a need for increased farm income. Limited resource partnerships, joint operations, cooperatives, or corporations must meet some of the same eligibility requirements as individual applicants. Your FmHA county office can explain the eligibility rules in detail.

What May Loans Be Used For?

- To provide essential service buildings, land, and facilities for the nonfarm enterprise;

- To buy, rent, lease, or repair necessary tools, equipment, facilities and furnishings;

- To pay operating expenses;

- To refinance debts, pay loan closing costs and other necessary expenses;

- To purchase inventories and supplies;

- To pay the costs of organizing the nonfarm enterprise;

- To develop water and waste disposal systems essential to the operation; and

- To construct roads, ditches, or power, gas, and water lines on land where easements or right-of-way are obtained.

What Security is Required?

Intermediate-term credit may be secured by liens on inventory, equipment, real estate, and fixtures. Each long-term loan will be adequately secured by real estate to protect the interests of the U.S. Government.

What are the Loan Limits and Terms of Repayment?

The amount of credit depends on the applicant's needs and ability to repay the loan as indicated in a plan developed with the FmHA county supervisor.

FmHA can make intermediate-term loans of up to $200,000 and can guarantee loans of up to $400,000 made by banks and other authorized lenders for the purposes of financing equipment and operating expenses. Repayments are scheduled over 1 to 7 years and, in exceptional cases, may be rescheduled for up to 15 additional years.

Long-term loans also are available for real estate purposes, including the purchase and construction of buildings. For these long-term loans, the maximum outstanding principal balance for FmHA loans is $200,000 and for guaranteed loans the limit is $300,000. In addition, the loan may not exceed the market value of the security, minus any liens against the property that will remain outstanding. The maximum repayment term is 40 years.

The interest rate for FmHA nonfarm enterprise loans is set periodically based on the cost of borrowing to the U.S. Government.

A borrower may make large payments in years of high income to build a reserve that will keep the loan in good standing during years of low income. Each borrower must refinance the unpaid balance of the loan with private lenders when able to do so at reasonable rates and terms.

What Advisory Service is Available to Borrowers?

Supervision and technical assistance will be provided to borrowers in order to help them achieve the objectives of the loan. This assistance may involve planning and analyzing the nonfarm enterprise, recordkeeping, and managing the business.

Where and How are Applications Made?

Applications can be made at your local county office of the FmHA. The staff will be happy to discuss the nonfarm enterprise loan program and explain how to prepare a written application.

The Overseas Private Investment Corporation (OPIC)

If you are searching for a loan to conduct business overseas, a source your might wish to contact is the Overseas Private Investment Corporation (OPIC) which is a federal government agency that promotes economic growth by encouraging U. S. companies to invest in developing nations.

OPIC's programs include direct loans and loan guarantees that can be used to start or expand a business in a developing nation. Direct loans of $500,000 to $6 million are available. To qualify, a borrower must demonstrate a good credit rating as well as a solid track record in their industry. Loan guarantees require a participating lending institution, however, the full amount of the loan is guaranteed by the OPIC. Most of these loans range from $2 to $25 million, but can be as much as $50 million.

Another service that OPIC offers is its *Opportunity Bank* which searches computerized data to match U. S. businesses with foreign business interests. It's a great way to identify business opportunities overseas.

To be eligible for OPIC loans or guaranteed loans, overseas ventures must be located in a developing country, must be a positive factor in that country's social and economic development and cannot have an adverse impact on the U. S. economy.

For further information, including a list of nations served by OPIC, you can call their office at (202) 336-8400 or write OPIC, Information Officer, 1100 New York Avenue NW, Washington, DC 20527.

State, County and Community Loan Programs

In addition to the SBA's Certified Development Companies described earlier, many states, counties and communities offer loan and business services that entrepreneurs and small business owners are not aware of. The names of these programs vary, but they frequently include the word *development* to describe their services. For example: Small Business Development, Community Development, Rural Development, Economic Development and Capital Development Programs. The great majority of them offer loans and/or professional services to help small businesses with their finance, production, marketing, distribution and technical problems. These services are usually free or available at modest cost. To determine if such programs are available in your area, contact your state, county and city government offices.

If you are uncertain whether exporting would work for your business, or you feel that conducting business in export markets is confusing, The Oasis Press offers the book *Export Now: A Guide For Small Businesses*.

This guide helps you assess the practicalities of exporting; plan market strategies; and prepare the appropriate documents. *Export Now* also includes charts, forms, and sample documents. It is available by calling The Oasis Press at 1-800-228-2275.

Chapter 5
Private Investment In Your Business

The problem of finding money to start a business or even to expand one is universal. Most entrepreneurs and small business owners do not have the necessary savings, loan collateral or cash flow to adequately finance a new project through conventional methods. Even when they are able to secure the funds needed through a personal or business loan, the burden of repaying the principal and interest could prove overwhelming.

Venture Capital

The alternative is to secure financing from a private investor who is more interested in the *future prospects* of a new or existing business rather than its current situation. If the investment, albeit a risk, will contribute to the establishment of a successful enterprise or expand one, the opportunity for profits or appreciation in share value may far exceed any possible return earned through a more conventional investment or savings program.

Investors, by definition, are *risk takers* who evaluate business opportunities, invest in them and expect to make money. Usually, their investment decision is based upon the merits of a business plan and the ability of management to carry it out. Rarely will they invest in a project because they *like you*, although your friends and relatives may do so if they are inexperienced investors. Sometimes, family and close associates can be the worst sources of investment capital. Especially when the chips are down and a new business is not performing as planned. Relationships can become strained, even to the breaking point. Demands might be made that they *want to control the finances* or *run the company* and suddenly, your lifelong dream of building a business and your friendships can turn into a nightmare.

This is not to say that family and friends cannot be good lenders, investors or partners because they can be. Many new ventures would not have succeeded without their financial support, expertise and advice. However, and because they are usually inexperienced investors, it is important that you fully explain (and they understand) the risks involved before asking them for financial assistance or permitting them to invest their savings in your business.

When searching for venture capital, one must expect to give up a portion of the company's equity ownership to obtain it. The actual percentage will have to be negotiated, but keep in mind that equity ownership has a direct relationship to the amount you are asking someone to invest in your business and the risk they must assume if it fails.

If, for example, you need $100,000 to start a business and have only $10,000 of your own money to contribute, you may have to give up as much as 90 percent or as little as 10 percent of the ownership.

Much depends on the type of business, the business plan, the competition, your management expertise, projected profits and the overall investment risk.

Small Business Investment Companies (SBICs) on the other hand cannot, by law, directly or indirectly own more than 50 percent of the outstanding stock in a company they invest in or more than 25 percent if their share of the stock is as large or larger than that held by any other shareholder. Therefore, an SBIC may elect to invest a certain amount and loan the balance of the funds required. Other investors and some venture capital firms might not be so generous and may demand the lion's share of a company's equity in exchange for their investment — even if you have the expertise required to manage the business successfully.

Negotiation is the key word here and unless you are skilled in the art, hire a competent business lawyer to represent your best interests when attending meetings with prospective investors. After all, giving up an additional 5 percent in equity may not seem like much to get the investment capital you need, but it can make a BIG difference if the enterprise should become another IBM or XEROX!

Several venture capital companies and SBICs/SSBICs do invest in businesses nationwide. Some prefer to deal only with projects in their region, state or community. It is therefore a good idea to contact them by telephone or letter to determine their lending and industry preferences, and whether or not they make investments outside of the states where they are located. Although this information is provided in **Appendix E**, I still recommend contacting them first before mailing a copy of your business plan because they do, from time to time, change their investment policies and criteria.

A Word About Using A Money Finder

When searching for venture capital and loans, beware of individuals and firms that claim access to *hidden or private* lending/investment sources and then ask for an up-front fee to conduct a search for you. Some do represent private investors, but most do not have any more information than you do in this book. Should you decide to use a *money finder* or *money broker*, ask for the names of other entrepreneurs and firms they have helped and call them for verification. NEVER pay an up-front fee for such a service and make sure that any contract you sign spells out the terms of the agreement and the fees to be paid ONLY IF the investment or loan you need is actually secured through the *money finder's* efforts.

Although a sizable listing of lending institutions and investment firms can be found in the appendices of this edition, there are literally thousands of companies nationwide that focus primarily on financing local businesses. To find these sources, visit your public library and check the Yellow Pages telephone directories for each major city in your state — under the headings of *financing* and *loans*. A few hours of research, followed up by some phone calls to learn more about these prospective sources, could prove to be time well spent.

Public Stock Offerings

The sale of a company's stock to the public is state and federally regulated and requires the professional services of legal counsel, a certified public accountant and a participating underwriter or brokerage firm. Depending on the amount of money a company wants to raise in a public offering, the up-front expenses for legal, accounting, printing and underwriting services can range from $20,000 and up. It can be extremely costly and there are no guarantees that a stock issue will be sold. My advice is to discuss this option with your lawyer and an underwriter that specializes in Initial Public Offerings (frequently called *IPOs*) before making the decision to attempt one.

Private Stock Offerings

The private sale or private placement of a company's stock involves a limited number of investors as determined by state and federal regulating authorities. Generally speaking, a private placement offering of a company's stock is accomplished by using a *Private Placement Circular* which is a financing proposal or management memorandum used to attract a limited number of investors. Even though a private investment (in exchange for a negotiated percentage of a company's stock) is certainly less expensive and complicated than a public offering, legal counsel is strongly recommended. It can be a relatively quick and efficient way to raise financing when other methods do not appear feasible. Your banker, lawyer, broker, accountant, friends and relatives may know of individuals who would consider such a private

investment in your company. Since some states limit the actual number of solicitations one can make and the number of investors allowed, it is essential to determine if a prospect's interest is valid before presenting the circular, plan or memorandum. For complete information on this subject, contact your state's commerce or securities registration department.

Many Communities Want To Help You

If you have been unsuccessful in securing startup or expansion financing in your home town, city or state, you are not alone! The good news is, there are hundreds of villages, towns, large and small cities throughout the country that are searching for you!

If you own a business or have a good plan for one that will PROVIDE JOBS and, you or your associates can pledge some equity toward the enterprise, these communities are eager to help you arrange the financing required and to relocate. Yes, sometimes the grass is greener on the other side of the fence!

To determine who these communities are and where they are located, you might want to review the SBA Certified Development Companies listed in **Appendix C.** Should you find some areas of the country that look appealing, write to the CDCs that serve them. Ask for information about their programs and briefly describe your present situation. It could be the first step toward a great business relationship and a new home.

If you would like detailed information on business laws, regulations, and taxes in a particular state, The Oasis Press offers its *Starting and Operating a Business* book series, published for each state and the District of Columbia. Each book explains both federal and state laws in a clear, concise manner. The Oasis Press also publishes a wide array of books and software for small business owners. Call 1-800-228-2275 for more details.

Chapter 6
Alternative Sources Of Help

In addition to the SBA, FmHA, SCORE/ACE chapters, state and community business assistance programs and the listings presented in this book, there are several alternative sources of help that a determined entrepreneur can contact in his or her search for business financing.

The Informational Interview

Although seldom used today, the informational interview, if approached in the right way, can be an excellent source for advice, counsel and new financing prospects. We all need a mentor from time to time, and there is no better way to find one than to contact individuals we either know or don't know who may be able to help us. Individuals who are either experts in their respective fields or who have enjoyed a high level of business success. Here are some examples of the professionals I am referring to:

- Your bank or credit union's president and commercial loan officer
- CPAs and lawyers specializing in business law
- Local business clubs and organizations
- Successful business owners, company presidents and vice presidents
- Directors of small business incubators
- Business college professors
- Stock brokers who specialize in private placements

Everyone likes to give advice — especially when asked for it by someone who has a problem they can help solve. The secret is knowing how to ask for help without making the request seem like an ordeal that could be avoided. Here are some examples on how to set up an informational interview:

1. "Mr. Jones, my name is Tom Smith and I am a customer of your bank. I have developed a new business idea that needs the advice of an expert like you to determine the feasibility of the project. I'm wondering if we could set up a convenient appointment to briefly discuss it so that you could give me your assessment of the idea?"

2. "Mr. Stevens, my name is Tom Smith. The reason for my call is that you were referred to me as a lawyer who specializes in business law. I have developed a new business idea that needs the professional advice of an expert like you to determine the feasibility of the project. I haven't enlisted legal counsel at this point, but if you have some time open on your calendar, perhaps we could set up a brief appointment to get your opinion?"

3. "Mr. Brown, my name is Tom Smith. The reason for my call is that you were referred to me as one of the leading CPAs in town. I have

developed a new business idea that needs the advice of an expert like you to determine the feasibility of the project. I haven't enlisted the services of an accountant at this point, but I am wondering if we could set up a convenient appointment to briefly discuss it. I would certainly value your opinion."

Do you understand the idea? The appointment call is straight forward. It tells the professionals you know they are *experts* and would like their advice. You are promising to be brief, but you need their assessment. It also offers the possibility that you may use their services in the future.

Once you get the appointment, present a short talk about your plan using only 5 or 10 minutes at most. If you have prepared a financing proposal, offer a copy of it for the *expert* to review at a later time. Explain that you need a professional opinion about the project and whether or not he or she believes it is workable (even though you believe it is). Also mention that if he or she thinks the idea has merit, you plan to conduct a search for the necessary funds to finance it.

Then STOP TALKING and LISTEN! One of two things will happen. The *expert* will ask for time to review the proposal and promise to get back to you, or a lengthy conversation might develop. Either way, you are on the road to receiving valuable and free advice. If the conclusion is that your plan does have possibilities, ALWAYS ASK for the names of individuals who might have a financial interest in the project. There is nothing more precious

than a referred lead from a third party. It is even more precious when it comes from a respected professional who also believes in your plan or idea. Chances are the *expert* does know of someone who may be interested and will either give you the name or volunteer to forward a copy of your business proposal to that person. You won't always get a referral, but when you do, it will be worth the time and trouble you spent to get it. And, it just may be the financing source you have been searching for!

If you lack business contacts, informational interviews are a great way to begin accumulating them in your community. All it requires is a few telephone calls and one-on-one meetings to get the ball rolling. If you receive a referral, always report the results back to the source who gave it to you. Maybe the lead didn't pan out, but by keeping your source informed, he or she may be able to give you more leads to follow-up. It is a form of networking that REALLY WORKS!

Corporations Are Searching For Opportunities

If you have exhausted all other possible sources, you may consider presenting your business plan to selected corporations if you believe the project is compatible with their present operation and goals.

Most companies are searching for ideas that can be developed into new profit centers and while they may not be interested in financing your venture as a standalone business, they may be willing to invest in the project as a new division or department under your management. And, even though this is not the most ideal solution, since most entrepreneurs prefer to own and manage their own businesses, it is nevertheless a way to establish a product or service that might otherwise fail to get off the ground.

If such an agreement is equitable to all parties concerned and the compensation to be paid for your services is reasonable, the opportunity could far exceed your expectations for success. Yes, the trade-off might mean giving up a degree of independence and you probably would have to share in the management decisions, but the problem of financing would be solved and many of the typical small business headaches one normally encounters would vanish. Since the objective is to turn your vision into a reality, this viable option should not be overlooked as a last resort.

Insurance Companies

Many of the nation's insurance companies are willing to consider projects involving real estate and commercial development proposals where they can provide the mortgage financing required. Such projects might include: land for commercial development, apartment, office, manufacturing, warehouse, retail and medical buildings, nursing homes, retirement centers, hotels, motels, resorts and amusement parks to name a few. Several also provide mortgage loans for farms, ranches and homes. Usually, insurance companies will not provide venture capital for new

business startups, although most do invest in a broad portfolio of securities and in the stock and bond markets.

If you are searching for a loan to finance a real estate project, call the insurance firms in your area for information about their mortgage programs or visit your local library and compile a listing of prospective insurance companies that you can contact by phone or mail to request their lending guidelines.

Foundations

If you are planning to establish a non-profit organization (hopefully with the advice of a lawyer and public accountant), there are hundreds of foundations in the United States that offer *seed money* for starting a large variety of worthwhile projects. A good place to begin your search is at the public library where you can access detailed information about these foundations, their geographical funding preferences and grant making policies. An excellent reference source to review is *The Foundation Directory* published by the Foundation Center in New York. There are several other books and publications that furnish this information as well, plus a host of books offering grant writing tips and non-profit management advice.

Most foundations do not make grants or loans to individuals, but some do award direct educational aid and scholarships. A few will finance projects submitted by individuals if the grant or loan requested is for *seed money* to develop a new non-profit entity. Your public librarian can help you investigate these sources and the great multitude of programs they support.

Once you have prepared a list of prospective foundations, write to them and request their *guidelines* for submitting a grant proposal. You will find that writing for a grant is very similar to preparing a good business plan because it requires much of the same detail. Thousands of non-profit organizations received their initial funding from foundations interested in helping them get started. If you have a unique idea that could contribute to the improvement of our society, why not give it a try? Founding and managing a new non-profit organization could become the most rewarding and satisfying career choice of them all!

Small Business Development Centers

Many colleges, universities, private businesses, state and local governments throughout the United States offer a wide variety of professional help to entrepreneurs and established firms through a program called Small Business Development Centers (SBDCs).

Administered by the SBA, the SBDC program provides management assistance to current and prospective small business owners and offers one-stop information and guidance on any business subject. Since there are over 900 SBDC service locations nationwide and because their addresses, phone numbers, and contact persons change frequently, only the principal State Offices are listed in Appendix H. For the current address and phone number of a

nearby SBDC office in your state, contact the nearest SBA office listed in Appendix A or call The Oasis Press at (503) 479-9464 for this information.

You Are Not Alone

Did you know that the number of small businesses in the United States has increased 54 percent since 1980? There are approximately 20.5 million small businesses in this country. They include 4.5 million corporations, 1.7 million partnerships and 14.3 million sole proprietorships. Almost half of these businesses operate full time, the rest part-time. The 14.3 million sole proprietorships represent about 14 percent of all non-agricultural workers in America.

The number of new small businesses has continued to increase steadily during the past three decades and part-time entrepreneurs have increased five-fold in recent years. A trend that is rapidly accelerating due to the downsizing of our large corporations, merger mania and the growing desire for personal independence and opportunity.

Small businesses now employ 60 percent of the private work force, contribute 54 percent of all sales in the country, and are responsible for 50 percent of all private sector products. While the naysayers may *think* that new entrepreneurs can't compete or survive in our yo-yo economy anymore, don't believe it for a minute!

Despite the problems these enterprises routinely encounter in their day-to-day operations, most have learned (or are learning) how to cope with and manage them. And, as the foregoing U.S. Department of Labor statistics illustrate, they are proving that America is still the land of golden opportunity.

Are You An Investor or Lender?

If your company, bank, institution or investment group actively makes small business loans or operates as an equity investor, either locally, regionally or nationally, and would like a free listing in future editions of *The Money Connection*, The Oasis Press editors and I would like to hear from you. To receive a "Capital Source Questionnaire" send a postpaid, self-addressed #10 envelope to: Lawrence Flanagan, *The Money Connection*, P.O. Box 461, Excelsior, MN 55331. We reserve the right to reject a source that cannot provide evidence of making loans, equity investments or

both, and we do not list money finders or money brokers in this book.

Summing It Up

If there are three characteristics that stand out in all successful entrepreneurs, it has to be their *persistence*, their *willingness to do what others won't* and their *desire for financial independence*. Certainly the search for funds to start or expand one's business is not easy, but if you happen to possess these three attributes, you will go very far, my friend!

I sincerely hope the previous chapters have given you some insight on the subject of business finance and that the advice and capital sources presented herein will help make your quest an easier one.

Appendix A
U.S. Small Business Administration (SBA)
Regional, District, Branch, And Post Of Duty Offices

REGION I

Regional Office
155 Federal Street, 9th Floor
Boston, MA 02110
(617) 451-2023

District Office
10 Causeway St., Room 265
Boston, MA 02222
(617) 565-5590

District Office
40 Western Ave., Room 512
Augusta, ME 04330
(207) 622-8378

District Office
143 N. Main St., Suite 202
Concord, NH 03301
(603) 225-1400

District Office
330 Main St., 2nd Floor
Hartford, CT 06106
(203) 240-4700

District Office
87 State St., Room 205
Montpelier, VT 05602
(802) 828-4422

District Office
380 Westminister Hall, 5th Floor
Providence, RI 02903
(401) 528-4561

Branch Office
1550 Main St., Room 212
Springfield, MA 01103
(413) 785-0268

REGION II

Regional Office
26 Federal Plaza, Room 31-08
New York, NY 10278
(212) 264-1450

District Office
111 West Huron St., Room 1311
Buffalo, NY 14202
(716) 846-4301

District Office
60 Park Plaza, 4th Floor
Newark, NJ 07102
(201) 645-2434

District Office
26 Federal Plaza, Room 31-00
New York, NY 10278
(212) 264-2454

District Office
Carlos Chardon Ave., Suite 691
Hato Rey, PR 00918
(809) 766-5572

District Office
100 S. Clinton St., Suite 1071
Syracuse, NY 13260
(315) 423-5383

Branch Office
333 E. Water St., 4th Floor
Elmira, NY 14901
(607) 734-8130

Branch Office
35 Pinelawn Road, Room 207W
Melville, NY 11747
(516) 454-0750

REGION II (continued)

Branch Office
100 State St., Room 410
Rochester, NY 14614
(716) 263-6700

POD Office
Clinton and Pearl Streets, Suite 815
Albany, NY 12207
(518) 472-6300

POD Office
2600 Mt. Ephraim Avenue
Camden, NJ 08104
(609) 757-5183

POD Office
3013 Golden Rock
St. Croix, VI 00820
(809) 778-5380

POD Office
3800 Crown Bay
St. Thomas, VI 00802
(809) 774-8530

REGION III

Regional Office
475 Allendale Rd., Suite 201
King of Prussia, PA 19406
(215) 962-3700

District Office
10 S. Howard St., Suite 6220
Baltimore, MD 21201
(410) 962-4392

District Office
168 W. Main Street
Clarksburg, WV 26301
(304) 623-5631

REGION III (continued)

District Office
475 Allendale Rd., Suite 201
King of Prussia, PA 19406
(215) 962-3800

District Office
960 Penn Avenue, 5th Floor
Pittsburgh, PA 15222
(412) 644-2780

District Office
400 N. Eighth St., Room 3015
Richmond, VA 23240
(804) 771-2400

District Office
1110 Vermont Ave., NW, Suite 900
Washington, DC 20036
(202) 606-4000

Branch Office
550 Eagan Street, Room 309
Charleston, WV 25301
(304) 347-5220

Branch Office
100 Chestnut St., Room 309
Harrisburg, PA 17101
(717) 782-3840

Branch Office
20 N. Pennsylvania Ave., Rm. 2327
Wilkes-Barre, PA 18701
(717) 826-6497

Branch Office
920 N. King Street, Suite 412
Wilmington, DE 19801
(302) 573-6295

REGION IV

Regional Office
1375 Peachtree St., NE, 5th Floor
Atlanta, GA 30367
(404) 347-2797

District Office
1720 Peachtree Rd., NW, 6th Floor
Atlanta, GA 30309
(404) 347-4749

District Office
2121 8th Avenue North, Suite 200
Birmingham, AL 35203
(205) 731-1344

District Office
200 N. College St., Suite A2015
Charlotte, NC 28202
(704) 344-6563

District Office
1835 Assembly St., Room 358
Columbia, SC 29201
(803) 765-5377

District Office
101 West Capitol St., Suite 400
Jackson, MS 39201
(601) 965-4378

District Office
7825 Baymeadows Way, Suite 100-B
Jacksonville, FL 32256
(904) 433-1900

District Office
600 Dr. Martin Luther King, Jr. Place
Rm. 188
Louisville, KY 40202
(502) 582-5971

District Office
1320 S. Dixie Hwy., Suite 501
Coral Gables, FL 33146
(305) 536-5521

REGION IV (continued)

District Office
50 Vantage Way, Suite 201
Nashville, TN 37228
(615) 736-5881

Branch Office
One Hancock Plaza, Suite 1001
Gulfport, MS 39501
(601) 863-4449

POD Office
52 North Main St., Room 225
Statesboro, GA 30458
(912) 489-8719

POD Office
501 East Polk St., Suite 104
Tampa, FL 33602
(813) 228-2594

REGION V

Regional Office
300 S. Riverside Plaza, Suite 1975S
Chicago, IL 60606
(312) 353-5000

District Office
500 W. Madison St., Rm. 1250
Chicago, IL 60661
(312) 353-4528

District Office
1111 Superior Ave., Suite 630
Cleveland, OH 44144
(216) 522-4180

District Office
2 Nationwide Plaza, Suite 1400
Columbus, OH 43215
(614) 469-6860

REGION V (continued)

District Office
477 Michigan Ave., Room 515
Detroit, MI 48226
(313) 226-6075

District Office
429 N. Pennsylvania, Suite 100
Indianapolis, IN 46204
(317) 226-7272

District Office
212 E. Washington Ave., Rm. 213
Madison, WI 53703
(608) 264-5261

District Office
100 N. 6th St., Suite 610
Minneapolis, MN 55403
(612) 370-2324

Branch Office
525 Vine St., Suite 870
Cincinnati, OH 45202
(513) 684-2814

Branch Office
310 W. Wisconsin Ave., Suite 400
Milwaukee, WI 53203
(414) 297-3941

Branch Office
228 West Washington, Suite 11
Marquette, MI 49885
(906) 225-1108

Branch Office
511 W. Capitol St., Suite 302
Springfield, IL 62704
(217) 492-4416

REGION VI

Regional Office
8625 King George Dr., Bldg. C
Dallas, TX 75235
(214) 767-7633

District Office
625 Silver Ave., SW, Suite 320
Albuquerque, NM 87102
(505) 766-1870

District Office
4300 Amon Carter Blvd., Suite 114
Fort Worth, TX 76155
(817) 855-6500

District Office
10737 Gateway West, Suite 320
El Paso, TX 79935
(915) 540-5676

District Office
9301 Southwest Freeway, Suite 550
Houston, TX 77074
(713) 773-6500

District Office
2120 Riverfront Dr., Suite 100
Little Rock, AR 72202
(501) 324-5871

District Office
222 E. Van Buren St., Room 500
Harlingen, TX 78550
(512) 427-8533

District Office
1611 Tenth St., Suite 200
Lubbock, TX 79401
(806) 743-7462

District Office
365 Canal St., Suite 3100
New Orleans, LA 70130
(504) 589-6685

REGION VI (continued)

District Office
200 North West 5th St., Suite 670
Oklahoma City, OK 73102
(405) 231-5521

District Office
727 E. Durango, 5th Floor
San Antonio, TX 78206
(512) 229-5900

Branch Office
606 N. Carancahus, Suite 1200
Corpus Christi, TX 78476
(512) 888-3331

POD Office
300 E. 8th St., Room 967
Austin, TX 78701
(512) 482-5288

POD Office
505 E. Travis, Room 112
Marshall, TX 75670
(903) 935-5257

POD Office
401 Edward Street, Suite 916
Shreveport, LA 71101
(318) 676-3196

REGION VII

Regional Office
911 Walnut St., 13th Floor
Kansas City, MO 64106
(816) 426-3608

District Office
215 4th Avenue Rd., SW, Suite 200
Cedar Rapids, IA 52401
(319) 362-6405

REGION VII (continued)

District Office
210 Walnut St., Room 749
Des Moines, IA 50309
(515) 284-4422

District Office
323 West 8th St., Suite 501
Kansas City, MO 64105
(816) 374-6708

District Office
11145 Mill Valley Rd.
Omaha, NE 68154
(402) 221-4691

District Office
815 Olive St., Room 242
St. Louis, MO 63101
(314) 539-6600

District Office
100 E. English St., Suite 510
Wichita, KS 67202
(316) 269-6616

Branch Office
620 S. Glenstone St., Suite 110
Springfield, MO 65802
(417) 864-7670

REGION VIII

Regional Office
633 17th St., 7th Floor
Denver, CO 80202
(303) 294-7186

District Office
100 East "B" St., Room 4001
Casper, WY 82602
(307) 261-5761

REGION VIII (continued)

District Office
721 19th St., Room 426
Denver, CO 80202
(303) 844-3984

District Office
657 2nd Avenue North, Rm. 219
Fargo, ND 58108
(701) 239-5131

District Office
301 South Park, Room 334
Helena, MT 59626
(406) 449-5381

District Office
125 S. State St., Room 2237
Salt Lake City, UT 84138
(801) 524-5804

District Office
101 S. Main Avenue, Suite 200
Sioux Falls, SD 57102
(605) 330-4231

REGION IX

Regional Office
71 Stevenson St., 20th Floor
San Francisco, CA 94105
(415) 744-6402

District Office
2719 North Air Fresno Drive, Suite 107
Fresno, CA 93727
(209) 487-5189

District Office
300 Ala Moana Blvd., Rm. 2213
Honolulu, HI 96850
(808) 541-2990

REGION IX (continued)

District Office
301 E. Stewart St., Room 301
Las Vegas, NV 89125
(702) 388-6611

District Office
330 N. Brand Blvd., Suite 1200
Glendale, CA 91203
(818) 552-3210

District Office
2828 N. Central Ave., Suite 800
Phoenix, AZ 85004
(602) 640-2316

District Office
880 Front St., Suite 4-S-29
San Diego, CA 92188
(619) 557-7252

District Office
211 Main St., 4th Floor
San Francisco, CA 94105
(415) 744-6820

District Office
901 W. Civic Center Dr., Suite 160
Santa Ana, CA 92703
(714) 836-2494

Branch Office
238 Archbishop F. C. Flores St., 508
Agana, GM 96910
(671) 472-7277

Branch Office
660 "J" Street, Room 215
Sacramento, CA 95814
(916) 551-1426

POD Office
50 S. Virginia St., Room 238
Reno, NV 89505
(702) 784-5268

REGION IX (continued)

POD Office
300 W. Congress St., Room 7-H
Tucson, AZ 85701
(602) 670-4759

POD Office
6477 Telephone Rd., Suite 10
Ventura, CA 93003
(805) 642-1866

REGION X

Regional Office
2601 4th Ave., Room 500
Seattle, WA 98121
(206) 553-5676

District Office
222 West 8th Ave., Room A36
Anchorage, AK 99513
(907) 271-4022

District Office
1020 Main St., Suite 290
Boise, ID 83702
(208) 334-1696

District Office
222 S. West Columbia, Suite 500
Portland, OR 97201
(503) 326-2682

District Office
915 Second Ave., Room 1792
Seattle, WA 98174
(206) 220-6520

REGION X (continued)

District Office
West 601 First Ave., 10th Floor
Spokane, WA 99204

DISASTER AREA OFFICES

#1 DAO
360 Rainbow Blvd. S., 3rd Floor
Niagara Falls, NY 14303
(716) 282-4612

#2 DAO
One Baltimore Place, Suite 300
Atlanta, GA 30308
(404) 347-3771

#3 DAO
4400 Amon Carter Blvd., Suite 102
Ft. Worth, TX 76155
(817) 885-7600

#4 DAO
1825 Bell St., Suite 208
Sacramento, CA 95825
(916) 978-4571

COMMERCIAL LOAN SERVICING CENTER

CLSC Office
2719 North Air Fresno Drive
Fresno, CA 93727
(209) 487-5189

Appendix B
U.S. Department of Agriculture
Farmers Home Administration (FmHA)
State Offices

ALABAMA
Horace Horn
Sterling Center, Suite 401
4121 Carmichael Road
Montgomery, AL 36106-3683
(205) 279-3400

ALASKA
Ernest Brannon
634 S. Bailey, Suite 103
Palmer, AK 99645
(907) 745-2176

ARIZONA
Alan Stephens
3003 North Central Ave., Suite 900
Phoenix, AZ 85012
(602) 280-8700

ARKANSAS
Michael L. Dunaway
700 W. Capitol
P. O. Box 2778
Little Rock, AR 72203
(501) 324-6281

CALIFORNIA & NEVADA
Paul Rice
194 W. Main St., Suite F
Woodland, CA 95695
(916) 668-2000

COLORADO
Michael Reyna
655 Parfet St., Room E-100
Lakewood, CO 80215
(303) 236-2801

DELAWARE & MARYLAND
John Walls
4611 So. Dupont Highway
P.O. Box 400
Camden, DE 19934-9998
(302) 697-4300

FLORIDA
Jan Shadburn
4440 NW 25th Place
P.O. Box 147010
Gainesville, FL 32614-7010
(904) 338-3400

GEORGIA
Laura Jean Meadows
Stephens Federal Building
355 E. Hancock Avenue
Athens, GA 30610
(404) 546-2173

HAWAII
Francis Blanco
Federal Building, Room 311
154 Waianuenue Avenue
Hilo, HI 96720
(808) 933-3000

IDAHO
Loren Nelson
3232 Elder Street
Boise, ID 83705
(208) 334-1301

ILLINOIS
Wallace Furrow
Illini Plaza, Suite 103
1817 South Neil Street
Champaign, IL 61820
(217) 398-5235

INDIANA
John Thompson
5975 Lakeside Blvd.
Indianapolis, IN 46278
(317) 290-3100

IOWA
Ellen Huntoon
Federal Building, Room 873
210 Walnut Street
Des Moines, IA 50309
(515) 284-4663

KANSAS
Bill Kirk
1201 SW Summit Exec. Court
P. O. Box 4653
Topeka, KS 66604
(913) 271-7300

KENTUCKY
Rom Fern
771 Corporate Plaza, Suite 200
Lexington, KY 40503
(606) 224-7300

LOUISIANA
Austin Cormier
3727 Government Street
Alexandria, LA 71302
(318) 473-7920

MAINE
Seth Bradstreet
444 Stillwater Ave., Suite 2
P. O. Box 405
Bangor, ME 04402-0405
(207) 990-9106

MASSACHUSETTS, RHODE ISLAND & CONNECTICUT
William Bradley
451 West Street
Amherst, MA 01002
(413) 253-4300

MICHIGAN
Donald Hare
3001 Coolidge Road, Suite 200
East Lansing, MI 48823
(517) 337-6635

MINNESOTA
Janice Daley
410 Farm Credit Service Building
375 Jackson Street
St. Paul, MN 55101
(612) 290-3842

MISSISSIPPI
George E. Irvin
Federal Building, Room 831
100 W. Capitol Street
Jackson, MS 39269
(601) 965-4316

MISSOURI
William Shay
601 Business Loop 70 West
Parkade Center, Suite 235
Columbia, MO 65203
(314) 876-0976

MONTANA
Anthony Preite
900 Technology Blvd., Suite B
P.O. Box 850
Bozeman, MT 59771
(406) 585-2580

NEBRASKA
Stanley Foster
Federal Building, Room 308
100 Centennial Mall N
Lincoln, NE 68508
(402) 437-5551

NEVADA
Sarah Mersereau
1390 South Curry Street
Carson City, NV 89703-5405
(702) 887-1222

NEW JERSEY
Ernest Grunow
Tarnsfield Plaza, Suite 22
1016 Woodlane Road
Mt. Holly, NJ 08060
(609) 265-3600

NEW MEXICO
Steven Anaya
Federal Building, Room 3414
517 Gold Avenue, SW
Albuquerque, NM 87102
(505) 766-2462

NEW YORK
James Bay
The Galleries of Syracuse
441 W. Salina Street
Syracuse, NY 13202
(315) 477-6400

NORTH CAROLINA
James Kearney
4405 Bland Road, Suite 260
Raleigh, NC 27609
(919) 790-2731

NORTH DAKOTA
Charles Mertens
Federal Building, Room 208
3rd & Rosser
P.O. Box 1737
Bismarck, ND 58502
(701) 250-4781

OHIO
Linda Page
Federal Building, Room 507
200 North High Street
Columbus, OH 43215
(614) 469-5606

OKLAHOMA
Charles Rainbolt
USDA Agricultural Center
Stillwater, OK 74074
(405) 742-1000

OREGON
Scott Duff
Federal Building, Room 1590
1220 SW 3rd Avenue
Portland, OR 97204
(503) 326-2731

PENNSYLVANIA
Cheryl Cook
1 Credit Union Place, Suite 330
Harrisburg, PA 17110-2996
(717) 782-4476

PUERTO RICO
Ileana Echegoyen
New San Juan Office Bldg., Rm. 501
159 Carlos E. Chardon Street
Hato Rey, PR 00918-5481
(809) 766-5095

SOUTH CAROLINA
Bernie Wright
Strom Thurmond Federal Building
1835 Assembly Street, Room 1007
Columbia, SC 29201
(803) 765-5163

SOUTH DAKOTA
Dallas Tonsager
Federal Building, Room 308
200 4th Street SW
Huron, SD 57350
(605) 353-1100

TENNESSEE
David Seivers
3322 West End Avenue, Suite 300
Nashville, TN 37203-1071
(615) 783-1308

TEXAS
George Ellis
M.J. Pena
Federal Building, Suite 102
101 South Main
Temple, TX 76501
(817) 774-1301

UTAH
James Harvey
Federal Building, Room 5438
125 South State Street
Salt Lake City, UT 84138
(801) 524-4063

**VERMONT, NEW HAMPSHIRE
& VIRGIN ISLANDS**
Roberta Harold
City Center, 3rd Floor
89 Main Street
Montpelier, VT 05602
(802) 828-6001

VIRGINIA
Lloyd A. Jones
Culpepper Building, Suite 238
1606 Santa Rosa Road
Richmond, VA 23229
(804) 287-1550

WASHINGTON
George Aldaya
Federal Building, Room 319
301 Yakima Street
P.O. Box 2427
Wenatchee, WA 98807
(509) 664-0240

WEST VIRGINIA
Robert Lewis
75 High Street
P.O. Box 678
Morgantown, WV 26505
(304) 291-4791

WISCONSIN
Bryce Luchterhand
4949 Kirschling Court
Stevens Point, WI 54481
(715) 345-7625

WYOMING
Derrel L. Carruth
Federal Building, Room 1005
P.O. Box 820
Casper, WY 82602
(307) 261-5271

Appendix C
SBA Certified Development Companies

REGION I (CT, MA, ME, NH, RI & VT)

Androscoggin Valley Council of Governments
Bryce Johnston
125 Manley Road
Auburn, ME 04210
(207) 783-9186
SBA Office: Augusta
Area of Operation: Counties of Androscoggin, Franklin and Oxford

Bay Colony Development Corp.
David King
Watermill Center
800 South St., 4th Floor
Waltham, MA 02154
(617) 891-3594
SBA Office: Boston
Area of Operation: Throughout Mass. except Dukes and Nantucket Counties

Boston Local Development Corp.
John Dineen
43 Hawkins Street
Boston, MA 02111
(617) 635-3342
SBA Office: Boston
Area of Operation: City of Boston

Brattleboro Development Credit Corp.
Al Moulton
5 Grove Street
P. O. Box 1177
Brattleboro, VT 05301
(802) 257-7731
SBA Office: Montpelier
Area of Operation: Windham and Windsor Counties

Bridgeport Economic Development Corp.
Roy O'Neil
10 Middle Street, 14th Floor
Bridgeport, CT 06604-4229
(203) 355-3800
SBA Office: Hartford
Area of Operation: City of Bridgeport

Bristol County Chamber Local Develop. Corp.
President
654 Metacom Avenue
P. O. Box 250
Warren, RI 02885
(401) 245-0851
SBA Office: Providence
Area of Operation: Bristol County, RI

Central Vermont Economic Development Corp.
Donald C. Rowan
P. O. Box 1439
Montpelier, VT 05601
(802) 223-4654
SBA Office: Montpelier
Area of Operation: Washington County plus part of northern Orange County

Coastal Enterprises, Inc.
Ronald L. Phillips
P. O. Box 268
Wiscasset, ME 04578
(207) 882-7552
SBA Office: Augusta
Area of Operation: Counties of Cumberland, Knox, Lincoln, Sagadahoc and York

Concord Regional Development Corp.
Niel Cannon
P. O. Box 664
Concord, NH 03301
(603) 228-1872
SBA Office: Concord
Area of Operation: Belknap, Grafton, Merrimack and Sullivan Counties

Connecticut Business Development Corp.
Vincent Pellegrino
845 Brook Street
Rocky Hill, CT 06067
(203) 258-7855
SBA Office: Hartford
Area of Operation: Statewide

REGION I (continued)

East Boston Local Development Corp.
Salvatore Colombo
72 Marginal Street, 6th Floor
East Boston, MA 02128
(617) 569-7174
SBA Office: Boston
Area of Operation: East Boston and its North
Shore Environs of Chelsea, Revere & Winthrop

Eastern Maine Development District
Charles Rowndy
One Cumberland Place, #300
P. O. Box 2579
Bangor, ME 04401
(207) 942-6389
SBA Office: Augusta
Area of Operation: Hancock, Kennebec, Knox,
Penobscot, Piscataquis, Somerset, Waldo and
Washington Counties

Granite State Economic Development Corp.
Alan Abraham
126 Daniel Street
P. O. Box 1491
Portsmouth, NH 03801
(603) 436-0009
SBA Office: Concord
Area of Operation: Statewide

**Greater Hartford Business Development
Center, Inc.**
Warren Leuteritz
c/o HEDCO
15 Lewis Street
Hartford, CT 06103
(203) 527-1301
SBA Office: Hartford
Area of Operation: County of Hartford

Housatonic Industrial Development Corp.
Charles E. Wrinn
57 North Street, #407
Danbury, CT 06810
(203) 743-0306
SBA Office: Hartford
Area of Operation: West of Connecticut River

Lewiston Development Corp.
Stephen A. Heavener
37 Park Street
P. O. Box 1188
Lewiston, ME 04243
(207) 783-3505
SBA Office: Augusta
Area of Operation: City of Lewiston

Lynn Capital Investment Corp.
Peter M. DeVeau
One Market Street, #4
Lynn, MA 01901
(617) 592-2361
SBA Office: Boston
Area of Operation: City of Lynn

Massachusetts Certified Development Corp.
Elizabeth C. DiSabatino
One Liberty Square
Boston, MA 02109
(617) 350-8877
SBA Office: Boston
Area of Operation: Statewide

New Haven Community Investment Corp. LDC
Faron Lawrence
770 Chapel Street, #B31
New Haven, CT 06510-3101
(203) 787-6023
SBA Office: Hartford
Area of Operation: New Haven County

North Central Massachusetts Develop. Corp.
Mark A. Goldstein
110 Erdman Way
Leominster, MA 01453
(508) 840-4300
SBA Office: Boston
Area of Operation: Cities & towns in northern
Worcester County & western Middlesex County

REGION I (continued)

Northeastern Mass. Development Corp.
John A. Wells
28½ Peabody Square
Peabody, MA 01960
(508) 531-0454
SBA Office: Boston
Area of Operation: Essex County and a portion
of Eastern Middlesex County

Northern Community Investment Corp.
Carl J. Garbelotti
20 Main Street
St. Johnsbury, VT 05819
(802) 748-5101
SBA Office: Montpelier
Area of Operation: Caledonia, Essex and Orleans
Counties in Vermont; also Coos, Carroll and
Grafton Counties in New Hampshire

Northern Maine Dev. Commission, Inc.
Duane Walton
Main Street
P. O. Box 779
Caribou, ME 04736
(207) 498-8736
SBA Office: Augusta
Area of Operation: Aroostock, 19 unorganized
townships in Pescatiguis County, 6 communities
in Penobscot and 1 in Washington County

Ocean State Business Development Authority
Henry A. Violet
155 South Main Street, #301
Providence, RI 02903
(401) 454-4560
SBA Office: Providence
Area of Operation: Counties of Providence, Kent,
Washington and Newport

Pittsfield Economic Revitalization Corp.
Kenneth E. Walto
70 Allen Street
Pittsfield, MA 01201
(413) 499-9371
SBA Office: Boston
Area of Operation: County of Berkshire

Riverside Development Corp.
Richard Courchesne
70 Lyman Street
Holyoke, MA 01040
(413) 533-7102
SBA Office: Boston
Area of Operation: City of Holyoke

South Eastern Economic Development Corp.
Maria Gooch
88 Broadway
Taunton, MA 02780
(508) 822-1020
SBA Office: Boston
Area of Operation: Counties of Barnstable, Bristol,
Dukes, Nantucket and Plymouth

South Shore Economic Development Corp.
Tricia Fell
36 Miller Stile Road
Quincy, MA 02169
(617) 479-1111
SBA Office: Boston
Area of Operation: Plymouth & Norfolk Counties

Vermont 503 Corp.
Thomas A. Porter
56 East State Street
Montpelier, VT 05602
(802) 479-8066
SBA Office: Montpelier
Area of Operation: Statewide

Western Mass. Small Business Assistance, Inc.
Bob Reavey
1350 Main Street, 3rd Floor
Boston, MA 01103
(413) 787-1553
SBA Office: Boston
Area of Operation: Counties of Hampden,
Hampshire and Franklin

Worchester Business Development Corp.
William E. Purcell
33 Waldo Street
Worchester, MA 01608
(617) 753-2924
SBA Office: Boston
Area of Operation: Worchester County

REGION II (NJ, NY & PR)

Andirondack Economic Development Corp.
Ernest S. Hohmeyer
30 Main Street
Saranac Lake, NY 12983
(518) 891-2020
SBA Office: Syracuse
Area of Operation: Counties of Clinton, Essex
and Franklin

Advancer Local Development Corp.
Luz Celenia Castellano
403 Del Parque St., #352, #202
Santurce, PR 00912
(809) 721-6797
SBA Office: Hato Rey, PR
Area of Operation: Island of Puerto Rico, except
Municipality of Las Marias

Albany Local Development Corp.
George Leveille
City Hall, 4th Floor
Albany, NY 12207
(518) 434-5133
SBA Office: Syracuse
Area of Operation: City of Albany

Buffalo Enterprise Development Corp.
Dick Velez
300 Pearl St., Olympic Towers, #452
Buffalo, NY 14202
(716) 842-3020
SBA Office: Buffalo
Area of Operation: City of Buffalo

Burlington County 503 Development Corp.
George Fekete
49 Rancocas Road
Mt. Holly, NJ 08060
(No telephone listing)
SBA Office: Newark
Area of Operation: County of Burlington

Caciques Development Corp.
Robert Hughes
P.O. Box 1626
Orocovis, PR 00720
(809) 876-2520
SBA Office: Hato Rey
Area of Operation: Puerto Rico

Corp. for Business Assistance in New Jersey
Eugene Bukowski
Capital Place One #600-CN991
200 South Warren Street
Trenton, NJ 08625
(609) 633-7737
SBA Office: Newark
Area of Operation: Statewide

**Corp. para el Fomento Economico de la
Ciudad Capital**
Robert Ramirez, Jr.
Chardon Ave., P. O. Box 1791
Hato Rey, PR 00919
(809) 756-5080
SBA Office: Hato Rey, PR
Area of Operation: City of San Juan

Economic Development Corp. of Essex County
Ellisworth Salisbury
443 Northfield Avenue
West Orange, NJ 07052
(201) 731-2772
SBA Office: Newark
Area of Operation: Essex County

Empire State Certified Development Corp.
Robert Lazar
41 State Street
P. O. Box 738
Albany, NY 12207
(518) 463-2268
SBA Office: Syracuse
Area of Operation: Statewide

Greater Syracuse Business Development Corp.
Richard Arciero
572 South Salina Street
Syracuse, NY 13202
(315) 470-1800
SBA Office: Syracuse
Area of Operation: County of Onondaga

REGION II (continued)

Hudson Development Corp.
Lynda Davidson
444 Warren Street
Hudson, NY 12534
(518) 828-3373
SBA Office: New York
Area of Operation: Columbia County

La Marketing Development Corp.
Julio C. Morillo-Limardo
P. O. Box 3824
San Juan, PR 00919
(809) 783-1646
SBA Office: Hato Rey, PR
Area of Operation: The Commonwealth of Puerto
Rico except the Municipalities of Vieques and
Culerbra

Long Island Development Corp.
Roslyn Goldmacher
255 Glen Cove Road
Carle Place, NY 11514
(516) 741-5690
SBA Office: New York
Area of Operation: Counties of Nassau, Suffolk
and environs

Metropolitan Business Assistance, LTD
President
c/o Finance Services Corp.
110 William Street
New York, NY 10038
(212) 566-1358
SBA Office: New York
Area of Operation: 5 Boroughs of New York —
Bronx, Brooklyn, Manhattan, Queens and
Staten Island

Middlesex County Certified Local Dev. Corp.
Angel Guikoff
303 George Street, #304
New Brunswick, NJ 08901
(908) 745-4005
SBA Office: Newark
Area of Operation: Middlesex County

Mohawk Vallery Certified Development Corp.
Michael Reese
26 West Main Street
P. O. Box 69
Mohawk, NY 13407
(315) 866-4671
SBA Office: Syracuse
Area of Operation: Oneida, Herkimer, Fulton,
Montgomery and Schoharie Counties

Monroe County Industrial Development Corp.
Judy Seil
1 W. Main Street, #600
Rochester, NY 14614-1481
(716) 28-5260
SBA Office: Syracuse
Area of Operation: Monroe County

N. F. C. Development Corp.
Sam Ferraro
745 Main Street
Niagara Falls, NY 14302
(716) 286-4472
SBA Office: Buffalo
Area of Operation: City of Niagara Falls

No. Puerto Rico Local Development Co., Inc.
Jose A. Franceschini
Mercantil Plaza, #801
Hato Rey, PR 00918
(809) 754-7474
SBA Office: Hato Rey, PR
Area of Operation: Island of Puerto Rico

Operation Oswego County, Inc.
L. Michael Treadwell
East 2nd and Schuyler Streets
P. O. Box 4067
Oswego, NY 13126
(315) 343-1545
SBA Office: Syracuse
Area of Operation: Oswego County

REGION II (continued)

Port Jervis Development Corp.
Sally T. Martinez
14 - 20 Hammond Street
P. O. Box 3105
Port Jervis, NY 12771
(914) 856-8358
SBA Office: New York
Area of Operation: Orange County

Rochester Economic Development Corp.
Charlie Andrus
30 Church Street
Rochester, NY 14614
(716) 428-6808
SBA Office: Syracuse
Area of Operation: City of Rochester

Syracuse Economic Development Corp.
Michael F. Rosanio
233 City Hall
Syracuse, NY 13202
(315) 473-2870
SBA Office: Syracuse
Area of Operation: City of Syracuse

Tier Information & Enterprise Resources, Inc.
Richard McCormick
46 S. Washington Street
Binghamton, NY 13903-1712
(607) 724-1327
SBA Office: Syracuse
Area of Operation: Broome, Chenango, Cortland, Delaware, Otsego, Schoharie, Tioga and Tompkins Counties

Trenton Business Assistance Corp.
Arthur H. Anderson, III
City Hall Annex
319 East State Street
Trenton, NJ 08608
(609) 989-3507
SBA Office: Newark
Area of Operation: Citywide in Trenton

Union County Economic Development Corp.
Ralph S. Klopper
3999 Westfield Avenue
Elizabeth, NJ 07208
(201) 527-1166
SBA Office: Newark
Area of Operation: Union County, NJ

REGION III (DC, DE, MD, PA, VA & WV)

4-C Certified Development Company
John Hunt
214 Main Street
Oak Hill, WV 25901
(304) 465-0585
SBA Office: Clarksburg
Area of Operation: Fayette, Nicholas, Raleigh and Summers Counties

Allentown Economic Development Corp.
Janice Gubich
801 Hamilton Mall, #200
Allentown, PA 18101
(215) 435-8890
SBA Office: Philadelphia
Area of Operation: Lehigh County

Altoona Enterprises, Inc.
Robert A. Halloran
1212 Twelfth Avenue
Altoona, PA 16601
(814) 944-6113
SBA Office: Pittsburgh
Area of Operation: Counties of Blair and Bedford, PA

BEDCO Development Corp.
Carolyn Boozer
Suite 1600 Charles Center South
36 South Charles Street
Baltimore, MD 21201
(301) 837-9305
SBA Office: Baltimore
Area of Operation: Citywide Baltimore

REGION III (continued)

Community Dev.Corp. of Butler County
George B. Howley
100 North Main Street
P. O. Box 1082
Lynchburg, VA 24502
Butler, PA 16003-1082
(412) 283-1961
SBA Office: Pittsburgh
Area of Operation: Butler County

Crater Development Company
James McClure
1964 Wakefield Street
P.O. Box 1808
Petersburg, VA 23805
(804) 861-1668
SBA Office: Richmond
Areas of Operation: Cities of Colonial Heights,
Emporia, Hopewell & Petersburg; Chesterfield,
Dinwiddie, Greensville, Prince George, Surry
and Sussex Counties

**Cumberland-Allegany County Industrial
Foundation, Inc.**
John Kirby
1 Commerce Drive
Cumberland, MD 21502
(301) 777-5968
SBA Office: Baltimore
Area of Operation: Cumberland and
Allegany Counties

Delaware Development Corporation
Gary Smith
99 Kings Highway
P.O. Box 1401
Dover, DE 19903
(302) 739-4271
SBA Office: Philadelphia
Area of Operation: Statewide

James River Certified Development Corp.
Frederick Minton
1111 East Main Street, 18th Floor
P.O. Box 27025
Richmond, VA 23261-7025
(804) 788-6966
SBA Office: Richmond
Areas of Operation: Richmond and Counties
of Charles City, Goochland, Hanover, Henrico,
James City, New Kent, Powhatan and York

**Johnstown Area Regional Industries
Certified Development Corp.**
Richard M. Uzelac
551 Main Street
East Building, #203
Johnstown, PA 15901
(814) 535-8675
SBA Office: Pittsburgh
Area of Operation: Cambria and Somerset Counties

Keystone Small Business Assistance Corp.
John Hoishik
311 North Broad Street
P.O. Box 407
Lansdale, PA 19446
(215) 368-4880
SBA Office: Philadelphia
Area of Operation: Bucks and Montgomery Counties

Lake County Development Corp.
Deborah Doyle
123 S. Mecklenburg Avenue
P. O. Box 150
South Hill, VA 23970
(804) 447-7101
SBA Office: Richmond
Area of Operation: Counties of Brunswick,
Mecklenburg and Halifax — Cities of South Hill
and South Boston

MetroAction, Inc.
John Walsh
222 Mulberry Street
Scranton, PA 18501
(717) 342-7713
SBA Office: Wilkes-Barre
Area of Operation: Lackawanna, Luzerne and
Morrow Counties

Mid-Atlantic Certified Development Co. (The)
Robert Klepper
2 Hopkins Plaza, 9th Floor
Baltimore, MD 21201-2911
SBA Office: Baltimore
Area of Operation: State of Maryland except
Allegany County and City of Baltimore

REGION III (continued)

New Castle County Economic Dev. Corp.
Ted Lambert
536 First Federal Plaza
704 King Street
Wilmington, DE 19801
(302) 656-5050
SBA Office: Philadelphia
Area of Operation: New Castle County, DE

New River Valley Development Corp.
Wayne Carpenter
1612 Wadsworth Street
P. O. Box 3726
Radford, VA 24143
(703) 639-9314
SBA Office: Richmond
Area of Operation: New River Valley Planning
District; City of Radford, Counties of Floyd, Giles,
Montgomery and Pulaski

OVIBDC CDC, Inc.
Terry Burkhart
12th and Chapline Streets
P.O. Box 1029
Wheeling, WV 26003
(304) 232-7722
SBA Office: Clarksburg
Area of Operation: Ohio, Marshall and
Wetzel Counties

PIDC Local Development Corp.
William Hankowsky
2600 Centre Square West
1500 Market Street
Philadelphia, PA 19109-2126
(215) 496-8020
SBA Office: Philadelphia
Area of Operation: City and County of
Philadelphia

Pittsburgh Countywide Corp., Inc.
Steven Mahaven
437 Grant Street
Frick Building, #1220
Pittsburgh, PA 15219
(412) 471-1030
SBA Office: Pittsburgh
Area of Operation: Counties of Allegheny,
Armstrong, Beaver, Butler, Fayette, Greene,
Indiana, Washington and Westmoreland

Pocono Northeast Enterprise Development Corp.
Len Ziolkowski
1151 Oak Street
Pittston, PA 18640
(717) 655-5587
SBA Office: Philadelphia
Area of Operation: Carbon, Lackawanna, Luzerne,
Monroe, Pike, Schuylkill and Wayne Counties

Portsmouth Certified Development Corp.
Philip Tuning
801 Crawford Street
Portsmouth, VA 23704
(804) 393-8989
SBA Office: Richmond
Area of Operation: City of Portsmouth

Prince George's County Financial Services Corp.
Joseph R. Timer
9200 Basil Court, #200
Landover, MD 20785
(301) 386-5600
SBA Office: District of Columbia
Area of Operation: Prince George's County, MD

Quaker State Business Finance Corp.
Ira P. Lutsky
Jefferson House, #C-91
3900 City Line Avenue
Philadelphia, PA 19131
(215) 871-3770
SBA Office: Philadelphia
Area of Operation: Philadelphia, Montgomery,
Bucks, Delaware and Chester Counties

Rappahannock Economic Development Corp.
Kathy Beard
904 Princess Anne Street
P.O. Box 863
Fredericksburg, VA 22401
(703) 373-2897
SBA Office: Richmond
Area of Operation: Caroline, King George,
Stafford and Spotsylvania Counties and the
City of Fredericksburg

REGION III (continued)

SEDA-COG Local Development Corp.
Jerry Bohinski
R.D. #1
Lewisburg, PA 17837
(717) 524-4491
SBA Office: Philadelphia
Area of Operation: Adams, Centre, Clinton,
Columbia, Cumberland, Dauphin, Franklin,
Juniata, Lancaster, Lebanon, Lycoming, Mifflin,
Montour, Northumberland, Perry, Snyder,
Union and York Counties

South Eastern Economic Dev. Co. of PA.
Gary Smith or Lisa Taylor
750 Pottstown Pike
Exton, PA 19341
(215) 363-6110
SBA Office: Philadelphia
Area of Operation: Chester County

Uniform Region Nine Certified Dev. Co.
Dale Massie
614 Eleventh Street
Franklin, PA 16323
(814) 437-3024
SBA Office: Pittsburgh
Area of Operation: Clarion, Crawford, Erie,
Forest, Lawrence, Mercer, Venango and
Warren Counties

Urban Business Development Corp.
Thomas Marino
201 Granby Street, #1000
Norfolk, VA 23510
(804) 623-2691
SBA Office: Richmond
Area of Operation: Cities of Norfolk,
Virginia Beach and Chesapeake

Urban Local Development Corp. c/o PCDC
John Lenahan
1315 Walnut, 6th Floor
Philadelphia, PA 19107
(215) 790-2200
SBA Office: Philadelphia
Area of Operation: Philadelphia County, PA

Virginia Asset Financing Corp.
Kathleen Strawhacker
12020 Sunrise Valley Drive, #260
Reston, VA 22091
(703) 476-0504
SBA Office: District of Columbia
Area of Operation: Alexandria, Arlington, Clarke,
Fairfax, Falls Church, Frederick, Loudoun,
Manassas, Manassas Park, Page, Prince William,
Shenandoah, Warren and Winchester

Virginia Economic Development Corp.
James Skove
413 East Market Street, #102
Charlottesville, VA 22901
(804) 972-1720
SBA Office: Richmond
Area of Operation: Albemarle, Fluvanna, Greene,
Louisa and Nelson Counties, and the City of
Charlottesville

Washington, D.C. Local Development Corp.
John Ford
1201 Pennsylvania Avenue, 4th Floor
Washington, DC 20004
Norfolk, VA 23510
(202) 626-6890
SBA Office: District of Columbia
Area of Operation: Washington, DC

Wilmington Local Development Corp.
Ted Nutter
605 A Market Street Mall
Wilmington, DE 19801
(302) 571-9087
SBA Office: Wilmington
Area of Operation: Citywide Wilmington

West Virginia Certified Development Corp.
Timothy A. Bailey
State Capitol Complex
Building 6, Room 525
Charleston, WV
(304) 558-3691
SBA Office: Clarksburg
Area of Operation: Statewide

REGION IV (AL, FL, GA, KY, NC, SC & TN)

Advancement, Inc.
Robert Herring
711 North Cedar Street
Lumberton, NC 28358
(919) 738-4851
SBA Office: Charlotte
Area of Operation: Anson, Bladen, Columbus,
Harnett, Hoke, Moore, Richmond, Robeson,
Sampson and Scotland

Alabama Community Development Corp.
Diane Roerig
No. 3 Office Park Circle, #300
Mountain Brook, AL 35223
(205) 870-3360
SBA Office: Birmingham
Area of Operation: State of Alabama except
Sumter, Choctaw and Washington Counties

Albemarle Development Authority, Inc.
Jane Miller
512 South Church Street
P.O. Box 646
Hertford, NC 27944
(919) 426-5755
SBA Office: Charlotte
Area of Operation: Camden, Chowan, Currituck,
Dare, Gates, Hyde and Washington Counties

Appalachian Development Corp.
Robert M. Strother
50 Grand Avenue
P.O. Box 6668
Greenville, SC 29606
SBA Office: Greenville
Area of Operation: Anderson, Cherokee,
Greenville, Oconee, Pickens and Spartanburg
Counties

Areawide Development Corp.
Don Woods
5616 Kingston Pike
P.O. Box 19806
Knoxville, TN 37919
(615) 588-7972
SBA Office: Nashville
Area of Operation: Scott, Campbell, Claiborne,
Anderson, Union, Morgan, Roane, Loudon,
Monroe, Blount, Knox, Grainger Hamblen,
Jefferson, Cocke and Sevier

Asheville-Buncombe Development Corp.
Robert C. Kendrich
P.O. Box 1010
Asheville. NC 28802-1011
(704) 258-0317
SBA Office: Charlotte
Area of Operation: The County of Buncombe
and its Municipalities

Atlanta Local Development Company
Walter R. Huntley, Jr.
230 Peachtree Street, NW, #1650
Atlanta, GA 30303
(404) 658-7000
SBA Office: Atlanta
Area of Operation: Citywide Atlanta

Barren River Development Council
Jack Eversole
740 East 10th Street
Bowling Green, KY 42102
(502) 781-2381
SBA Office: Louisville
Area of Operation: Allen, Barren, Butler,
Edmonson, Hart, Logan, Metcalfe, Monroe,
Simpson and Warren Counties, and
Southcentral Kentucky

Birmingham Citywide Local Development Co.
Mike Vance
North 20th Street
Birmingham, AL 35203
(205) 254-2799
SBA Office: Birmingham
Area of Operation: Citywide Birmingham,
Jefferson and Shelby Counties of Alabama

Buffalo Trace Area Development District, Inc.
Robert Money
327 West Second Street
Maysville, KY 41056
SBA Office: Louisville
Area of Operation: Bracken, Fleming, Lewis,
Mason and Robertson Counties

REGION IV (continued)

Business Development Corporation of Northeast Floride, Inc.
Patricia A. Ferm
9143 Phillips Highway, #350
Jacksonville, FL 32256
Phone: Contact SBA in Jacksonville
SBA Office: Jacksonville
Area of Operation: Florida counties of Nassau, Baker, Clay, St. Johns, Flagler, Putnam, and Duval (except for the City of Jacksonville)

Business Growth Corp. of Georgia (The)
Vicki M. Schoen
4000 Cumberland Parkway, #1200A
Atlanta, GA 30339
(404) 434-0273
SBA Office: Atlanta
Area of Operation: Statewide

Capital Economic Development Corp.
Kelley Ferrante
805 New Bern Avenue
P. O. Box 1443
Raleigh, NC 27610
(919) 832-4524
SBA Office: Charlotte
Area of Operation: Durham, Wake and Orange Orange Counties

Catawba Regional Development Corp.
Elaine Fairman
P. O. Box 862
Rock Hill, SC 29730
(803) 324-3161
SBA Office: Columbia
Area of Operation: Chester, Lancaster, Union and York Counties

Central Mississippi Development Co., Inc.
Thelman Larry Anderson
1170 Lakeland Drive
Jackson, MS 39216
(601) 981-1625
SBA Office: Jackson
Area of Operation: Copiah, Hinds, Madison, Rankin, Simpson, Warren and Yazoo Counties

Centralina Development Corp., Inc.
Paul K. Herringshaw
P. O. Box 35008
Charlotte, NC 28235
(704) 372-2416
SBA Office: Charlotte
Area of Operation: Cabarrus, Gaston, Iredell, Lincoln, Mecklenburg, Rowan, Stanly and Union Counties

Certified Development Co. of Georgia, Inc.
Chris McGahee
305 Research Drive
Athens, GA 30610
(404) 369-5650
SBA Office: Atlanta
Area of Operation: Barrow, Clarke, Elbert, Greene, Jackson, Madison, Morgan, Oconee, Oglethorpe and Walton Counties

Certified Development Corp. of South Carolina
Vern F. Amick
P.O. Box 21823
Columbia, SC 29221
SBA Office: Columbia
Area of Operation: Statewide

Charleston Citywide Local Development Corp.
Sharon A. Brennan
496 King Street
Charleston, SC 29403-5527
(803) 724-3796
SBA Office: Columbia
Area of Operation: Citywide Charleston

Charlotte Certified Development Corp.
Fred Miller
City Hall — 600 East 4th St., 5th Floor
Charlotte, NC 28202-2859
(704) 336-2114
SBA Office: Charlotte
Area of Operation: Mecklenburg County

REGION IV (continued)

City of Spartanburg Development Corp.
Tim Kuether
145 Broad Street
P.O. Box 1749
Spartanburg, SC 29304
(803) 596-2108
SBA Office: Columbia
Area of Operation: City of Spartanburg

Coastal Area District Dev. Authority, Inc.
Vernon D. Martin
1313 Newcastle Street, 2nd Floor
Brunswick, GA 31520
(912) 261-2500
SBA Office: Atlanta
Area of Operation: Effingham, Chatham, Bryan,
Long, Liberty, McIntosh, Glynn and Camden
but not Savannah City

Commonwealth Small Business Dev. Corp.
Theresa Middleton
2400 Capital Plaza Tower
Frankfort, KY 40601
(502) 564-4554
SBA Office: Louisville
Area of Operation: Statewide

CSRA Local Development Corp.
Randy Griffin
2123 Wrightsboro Road
P. O. Box 2800
Augusta, GA 30904
(404) 737-1823
SBA Office: Atlanta
Area of Operation: Burke, Columbia, Emanuel,
Glascock, Jefferson, Jenkins, Lincoln, McDuffie,
Richmond, Screven, Taliaferro, Warren, Wilkes,
Johnson, Washington and Hancock Counties

Cumberland Area Investment Corp.
Freda Wakefield
1225 Burgess Falls Road
Cookeville, TN 38501
(615) 432-4115
SBA Office: Nashville
Area of Operation: Cannon, Clay, Cumberland,
DeKalb, Fentress, Jackson, Macon, Overton,
Pickett, Putman, Smith, Van Buren Warren and
White Counties

Development Corp. of Middle Georgia
Clayton Black
600 Grand Building
Mulberry Street
Macon, GA 31201
(912) 751-6160
SBA Office: Atlanta
Area of Operation: Bibb, Crawford, Houston,
Jones, Monroe, Peach and Twigg Counties

Economic Development Corp. of Fulton County
Ed Nelson
141 Pryor Street, #5001
Atlanta, GA 30303
(404) 730-8076
SBA Office: Atlanta
Area of Operation. Fulton County

Economic Development Corp. of East Kentucky
Avalon Haight
3000 Louisa Street
Catlettsburg, KY 41129
(606) 739-5191
SBA Office: Louisville
Area of Operation: The FIVCO area consisting
of four rural and one urban area (Boyd,
Elliott, Greenup, Carter & Lawrence Counties)

Financial Services Corp. of Southeast Georgia
Kenneth Hayes
3395 Harris Road
Waycross, GA 31501
(912) 285-6097
SBA Office: Atlanta
Area of Operation: Atkinson, Bacon, Brantley,
Charlton, Clinch, Coffee, Pierce, and Ware Counties

First Tennessee Economic Dev. Corp.
Stephen B. Holt
207 North Boone Street, #800
Johnson City, TN 37604
(615) 928-0224
SBA Office: Nashville
Area of Operation: Carter, Greene, Hancock,
Hawkins, Johnson, Sullivan, Unicoi and
Washington Counties

REGION IV (continued)

Florida Business Development Corp.
Jerry Abraham
6801 Lake Worth Road, Room 209
Lake Worth, FL 33469
(407) 433-0233
SBA Office: Miami
Area of Operation: Dade, Broward, Palm Beach,
St. Lucie, Martin, Indian River, Brevard,
Osceola, Orange, Polk, Pinellas and Manatee

Florida First Capital Finance Corp., Inc.
Danny Warren
Collins Building
107 West Gaines Street, #443
Tallahassee, FL 32399-2000
(904) 487-0466
SBA Office: Jacksonville
Area of Operation: Statewide

**Georgia Mountains Regional Economic
Development Corp.**
Sam Dayton
P. O. Box 1720
Gainesville, GA 30503
(404) 532-6541
SBA Office: Atlanta
Area of Operation: Banks, Dawson, Forsyth,
Franklin, Habersham, Hall, Hart, Lumpkin,
Rabun, Stephens, Towns, Union and White
Counties

Greater Mobile Development Corp.
Teresa Jacobs
One St. Louis Centre, #1001
Mobile, AL: 36602
(205) 661-9051
SBA Office: Birmingham
Area of Operation: County of Mobile

Gulf-Certco, Inc.
La Nelle C. Johnson
218 Downtown Building
P. O. Box 59
Gulfport, MS 39502
(601) 864-5657
SBA Office: Jackson
Area of Operation: Corporate limits of Gulfport
and ten miles outside of city limits

Heart of Georgia Area Development Corp.
Nicky Cabero
501 Oak Street
Eastman, GA 31023
(912) 374-4771
SBA Office: Atlanta
Area of Operation: Bleckley, Dodge, Laurens,
Montgomery, Pulaski, Talfair, Treutlen, Wheeler
and Wilcox Counties

Intercounty Development, Inc.
Jack Kendree
Horry-Georgetown Technical College
Highway 501
P. O. Box 1288
Conway, SC 29526
(803) 347-4604
SBA Office: Columbia
Area of Operation: Georgetown, Williamsburg
and Horry Counties

Jacksonville Economic Development Co., Inc.
James Taylor
Florida Theatre Building, #500
128 E. Forsyth Street
Jacksonville, FL 32206
(904) 630-1458
SBA Office: Jacksonville
Area of Operation: Citywide Jacksonville,
Duval County, FL

Lowcountry Regional Development Corp.
Thomas McTeer
I-95 at Point South
P.O. Box 98
Yemassee, SC 29945
(803) 726-5536
SBA Office: Columbia
Area of Operation: Lowcountry Region,
including Beaufort, Colleton, Hampton and
Jasper Counties

REGION IV (continued)

Lower Savannah Regional Development Corp.
Donna Scotten
2748 Wagner Road — 302 North
P. O. Box 850
Aiken, SC 29801
(803) 649-7985
SBA Office: Columbia
Area of Operation: Aiken, Calhoun, Orangeburg, Bamberg, Barnwell and Allendale Counties

Memphis Area Investment Corp.
Linda Burrell
157 Poplar Avenue, #B150
Memphis, TN 38103
(901) 576-4610
SBA Office: Nashville
Area of Operation: Fayette, Lauderdale,Shelby, and Tipton Counties

Metropolitan Capital Access Corp.
Randall McKenzie
200 Brown & Williamson Tower
401 South 4th Avenue
Louisville, KY 40202-4370
(502) 625-3051
SBA Office: Louisville
Area of Operation: Jefferson County, Kentucky

Mid-Carolina Regional Dev. Authority, Inc.
Roger Sheats
130 Gillespie Street
P. O. Drawer 1510
Fayetteville, NC 28302
(919) 323-4191
SBA Office: Charlotte
Area of Operation: Chatham, Cumberland, Harnett, Lee and Sampson Counties of NC

Mid-Cumberland Area Development Corp.
Douglas A. Remke
Stalman Building, 7th Floor
211 Union Street, #233
Nashville, TN 37201-1502
(615) 862-8855
SBA Office: Nashville
Area of Operation: Cheatham, Davidson, Dickson, Houston, Humphreys, Montgomery, Robertson, Rutherford, Stewart, Sumner, Trousdale, Williamson and Wilson

Mid-East Certified Development Corp., Inc.
Thomas Combs
P. O. Box 1787
Washington, NC 27889
(919) 946-1038
SBA Office: Charlotte
Area of Operation: Counties of Beaufort, Bertie, Martin and Hertford

Middle Flint Area Development Corp.
Bobby Lowe
P. O. Box 6
Ellaville, GA 31806
(912) 937-2561
SBA Office: Atlanta
Area of Operation: Crisp, Dooly, Macon, Marion, Schley, Sumter, Taylor and Webster Counties

Mississippi Business Finance Corp.
Vernon Sith
1201 Walter Sillers Building
P. O. Box 849
Jackson, MS 39205
(601) 359-6710
SBA Office: Jackson
Area of Operation: Statewide

Neuse River Development Authority, Inc.
Robert Quinn
233 O'Marks Square
P. O. Box 1717
New Bern, NC 28563
(919) 638-6724
SBA Office: Charlotte
Area of Operation: Carteret, Craven, Duplin, Greene, Johnston, Jones, Lenoir, Onslow, Pamlico and Wayne Counties

North Central Florida Areawide Dev. Co. Inc.
Ms. Conchi Ossa
2009 NW 67th Place
Gainesville, FL 32606
(904) 336-2199
SBA Office: Jacksonville
Area of Operation: Alachua, Bradford, Columbia, Dixie, Gilchrist, Hamilton, Lafayette, Madison, Suwannee, Taylor and Union Counties

REGION IV (continued)

North Georgia Certified Development Co.
Gloria Hausser
503 West Waugh Street
Dalton, GA 30720
(404) 226-1110
SBA Office: Atlanta
Area of Operation: Cherokee, Fannin, Gilmer,
Murray, Pickens and Whitfield Counties

**Northeast Mississippi Economic Development
Company, Inc.**
Thomas M. Coleman
P. O. Box 600
Booneville, MS 38829
(601) 728-6228
SBA Office: Jackson
Area of Operation: Alcorn, Benton, Marshall,
Prentiss, Tippah and Tishomingo Counties

Northern Kentucky Area Dev. District, Inc.
Morag Adton
16 Spiral Drive
Florence, KY 41022-0688
(606) 283-1885
SBA Office: Louisville
Area of Operation: Kenton, Campbell, Boone,
Carroll, Gallatin, Grant, Owen and Pendleton
Counties

Northwest Piedmont Development Corp., Inc.
Denice Allen
280 South Liberty Street
Winston-Salem, NC 27101
(919) 722-9348
SBA Office: Charlotte
Area of Operation: Davie, Forsyth, Stokes, Surry
and Yadkin Counties

Pee Dee Regional Development Corp.
Phillip C. Goff
U. S. Highway 52
P. O. Box 5719
Florence, SC 29502
(803) 669-3139
SBA Office: Columbia
Area of Operation: Chesterfield, Darlington,
Dillon, Florence, Marion and Marlboro Counties

Pennyrile Area Development District, Inc.
Dan Bozarth
609 Hammond Plaza
Ft. Campbell Blvd.
Hopkinsville, KY 42240
(502) 886-9484
SBA Office: Louisville
Area of Operation: Caldwell, Christian,
Crittenden, Hopkins, Livingston, Lyon, Mulenberg,
Todd and Trigg Counties

**Pitt County Dev. Commission Certified
Development Company**
John D. Chaffee
111 South Washington Street
Greenville, NC 27835-0837
(919) 758-0802
SBA Office: Charlotte
Area of Operation: Pitt County

Purchase Area Development District
Henry Hodges
Highway 45 North
P. O. Box 588
Mayfield, KY 42066
(502) 247-7175
SBA Office: Louisville
Area of Operation: Ballard, Calloway, Carlisle,
Fulton, Graves, Hickman, Marshall and
McCracken Counties

Region C Development Corp., Inc.
Ed Ghent
101 West Court Street
P. O. Box 841
Rutherfordton, NC 28139
(704) 652-3535
SBA Office: Charlotte
Area of Operation: Cleveland, McDowell, Polk,
and Rutherford Counties

Region D Certified Dev. Corp., Inc.
Rick Herndon
Executive Arts Building, Furman Road, #11
P. O. Box 1820
Boone, NC 28607
(704) 265-5437
SBA Office: Charlotte
Area of Operation: Alleghany, Ashe, Avery,
Mitchell, Watauga, Wilkes and Yancy

REGION IV (continued)

Region E Development Corp.
James E. Chandler
317 First Avenue, NW
Hickory, NC 28601
(704) 322-9191
SBA Office: Charlotte
Area of Operation: Counties of Alexander, Burke,
Caldwell and Catawba

Region K Certified Development Co., Inc.
Tommy Marrow
238 Orange Street
P. O. Box 709
Henderson, NC 27536
(919) 492-2538
SBA Office: Charlotte
Area of Operation: Granville, Franklin, Person,
Vance and Warren Counties

Santee-Lynches Regional Development Corp.
Dave Mueller
115 N. Harvin Street, 4th Floor
P. O. Box 1837
Sumter, SC 29150
(803) 775-7381
SBA Office: Columbia
Area of Operation: Clarendon, Kershaw, Lee
and Sumter Counties

Savannah Certified Development Corp.
Tony O'Reilly
31 W. Congress Street, #100
Savannah, GA 31401
(912) 232-4700
SBA Office: Atlanta
Area of Operation: Chatham County

Self-Help Ventures, Inc.
Jim Overton
409 E. Chapel Hill Street
Durham, NC 27701
(919) 683-3016
SBA Office: Charlotte
Area of Operation: Statewide

Smokey Mountain Development Corp.
Thomas Fouts
100 Industrial Park Drive
Waynesville, NC 28786
(704) 452-1967
SBA Office: Charlotte
Area of Operation: Madison, Haywood, Graham,
Cherokee, Clay, Macon, Jackson, Transylvania,
Henderson and Swain Counties

South Central Tennessee Business Dev. Corp.
Douglas Williams
815 South Main Street
P. O. Box 1346
Columbia, TN 38402
(615) 381-2041
SBA Office: Nashville
Area of Operation: Bedford, Coffee, Franklin,
Giles, Hickman, Lawrence, Lewis, Lincoln,
Marshall, Maury, Moore, Perry and Wayne
Counties

South Georgia Area Development Corp.
Don Chancey
327 W. Savannah Avenue
P. O. Box 1223
Valdosta, GA 31601
(912) 333-5277
SBA Office: Atlanta
Area of Operation: Bell Hill, Berrien, Brooks,
Cook, Echols, Irwin, Lanier, Lowndes,
Tift and Turner Counties

Southeast Local Development Corp.
Tom McAutey
25 Cherokee Blvd.
P.O. Box 4757
Chattanooga, TN 37405-0757
(615) 266-5781
SBA Office: Nashville
Area of Operation: 60 mile radius from
Hamilton County Courthouse, TN

Southern Development Council
James B. Allen, Jr.
401 Adams Avenue, #680
Montgomery, AL 36130
(205) 264-5441
SBA Office: Birmingham
Area of Operation: Statewide

REGION IV (continued)

Southern Mississippi Economic Dev. Co., Inc.
C.J. Tennant
1020 32nd Avenue
Gulfport, MS 39501
(601) 868-2312
SBA Office: Jackson
Area of Operation: Covington, Forrest, George, Hancock, Harrison, Jackson, Jefferson Davis, Jones, Lamar, Marion, Pearl Riv, Perry, Stone and Wayne

Sowega Economic Development Corp.
Roborett Murrah, Jr.
30 E. Broad Street
P. O. Box 346
Camilla, GA 31730
(912) 336-5617
SBA Office: Atlanta
Area of Operation: Baker, Calhoun, Colquitt, Decatur, Dougherty, Early, Grady, Lee, Miller, Mitchell, Seminole, Terrell, Thomas and Worth Counties

St. Petersburg Certified Dev. Co., Inc.
Timothy McDowell
P. O. Box 2842
St. Petersburg, FL 33731
(813) 892-5108
SBA Office: Miami
Area of Operation: Citywide St. Petersburg

Tampa-Bay Economic Development Corp.
George Unanue
306 E. Jackson Street, 7th Floor
Tampa, FL 33601-3330
(813) 223-2311
SBA Office: Miami
Area of Operation: Hillsborough County

Three Rivers Local Development Co., Inc.
Vernon R. Kelley, III
P. O. Drawer B
Pontotoc, MS 38863
(601) 489-2435
SBA Office: Jackson
Area of Operation: 41 Counties located in northern half of Mississippi

Troup County Local Development Corp.
Alesia Nixon
900 Dallis Street
P. O. Box 1107
LaGrange, GA 30241
(404) 884-4605
SBA Office: Atlanta
Area of Operation: Troup County

United Local Development Corp.
John Holliday
c/o Bank of Mississippi
One MS Plaza
P. O. Box 789
Tupelo, MS 38801
(601) 842-7140
SBA Office: Jackson
Area of Operation: Alcorn, Lee, Prentiss, Desoto, Itawamba, Monroe, Pontotoc, Union, Chichasaw and Calhoun Counties

Uptown Columbus, Inc.
Shelley Montgomery
10001 Front Avenue
P.O. Box 1237
Columbus, GA 31902
(706) 571-6057
SBA Office: Atlanta
Area of Operation: City of Columbus

Urban County Community Dev. Corp.
President
200 East Main Street
Lexington, KY 40507
(606) 258-3100
SBA Office: Louisville
Area of Operation: Fayette County

Wilmington Industrial Development, Inc.
Wayne Zeigler
508 Market Street
P. O. Box 1698
Wilmington, NC 28401
(919) 763-8414
SBA Office: Charlotte
Area of Operation: City of Wilmington and Counties of New Hanover, Pender and Brunswick

REGION V (IL, IN, MI, MN, OH, & WI)

Ashtabula County 503 Corp.
Duane Feher
25 West Jefferson Street
Jefferson, OH 44047
(216) 570-2040
SBA Office: Cleveland
Area of Operation: County of Ashtabula

Brown County Development Corp.
Dennis Sreneski
835 Potts Avenue
Green Bay, WI 54304
(414) 499-6444
SBA Office: Madison
Area of Operation: Brown County

Business Development Corp. of South Bend, Mishawaka, St. Joseph County, Indiana
Donald Inks
City of South Bend, Dept. of Development
1200 County-City Building
South Bend, IN 46601
(219) 284-9278
SBA Office: Indianapolis
Area of Operation: St. Joseph County

CANDO City-Wide Development Corp.
Ted Wysocki
343 S. Dearborn Street, #910
Chicago, IL 60604-3808
(312) 939-7171
SBA Office: Chicago
Area of Operation: City of Chicago

Cascade Certified Development Corp.
Deborah Victory
One Cascade Plaza, 8th Floor
Akron, OH 44308
(216) 376-5550
SBA Office: Cleveland
Area of Operation: Ashland, Holmes, Portage, Medina, Summit and Wayne Counties

Central Minnesota Development Co.
Kristin Wood
P.O. Box 33346
Coon Rapids, MN 55433
(612) 755-2304
SBA Office: Minneapolis
Area of Operation: City of Coon Rapids, County of Anoka

1 Step, Inc.
Dave Scaife
2415 14th Avenue South
Escanaba, MI 49829
(906) 786-9234
SBA Office: Detroit
Area of Operation: Alger, Schoolcraft, Marquette, Delta, Dickinson and Menominee Counties

Certified Development Company of Butler County, Inc.
Daniel E. Walsh
130 High Street
Hamilton, OH 45011
(513) 887-3000
SBA Office: Columbus
Area of Operation: Butler County

Certified Dev. Corp. of Warren County, Inc.
Bernard F. Eichholz
22 East 5th Street
Franklyn, OH 45005
(513) 748-1041
SBA Office: Columbus
Area of Operation: Warren County, OH

Certified Economic Development Foundation
Charles Krupp
300 Monroe, NW
Grand Rapids, MI 49503
(616) 456-3167
SBA Office: Detroit
Area of Operation: Kent County

Cincinnatti Local Development Co.
Gloria Simmons
805 Central Avenue, 7th Floor, #710
Cincinnati, OH 45202
(513) 352-1958
Office: Columbus
Area of Operation: Citywide Cincinnati

REGION V (continued)

Citywide Small Business Development Corp.
Robert Murray, Jr.
8 North Main Street
Dayton, OH 45402-1916
(513) 226-0457
SBA Office: Columbus
Area of Operation: City of Dayton & environs

Clark County Development Corp.
John M. Harris
300 East Auburn Avenue
Springfield, OH 45505
(513) 322-8685
SBA Office: Columbus
Area of Operation: Clark County

Cleveland Area Dev. Finance Corp.
Gerald H. Meyer
200 Tower City Center
50 Public Square
Cleveland, OH 44113-2291
(216) 241-1166
SBA Office: Cleveland
Area of Operation: Cuyahoga, Lake, Geauga,
Lorain, Medina, Portage and Summit Counties

Cleveland Citywide Development Corp.
George V. Voinovich
601 Lakeside, Room 210
Cleveland, OH 44114
(216) 664-2406
SBA Office: Cleveland
Area of Operation: City of Cleveland

Columbus Countywide Development Corp.
Mark Barbash
941 Chatham Lane, #207
Columbus, OH 43221
(614) 645-6171
SBA Office: Columbus
Area of Operation: Delaware, Fairfield, Fayette,
Franklin, Licking, Madison, Perry, Pickaway
and Union Counties

Community Dev. Corp. of Fort Wayne
Linda Doeden
Dept. of Economic Development
840 City-County Building
Fort Wayne, IN 46802
(219) 427-1127
SBA Office: Indianapolis
Area of Operation: Allen County

County Development Corp.
Marlene J. Flagel
1600 Miami Valley Tower
40 West 4th Street
Dayton, OH 45402
(513) 225-6328
SBA Office: Columbus
Area of Operation: Darke, Miami, Montgomery
and Preble Counties

Detroit Economic Growth Dev. Co. Corp.
Joe Vassallo
John W. Maden Bldg., #1500
151 West Jefferson
Detroit, MI 48226
(313) 963-2940
SBA Office: Detroit
Area of Operation: City of Detroit

East Central Michigan Development Corp.
Harold A. Steinke
3535 State Street
Saginaw, MI 48602
(571) 797-0800
SBA Office: Detroit
Area of Operation: Arenac, Bay, Clare, Gladwin,
Gratiot, Huron, Iosco, Isabella, Midland,
Ogemaw and Roscommon

Eau Claire County Economic Dev. Corp.
Brenda Blanchard
505 Dewey Street South, #101
Eau Claire, WI 54701-3707
(715) 834-0070
SBA Office: Madison
Area of Operation: Eau Claire County and the City
of Eau Claire

REGION V (continued)

Forward Development Corp.
Mark Sullivan
1101 Beach Street
Flint, MI 48502
(313) 257-3010
SBA Office: Detroit
Area of Operation: Genesee County

Greater Gratiot Development, Inc.
Donald C. Schurr
136 South Main
Ithaca, MI 48847
(517) 875-2083
SBA Office: Detroit
Area of Operation: Gratiot County

Greater Metropolitan Chicago Development
Howard Mullin
2725 Alison Street Road
Wilmette, IL 60091-2101
(708) 251-2756
SBA Office: Chicago
Area of Operation: Cook, Lake, McHenry, Kane, DuPage, Kendall, Will and Grundy Counties

Greater Muskegon Industrial Fund, Inc.
Ronald Keur
349 West Webster Avenue
Muskegon, MI 49440
(616) 726-4848
SBA Office: Detroit
Area of Operation: Muskegon County

Greater North-Pulaski Local Dev. Corp
James S. Lemonides
4054 West North Avenue
Chicago, IL 60639
(312) 384-7074
SBA Office: Chicago
Area of Operation: Chicago Ave. S., Belmont Ave. N., Western Ave. E. and Cicero Ave. W.

Greater Northwest Regional Dev. Corp. (The)
Richard J. Beldin
2200 Dendrincos Drive
Traverse City, MI 49684
(616) 929-5010
SBA Office: Detroit
Area of Operation: Antrim, Benzie, Clarlevoix, Emmet, Grand Traverse, Kalkaska, Leelanau, Manistee, Missaukee and Wexford Counties

Growth Finance Corp.
Lora Swenson
West Building 115
330 Oak Street
Big Rapids, MI 49307
SBA Office: Columbus
Area of Operation: Allegan, Ionia, Kent, Lake, Mason, Mecosta, Montcalm, Newaygo and Osceola Counties

Hamilton County Development Co., Inc.
David K. Main
1776 Mentor Avenue
Cincinnati, OH 45212
(513) 632-8292
Area of Operation: Hamilton County, OH (except for the City of Cincinnati)

Hammond Development Corp.
Mark McLaughlin
Office of Economic Development
649 Conkey Street
Hammond, IN 46324
(219) 853-6399
SBA Office: Indianapolis
Area of Operation: City of Hammond

Illinois Business Financial Services
Floyd Barlow, Jr.
331 Fulton Street, #405
Peoria, IL 61602
(309) 674-7437
SBA Office: Springfield
Area of Operation: Citywide in Peoria, Counties of Peoria, Tazewell and Woodford

REGION V (continued)

Illinois Small Business Growth Corp.
Douglas Kinley
403 E. Adams Street
Springfield, IL 62701
(217) 522-2772
SBA Office: Springfield
Area of Operation: Statewide

Indiana Statewide Certified Development Corp.
Jean Wojtowicz
8440 Woodfield Crossing Blvd., #315
Indianapolis, IN 46240-4300
(317) 469-6166
SBA Office: Indianapolis
Area of Operation: Statewide

Jackson Local Development Co. (The)
Duane Miller
City Hall, 8th Floor
161 West Michigan
Jackson, MI 49201
(517) 788-4187
SBA Office: Detroit
Area of Operation: Jackson County

Kenosha Area Development Corp.
Cecilia Lucas
5455 Sheridan Road, #101
Kenosha, WI 53140
(414) 654-7134
SBA Office: Madison
Area of Operation: Countywide

Lake County Economic Development Corp.
Margo Nelson
18 North County Street
Waukegan, IL 60085
(708) 360-6350
SBA Office: Chicago
Area of Operation: Lake County, IL

Lake County Small Business Assistance Corp.
Lawrence Kramer
Camelot Building
Lakeland Community College
Mentor, OH 44060
(216) 951-1290
SBA Office: Cleveland
Area of Operation: Lake County

Lapeer Development Corp.
Patricia Crawford-Lucas
449 McCormick Drive
Lapeer, MI 48446
(313) 667-0080
SBA Office: Detroit
Area of Operation: Lapeer County

Lucas County Improvement Corp.
James Holzemer
218 Huron Street
Toledo, OH 43404
(419) 245-4500
SBA Office: Cleveland
Area of Operation: Lucas County

Madison Development Corp.
David Scholtens
550 W. Washington Avenue
Madison, WI 53703
(608) 256-2799
SBA Office: Madison
Area of Operation: Dane County

Mahoning Valley Economic Development Corp.
Joe Burkey
4319 Belmont Avenue
Youngstown, OH 44505-1005
(216) 759-3668
SBA Office: Cleveland
Area of Operation: Mahoning, Columbiana and
Trumbull Counties

Mentor Economic Assistance Corp.
Elaine Lane
8500 Civic Center Blvd.,
Mentor, OH 44060
(216) 255-1100
SBA Office: Cleveland
Area of Operation: City of Mentor

Metropolitan Milwaukee Enterprise Corp.
Evelyn Beale
809 North Broadway
P. O. Box 324
Milwaukee, WI 53201
(414) 223-5812
SBA Office: Madison
Area of Operation: Milwaukee, Ozaukee,
Washington and Waukesha Counties

REGION V (continued)

Metropolitan Growth & Dev. Corp
Majorie Whittemore
Wayne County Building
600 Randolph, Room 323
Detroit, MI 48152
(313) 224-0750
SBA Office: Detroit
Area of Operation: Wayne County

Metro Small Business Assistance Corp.
Deborah Lutz
306 Civic Center Complex
1 NW Martin Luther King Blvd.
Evansville, IN 47708
(812) 426-5857
SBA Office: Indianapolis
Area of Operation: Posey, Gibson and
Vanderburgh Counties

Michigan Certified Development Corp.
Larry Schrauben
Law Building, 3rd Floor
525 W. Ottawa St.
Lansing, MI 48933
(517) 373-6378
SBA Office: Detroit
Area of Operation: Statewide

Mid City Pioneer Corp.
Jane Eaton
320 N. Alabama Street, #250
Indianapolis, IN 46204
(317) 236-6241
SBA Office: Indianapolis
Area of Operation: Boone, Hancock,
Hendricks, Johnson, Marion,Morgan
and Shelby Counties

Minneapolis Economic Development Corp.
Gary Whepley
105 5th Avenue South, #600
Minneapolis, MN 55401
(612) 673-5176
SBA Office: Minneapolis
Area of Operation: Hennepin County

Minnesota Business Finance, Inc.
Paul Moe
500 Metro Square
121 7th Place East
St. Paul, MN 55101
(612) 370-0231
SBA Office: Minneapolis
Area of Operation: Statewide

Northeast Michigan Development Corp.
Janis Kellogg
123 West Main Street
P. O. Box 457
Gaylord, MI 49735
(517) 732-3551
SBA Office: Detroit
Area of Operation: Alcona, Alpena, Cheboygan,
Crawford, Montmorency, Oscoda, Otsego and
Presque Isle Counties

Northwest Indiana Business Development Corp.
Arthur Pena
4525 Indianapolis Blvd.
East Chicago, IL 46312
(219) 398-1600
SBA Office: Indianapolis
Area of Operation: Lake County

Northwest Indiana Business Development Corp.
Dennis Henson
6100 Southport Road
Portage, IN 46368
(219) 763-6303
SBA Office: Indianapolis
Area of Operation: Lake, LaPorte, Newton, Porter,
Pulaski and Storke Counties

Oakland County Local Development Co.
Cheryl Gault
1200 North Telegraph Road
Pontiac, MI 48341
(313) 858-0732
SBA Office: Detroit
Area of Operation: Oakland County

REGION V (continued)

Ohio Statewide Development Corp.
Bruce Lagner
30 East Broad Street
P.O. Box 1001
Columbus, OBH 43266-0101
(614) 466-5043
SBA Office: Columbus
Area of Operation: Statewide

Ottawa County Development Co., Inc.
Louis Hallacy
272 East 8th Street
P.O. Box 1888
Holland, MI 49422-1888
(616) 392-2389
SBA Office: Detroit
Area of Operation: Ottawa County

Prairieland Economic Development Corp.
Randy Jorgenson
2524 Broadway Avenue
P. O. Box 265
Slayton, MN 56172
(507) 836-8549
SBA Office: Minneapolis
Area of Operation: Cottonwood, Jackson,
Lincoln, Lyon, Murray, Nobles, Pipestone,
Redwood and Rock Counties

Racine County Business Development Corp.
Leonard Ziolkowski
4701 Washington Avenue, #215
Racine, WI 53406
(414) 638-0234
SBA Office: Madison
Area of Operation: Racine County

Red Cedar Certified Development Corp.
Roger Hamlin
201 UP & LA Building
East Lansing, MI 48826-1221
(517) 337-2853
SBA Office: Detroit
Area of Operation: East Lansing and Meridian
Township

Region Nine Development Corp.
Gina Feehan
410 S. Fifth Street
P. O. Box 3367
Mankato, MN 56001
(507) 387-5643
SBA Office: Minneapolis
Area of Operation: Blue Earth, Brown, Faribault,
Le Sueur, Martin, Nicollet, Sibley, Waseca and
Watonwan Counties

Rockford Local Development Corp.
Sanders W. Howse, Jr.
515 N. Court Street
Rockford, IL 61103
(815) 987-8127
SBA Office: Chicago
Area of Operation: City of Rockford

Saint Paul/Metro East Development Corp.
Connie Hilis
25 West Fourth Street
St. Paul, MN 55102
(612) 228-3306
SBA Office: Minneapolis
Area of Operation: Counties of Dakota, Ramsey
and Washington

The Small Business Finance Alliance
Debbie Groeteka
203 West Main Street
Collinsville, IL 62234
(618) 334-4080
SBA Office: Springfield
Area of Operation: Bond, Clinton, Madison,
Monroe, St. Clair, Randolph and Washington
Counties

Somercor 504, Inc.
Karen Lennon
Two East 8th Street
Chicago, IL 60605
(312) 360-3163
SBA Office: Chicago
Area of Operation: Cook, DuPage, Lake, Kane,
McHenry and Will Counties

REGION V (continued):

South Central IL Regional Planning and Development Commission
Fred Walker
120 DelMar Avenue, #A
Salem, IL 62881
(618) 548-4234
SBA Office: Springfield
Area of Operation: Counties of Effingham, Fayette and Marion; also Cities of Centralia and Wamac

South Towns Business Growth Corp.
Chris Cochrane
Governors State University
University Park, IL 60466
(708) 534-4924
SBA Office: Chicago
Area of Operation: South Suburban Cook County and Eastern Will County

Southeastern Minnesota 504 Development, Inc.
Dwayne Lee
220 S. Broadway, #100
Rochester, MN 55904
(507) 288-6442
SBA Office: Minneapolis
Area of Operation: Counties of Dodge, Fillmore, Freeborn, Goodhue, Houston, Mower, Olmstead, Rice, Wabasha, Winona and City of Blooming Prairie

Stark Development Board Finance Corp.
Roland L. Theriault
800 Savannah Avenue, NE
Canton, OH 44704
(216) 453-5900
SBA Office: Cleveland
Area of Operation: Stark County

Twin Cities-Metro Certified Development Co.
Robert Heck
Four Seasons Professional Building
4200 Lancaster Lane, #1200
Plymouth, MN 55441
(612) 551-1825
SBA Office: Minneapolis
Area of Operation: Carver, Dakota, Hennepin Ramsey, Scott and Washington Counties

Warren Redevelopment and Planning Corp.
Janice E. Scott
106 E. Market Street, #705
Warren, OH 44481-1103
(216) 841-2566
SBA Office: Cleveland
Area of Operation: City of Warren and Trumbull County

Western Wisconsin Development Corp.
Bob Ahlin
100 Digital Drive
Turtle Lake, WI 54009
(415) 986-4310
SBA Office: Madison
Area of Operation: Barron, Bayfield, Burnett, Chippewa, Dunne, Polk, Rusk, St. Croix, Sawyer, and Washburn Counties

Wisconsin Business Dev. Finance Corp.
John Giegel
P. O. Box 2717
Madison, WI 53701-2717
(608) 258-8830
SBA Office: Madison
Area of Operation: Statewide

Xenia-Greene County Small Business Dev. Co.
Joy L. Wright
61 Greene Street
Xenia, OH 45385
(513) 372-0444
SBA Office: Columbus
Area of Operation: Greene County

REGION VI (AR, LA, NM, OK & TX)

Ark-La-Tex Investment & Development Corp.
M. D. LeCompte
P. O. Box 37005
Shreveport, LA 71133
(318) 632-2086
SBA Office: New Orleans
Area of Operation: Parishes of Bienville,
Bossier, Caddo, Clairborne, Desoto, Lincoln,
Natchitoches, Red River, Sabine and Webster

Ark-Tex Regional Development Co., Inc.
Stephen O. Harris
P. O. Box 1967
Texarkana, TX 75504-1967
(903) 832-8636
SBA Office: Dallas
Area of Operation: Bowie, Cass, Delta, Franklin,
Hopkins, Red River, Lamar, Morris and Titus
Counties in Texas; also Miller County in Arkansas

Arkansas Certified Development Corp.
Sam Walls
221 West Second Street, #800
Little Rock, AR 72116
(501) 374-8841
SBA Office: Little Rock
Area of Operation: Statewide

Big Country Development Corp.
Rick Womble
1025 East North 10th Street
P. O. Box 3195
Abilene, TX 79604
(915) 672-8544
SBA Office: Lubbock
Area of Operation: Brown, Callahan, Coleman,
Comanche, Eastland, Fisher, Haskell, Jones, Kent,
Know, Mitchell, Nolan, Runnels, Scurry,
Shackelford, Stephens, Stonewall, Taylor
and Throckmortan Counties

Brenham Industrial Foundation, Inc.
Richard O'Malley
314 S. Austin
Brenham, TX 77833
(409) 836-8927
SBA Office: Houston
Area of Operation: City of Brenham and 2 miles
beyond the city limits

Brownsville Local Development Co., Inc.
Ken Medders
P. O. Box 911
Brownsville, TX 78520
(512) 548-6157
SBA Office: Lower Rio Grande Valley
Area of Operation: Citywide Brownsville
and its environs

Bryan-College State Certified Dev. Co.
Dennis H. Goehring
2706 Finfeather
Bryan, TX 77801
SBA Office: Houston
Area of Operation: Brazos County

Capital Certified Development Co.
Colleen Rowland
410 East Fifth Street
Austin, TX 78701
Lubbock, TX 79452-3730
(512) 320-9649
SBA Office: San Antonio
Area of Operation: Statewide

Caprock Local Development Company
Tim Pierce
1328 58th St.
P. O. Box 3730
Lubbock, TX 79452-3730
(806) 762-8721
SBA Office: Lubbock
Area of Operation: Baily, Cochran, Crosby,
Dickens, Floyd, Garza, Hale, Hockley, King, Lamb,
Lubbock, Lynn, Motley, Terry and Yoakum

Cen-Tex Certified Development Corp.
Randy Cosson
3700 Lake Austin Blvd.
Austin, TX 78703
(512) 469-6853
SBA Office: San Antonio
Area of Operation: 43 Central Texas Counties

REGION VI (continued)

Central Arkansas Certified Development Corp.
Charles Cummings
112 NE Front Street
P. O. Box 187
Lonoke, AR 72086
(501) 374-6976
SBA Office: Little Rock
Area of Operation: Saline, Faulkner, Pulaski, Lonoke, Prairie and Monroe Counties

Central Texas Certified Development Co.
Bruce Gaines
P.O. Box 154118
Waco, TX 76715
(817) 799-0259
SBA Office: Dallas
Area of Operation: Bell, Bosque, Corywell, Falls, Freestone, Hamilton, Hill, Limestone, McLennan, Milam, Navarro, Somervell and Robertson Counties

Dallas Business Finance Corp.
James R. Reid
1501 Beaumont
Dallas, TX 75215
(214) 428-7332
SBA Office: Dallas
Area of Operation: City of Dallas

Deep East Texas Regional Certified Dev. Corp.
Russell Phillips
274 East Larmor Street
Jasper, TX 75951
(409) 384-5704
SBA Office: Houston
Area of Operation: Angelina, Houston, Jasper, Nacogdoches, Newton, Polk, Sabine, San Augustine, San Jacinto, Shelby, Trinity and Tyler

East Arkansas Planning & Dev. District
Dolores Harrelson
1801 Stadium Blvd.
P. O. Box 1403
Jonesboro, AR 72403
(501) 932-3957
SBA Office: Little Rock
Area of Operation: Clay, Craighead, Crittenden, Cross, Greene, Lawrence, Lee, Mississippi, Phillips, Poinsette, Randolph & St. Francis Counties

East Texas Regional Development Co., Inc.
Wayne Smith
3800 Stone Road
Kilgore, TX 75662
(214) 984-8641
SBA Office: Dallas
Area of Operation: Anderson, Camp, Cherokee, Gregg, Harrison, Henderson, Marion, Panola, Rains, Rusk, Smith, Upshur, Van Zandt and Wood Counties

Enhancement Land Certified Development Co.
Peter Froning
625 Silver SW, #315
Albuquerque, NM 87102
(505) 843-9232
SBA Office: Albuquerque
Area of Operation: Statewide

Fort Worth Economic Development Corp.
Claude Bailey
410 W. 4th Street
Fort Worth, TX 76102-3705
(817) 336-6420
SBA Office: Dallas
Area of Operation: City of Fort Worth; Erath, Denton, Ellis, Hood, Kaufman, Palo Pinto, Dallas, Tarrant, Wise, Parker and Johnson Counties — excluding the cities of Dallas and Garland

Garland Local Development Corp., Inc.
Harry Swanson
2734 W. Kingsley Road, #J4
Garland, TX 75041
(214) 271-9993
SBA Office: Dallas
Area of Operation: Cities of Garland, Mesquite, Plano and Richardson; and an area of Northeast Dallas City

Houston-Galveston Area Local Dev. Corp.
Richard A. Wiltz
3555 Timmons Lane, #500
Houston, TX 77027
SBA Office: Houston
Area of Operation: Austin, Brazoria, Chambers, Colorado, Fort Bend, Galveston, Harris, Liberty, Matagorda, Montgomery, Walker, Waller and Wharton Counties

REGION VI (continued)

JEDCO Development Corp.
M. Carol Ward
3330 N. Causeway Blvd., #430
Matairie, LA 70002
(504) 830-4860
SBA Office: New Orleans
Area of Operation: Jefferson Parish

Kisatchie-Delta Reg. Planning & Dev. Dist., Inc.
Lawrence Jeansonne
5212 Rue Verdun Street
P. O. Box 12248
Alexandria, LA 71315-2248
(318) 487-5454
SBA Office: New Orleans
Area of Operation: Parishes of Avoyelles,
Catahoula, Concordia, Grant, La Salle, Rapides,
Vernon and Winn

Louisiana Capital Certified Dev. Co. Inc.
Al Hodge
2014 W. Pinhook Road, #100
P.O. Box 3802
Lafayette, LA 70502
(318) 234-2977
SBA Office: New Orleans
Area of Operation: Lafayette Parish

Lower Rio Grande Valley Cert. Dev. Corp. (The)
Kenneth N. Jones, Jr.
4900 N. 23rd Street
McAllen, TX 78504
(512) 682-1109
SBA Office: Lower Rio Grande Valley
Area of Operation: Cameron, Hidalgo and
Willacy Counties

Metro Area Development Corp.
Richard L. Hess
708 NE 42nd Street
Oklahoma City, OK 73105
(405) 424-5181
SBA Office: Oklahoma City
Area of Operation: Canadian, Cleveland and
Oklahoma Counties

**New Orleans Regional Business
Development Loan Corp.**
Kevin E. Williams
301 Camp Street, #210
New Orleans, LA 70130
(504) 524-6172
SBA Office: New Orleans
Area of Operation: Parishes of Assumption,
Jefferson, Lafourche, Orleans, Plaquemines,
St. Bernard, St. Charles, St. James, St. John
the Baptist, St. Tammany, Tangipahoe,
Terrebonne and Washington

North Texas Certified Development Corp.
Lewis Donaghey
106 N. Hamilton Street, Room 101- A
Trenton, TX 75490
(708) 989-2720
SBA Office: Dallas
Area of Operation: Grayson, Ranes, Fannin,
Hunt, Collin, Cooke and Rockwell Counties

North Texas Regional Development Corp.
Dennis Wilde
The Galaxy Center, #200
4309 Jacksboro Highway
Wichita Falls, TX 76307-5144
(817) 322-5281
SBA Office: Dallas
Area of Operation: Archer, Baylor, Childress,
Clay, Cottle, Ford, Hardeman, Jack, Mantague,
Wichita, Wilbarger and Young Counties

REGION VI (continued)

Northeast Louisiana Industries, Inc.
Gerald E. McDonald
Route 3, Box 182
Monroe, LA 71203
(318) 345-0878
SBA Office: New Orleans
Area of Operation: Ouachita, Union,
Morehouse, Richland, Caldwell, Jackson,
Franklin, Tensas, East Carroll, West
Carroll and Madison Parishes

Northwest Arkansas Certified Dev. Company
Donald Raney
1313 Highway 62-65
P.O. Box 190
Harrison, AR 72601
(501) 741-8009
SBA Office: Little Rock
Area of Operation: Benton, Carroll, Boone,
Baxter, Marion, Washington, Madison, Newton
and Searcy Counties

Rural Enterprises, Inc.
Sherry Harlin
422 Cessna Street
Durant, OK 74702
(405) 924-5094
SBA Office: Oklahoma City
Area of Operation: Atoka, Bryan, Carter,
Choctaw, Coal, Creek, Garvin, Love, Haskell,
Hughes, Johnston, Latimer, LeFlore, McCurtain,
Logan, Lincoln, Marshall, Murray, Payne,
Pottawatomie, Okfuskee, Pittsburg, Pontotoc,
Pushmataha and Seminole

S-Tex Asset Financing Corp.
Bryan Beverly
539 N. Carancahua
Corpus Christi, TX 78401
(512) 880-6204
SBA Office: Houston
Area of Operation: The 44 South Texas Counties
served by Central Power and Light Company

San Antonio Local Development Corp.
Mike Mendoza
P. O. Box 830505
San Antonio, TX 78283-0505
(512) 299-8080
SBA Office: San Antonio
Area of Operation: Gillespie, Kerr, Kendall,
Comal, Guadalupe, Bandera, Bexar, Medina,
Wilson, Karnes, Atascosa and Frio Counties

Small Business Capital Corp.
Peggy Smith
616 South Boston
Tulsa, OK 74119
(918) 585-1201
SBA Office: Oklahoma City
Area of Operation: Osage, Tulsa, Creek and
Washington Counties

Southeast Texas Economic Dev. Corp.
James M. Stokes
450 Bowie
P. O. Box 3150
Beaumont, TX 77704
(409) 838-6581
SBA Office: Houston
Area of Operation: Jefferson and Orange Counties

Southwest Arkansas Reg.Development Corp.
Marvin Flincher
600 Bessie Street
P. O. Box 767
Magnolia, AR 71753
(501) 234-4039
SBA Office: Little Rock
Area of Operation: Calhoun, Columbia, Dallas,
Hempstead, Howard, Lafayette, Little River,
Miller, Nevada, Quachita, Seiver and Union
Counties

SWODA Development Corp.
Gary Gorshing
P. O. Box 562
Burns Flat, OK 73624
(405) 562-4886
SBA Office: Oklahoma City
Area of Operation: Beckham, Custer, Greer,
Harmon, Jackson, Kiowa, Roger Mills and
Washita Counties

REGION VI (continued)

Texas Certified Development Co., Inc.
Ernest Perales
909 Northeast Loop 410, #300
San Antonio, TX 78209
(512) 841-5668
SBA Office: San Antonio
Area of Operation: Area under jurisdiction
of SBA's San Antonio and Harlingen District
Offices, the Corpus Christi Branch Office
and Burleson County (under the jurisdiction
of the SBA's Houston District Office)

Texas Panhandle Regional Dev. Corp.
Perna Strickland
P.O. Box 9257
Amarillo, TX 79105-9257
(806) 372-3381
SBA Office: Lubbock
Castro, Collingsworth, Deaf Smith, Dallam,
Donley, Gray, Hall, Hansford, Hutchinson,
Hartley, Hemphill, Lipscomb, Moore, Ochiltree,
Randall, Oldham, Parmer, Potter, Roberts,
Sherman, Swisher and Wheeler

Tulsa Economic Development Corp.
Joyce Ann Topper
130 N. Greenwood
Tulsa, OK 74120
(918) 585-8332
SBA Office: Oklahoma City
Area of Operation: Citywide Tulsa

Upper Rio Grande Development Corp.
Louie Alfaro
1014 N. Stanton Street, #100
El Paso, TX 79902-4109
(915) 533-1875
SBA Office: El Paso
Area of Operation: El Paso, Hudspeth, Culberson,
Jeff Davis, Presidio and Brewster Counties

Verd-Ark-Ca Development Corp.
L. V. Watkins
600 Emporia, #A
Muskogee, OK 74401-6043
(918) 683-4634
SBA Office: Oklahoma City
Area of Operation: Adair, Cherokee, McIntosh,
Muskogee, Okmulgee, Wagoner, Rogers, Mayes,
Haskell, Sequoyah, Nowata, Le Flore, Craig,
Washington, Ottawa, Delaware and Tulsa

**West Central Arkansas Planning and
Development District, Inc.**
Patricia Heusel
ABT Towers, #502
P. O. Box 1558
Hot Springs, AR 71901
(501) 624-1036
SBA Office: Little Rock
Area of Operation: Johnson, Pope, Conway,
Yell, Perry, Montgomery, Garland, Hot
Springs, Pike and Clark Counties

**Western Arkansas Planning and Development
District, Inc.**
John Guthrie
1109 South 16th Street
P. O. Box 2067
Fort Smith, AR 72901
(501) 785-2651
SBA Office: Little Rock
Area of Operation: Crawford, Franklin,
Sebastian, Logan, Scott and Polk Counties

White River Planning & Dev. District, Inc.
Van C. Thomas
Highway 25 North
P. O. Box 2396
Batesville, AR 72501
(501) 793-5233
SBA Office: Little Rock
Area of Operation: Cleburne, Fulton,
Independence, Izard, Jackson, Sharp, Stone,
Van Buren, White and Woodruff Counties

REGION VII (IA, IL, KS, MO & NE)

Avenue Area Inc.
Thomas M. Overby
753 State Avenue, #106
Kansas City, KS 66101
(913) 371-0065
SBA Office: Kansas City
Area of Operation: Downtown Kansas City, KS;
Wyandotte County, KS

Bi-State Business Finance Corp.
Gary Vallem
1504 Third Avenue
Rock Island, IL 61201
(309) 793-1181
SBA Office: Cedar Rapids
Area of Operation: Scott and Muscatine Counties
in IA; Henry, Mercer and Rock Island Counties
in IL

Big Lakes Certified Development Company
Betty Nelson
431 Houston Street
Manhattan, KS 66502-6136
(913) 776-0417
SBA Office: Wichita
Area of Operation: Clay, Geary, Marshall,
Pottawatomie and Riley Counties

Black Hawk County Econ. Dev. Committee, Inc.
Don Wade
8 West Fourth Street
Waterloo, IA 50701
(319) 232-1156
SBA Office: Cedar Rapids
Area of Operation: Blackhawk County

Business Finance Corp. of St. Louis County
Richard Palank
121 South Merramec, #412
St. Louis, MO 63105
(314) 889-7663
SBA Office: St. Louis
Area of Operation: St. Louis County

Central Ozarks Development, Inc.
James R. Dickinson
c/o Meramec Regional Planning Committee
101 West Tenth Street
Rolla, MO 65401
(314) 346-5692
SBA Office: St. Louis
Area of Operation:Camden, Laclede, Pulaski,
Pulaski, Miller and Morgan Counties

Citywide Dev. Corp. of Kansas City, KS., Inc.
J. Ray Barmby
701 North 7th Street, 7th Floor
Kansas City, KS 66101
(913) 321-4406
SBA Office: Kansas City
Area of Operation: Kansas City, KS

Clay County Development Corp.
Bill Conroy
2900 Rockcreek Parkway, #150
North Kansas City, MO 64117
(816) 472-5775
SBA Office: Kansas City
Area of Operation: Clay County

Corp. for Economic Dev. in Des Moines (The)
Harley L. Thorton
The Armory Building
East 1st & Des Moines St.
Des Moines, IA 50309
(515) 283-4161
SBA Office: Des Moines
Area of Operation: Citywide Des Moines

Crawford County Industrial Dev. Corp.
Russ Ahrenholtz
1305 Broadway
Denison, IA 51442
(712) 263-5621
SBA Office: Des Moines
Area of Operation: Crawford County

REGION VII (continued)

E. C. I. A. Business Growth, Inc.
Jerry Schroeder
330 Nesler Center, #330
P. O. Box 1140
Dubuque, IA 52001-1140
(319) 556-4166
SBA Office: Cedar Rapids
Area of Operation: Cedar, Clinton, Delaware,
Dubuque and Jackson Counties and the cities
located therein

Eastern Kansas Economic Development, Inc.
Dr. Bartlett Finney
ESU Campus — Bos 4046
Emporia, KS 66801
(316) 342-7041
SBA Office: Wichita
Area of Operation: Chase, Clay, Coffey, Franklin,
Geary, Lyon, Marshall, Morris, Osage,
Pottawatomie, Riley and Wabaunsee Counties

Econ. Dev. Corp. of Jefferson County, MO (The)
Patrick Lamping
P.O. Box 623
Hillsboro, MO 63050
(314) 789-4594
SBA Office: St. Louis
Area of Operation: Jefferson County, MO

EDC Loan Corp.
Bill Sproull
1010 Petticoat Lane, #250
Kansas City, MO 64106
(816) 221-0636
SBA Office: Kansas City
Area of Operation: Kansas City

Enterprise Development Corp.
Michael Crist
1015 East Broadway, #210
P. O. Box 566
Columbia, MO 65201
(314) 875-8117
SBA Office: St. Louis
Area of Operation: Audrain, Boone, Callaway,
Cole, Cooper, Montgomery and Randolph
Counties

Four Rivers Development, Inc.
John R. Cyr
108 E. Main Street
Beloit, KS 67420
(913) 738-2210
SBA Office: Wichita
Area of Operation: Jewell, Republic, Washington,
Mitchell, Cloud, Lincoln, Ottawa, Ellsworth,
Dickinson and Saline Counties

Great Plains Development, Inc.
Ronald D. Nicholas
100 Military Plaza, #214
P. O. Box 1116
Dodge City, KS 67801
(316) 227-6406
SBA Office: Wichita
Area of Operation: Greeley, Wichita, Scott, Lane,
Ness, Hamilton, Kearny, Finney, Hodgeman,
Stanton, Grant, Haskell, Gray, Ford, Mortan,
Stevens, Seward, Meade, Clark, Barber,
Comanche, Kiowa, Pratt, Stafford, Edwards,
Barton, Rush and Pawnee

Green Hills Rural Development, Inc.
Michael R. Johns
909 Main Street
Trenton, MO 64683
(816) 359-5086
SBA Office: Kansas City
Area of Operation: Counties of Caldwell,
Daviess, Grundy, Harrison, Linn, Livingston,
Mercer, Putnam, Sullivan, Chariton and Carroll

Iowa Business Growth Company
Don J. Albertsen
505 5th Avenue
Des Moines, IA 50309
(515) 282-2164
SBA Office: Des Moines
Area of Operation: Statewide

REGION VII (continued)

Johnson County Certified Development Co.
David Long
Oak Park Bank Building
11111 W. 95th Street, #210
Overland Park, KS 66210
(913) 599-1717
SBA Office: Kansas City
Area of Operation: Johnson County

Leavenworth Area Economic Dev. Corp.
Gene Miller
518 Shawnee
P. O. Box 151
Leavenworth, KS 66048
(913) 682-6579
SBA Office: Kansas City
Area of Operation: Leavenworth County

Lee's Summit Economic Dev. Council (The)
Andrew M. Filla
600 Miller Street
P. O. Box 710
Lee's Summit, MO 64063
(816) 525-6617
SBA Office: Kansas City
Area of Operation: City of Lee's Summit, MO

McPherson County Small Business Dev. Assoc.
David O'Dell
222 E. Kansas Avenue
McPherson, KS 67460
(316) 241-3927
SBA Office: Wichita
Area of Operation: McPherson County

Meramec Regional Development Corp.
Jean Hentzel
101 West Tenth Street
Rolla, MO 65401
(314) 364-2993
SBA Office: Kansas City
Area of Operation: Philips, Dent, Crawford,
Washington, Gasconade and Maries Counties

Mid-America, Inc.
Nancy LeGrande
1501 S. Joplin
Pittsburg, KS 66762
(316) 231-8267
SBA Office: Kansas City
Area of Operation: Allen, Anderson, Bourbon,
Cherokee, Crawford, Labette, Lynn, Neosho,
Miami, Montgomery, Wilson and Woodson Counties

MO-KAN Development, Inc.
David Laurie
1302 Faraon Street
St. Joseph, MO 64501
(816) 234-0072
SBA Office: Kansas City
Area of Operation: Missouri Counties of Andrew,
Buchanan, Clinton and Dekalb; Kansas Counties
of Atchison, Brown and Daniphan

Nebraska Economic Development Corp.
Al Goodwin
2631 "O" Street
Lincoln, NE 68510-1340
(402) 346-23000
SBA Office: Omaha
Area of Operation: Statewide

Northeast Missouri Cert. Development Co.
David B. Shoush
346 East Jefferson
P.O. Box 246
Memphis, MO 63555
(816) 465-7281
SBA Office: Wichita
Area of Operation: Adair, Clark, Knox, Schuyler
and Scotland Counties

Pioneer Country Development, Inc.
Ned Webb
317 N. Pomercy Avenue
P.O. Box 248
Hill City, KS 67642
(913) 674-3488
SBA Office: Wichita
Area of Operation: Cheyenne, Decatur, Ellis, Gove,
Graham, Logan, Norton, Osborne, Phillips, Rawlins,
Rooks, Russell, Sherman, Sheridan, Smith, Thomas,
Trego and Wallace

REGION VII (continued)

Platte County Industrial Dev. Commission
Mary O. Olson
7505 NW Tiffany Springs Parkway
Kansas City, MO 64153
(816) 891-8770
SBA Office: Kansas City
Area of Operation: Platte County, MO

Rural Missouri, Inc.
Ken Lueckenotte
1014 Northeast Drive
Jefferson City, MO 65109
(314) 635-0136
SBA Office: St. Louis
Area of Operation: Statewide

Siouxland Economic Development Corp.
Kenneth Beekley
400 Orpheum Electric Building
Sioux City, IA 51101
(712) 279-6430
SBA Office: Des Moines
Area of Operation: Woodbury, Plymouth,
Cherokee, Ida, Monona and Union Counties
in IA; Dakota County in Nebraska; Union
and Clay Counties in SD

South Central Kansas Econ. Dev. District, Inc.
Jack Alumbaugh
151 N. Volutsia
Wichita, KS 67214-4695
(316) 683-4422
SBA Office: Wichita
Area of Operation: Butler, Chautauqua, Cowley,
Elk, Greenwood, Harper, Harvey, Kingman,
Marion, McPherson, Reno, Rice, Sedgquick and
Sumners Counties

St. Charles County Economic Dev. Council
Marsha Knuudtson
5988 Mid Rivers Mall Drive, #200
Saint Peters, MO 63376-4322
(314) 441-6881
SBA Office: St. Louis
Area of Operation: Counties of Franklin, Lincoln,
St. Charles and Warren

St. Louis County Local Dev. Company (The)
Larry Bushong
330 N. 15th, 3rd Floor
St. Louis, MO 63103
(314) 622-3400
SBA Office: St. Louis
Area of Operation: St. Louis County

Topeka/Shawnee County Dev. Corp., Inc.
J. Richard Pratt
515 S. Kansas Avenue, #405
c/o Community & Economic Development
Topeka, KS 66603
(913) 295-3711
SBA Office: Kansas City
Area of Operation: Shawnee County

Wakarusa Valley Development, Inc.
David L. Ross
734 Vermont Street, #104
Lawrence, KS 66044
(913) 749-2371
SBA Office: Kansas City
Area of Operation: Douglas County

REGION VIII (CO, MT, ND, SD, UT & WY)

Community Economic Dev. Co. of Colorado
John Burger
1111 Osage Street, #110
Denver, CO 80204
(303) 893-8989
SBA Office: Denver
Area of Operation: Statewide

Denver Urban Economic Dev. Corp.
Dick Jones
3003 Arapahoe Street
Denver, CO 80205
(303) 296-5570
SBA Office: Denver
Area of Operation: Countywide Denver;
Counties of Boulder, Adams, Arapahoe,
Jefferson and Douglas

**Greater Salt Lake Business District d/b/a
Deseret Certified Development Company**
Scott Davis
7050 Union Park Center, #570
Midvale, UT 84047
(801) 566-1163
SBA Office: Salt Lake City
Area of Operation: Statewide Utah; Uinta,
Lincoln, Sublette, Sweetwater and Teton
Counties in Western Wyoming

Economic Dev. Corp. of Yellowstone County
Jeff Leuthold
490 North 31st
Billings, MT 59101
(406) 245-5136
SBA Office: Helena
Area of Operation: Yellowstone County

Fargo-Cass Economic Development Corp.
John Kramer
417 Main Avenue
Fargo, ND 58103
(701) 237-6132
SBA Office: Fargo
Area of Operation: Statewide

First District Development Company
Roger Clark
124 First Avenue, NW
P. O. Box 1207
Watertown, SD 57201
(605) 886-7225
SBA Office: Sioux Falls
Area of Operation: Brookings, Clark, Codington,
Deuel, Grant, Hamlin, Kingsbury, Lake, Miner
and Moody Counties

Front Range Regional Economic Dev. Corp.
Rudolph Bianchi
P. O. Box 1059
Broomfield, CO 80038
(303) 232-5698
SBA Office: Denver
Area of Operation: Adams, Arapahoe, Boulder,
Denver, Douglas, Jefferson, Larimer, Morgan
and Weld Counties

Frontier Certified Development Company
Diane Johnston
232 East Second Street, #300
P. O. Box 3599
Casper, WY 82602
(307) 234-5352
SBA Office: Casper
Area of Operation: Statewide

Montana Community Finance Corp.
Robyn Young
555 Fuller Avenue
P. O. Box 916
Helena, MT 59624
(406) 443-3261
SBA Office: Helena
Area of Operation: Statewide

Northern Hills Community Dev., Inc.
Craig W. Johnston
2885 Spearfish Drive
P.O. Box 677
Spearfish, SD 57783
(605) 642-7106
SBA Office: Sioux Falls
Area of Operation: Butte, Lawrence, Meade
and Pennington Counties

REGION VIII (continued)

Pikes Peak Regional Development Corp.
Doug Adams
228 North Cascade Avenue, #208
Colorado Springs, CO 80903
(719) 471-2044
SBA Office: Denver
Area of Operation: El Paso County

SCEDD Development Company
Gil Baca
212 West 13th Street
Pueblo, CO 81002-3704
(719) 545-8680
SBA Office: Denver
Area of Operation: Alamosa, Baca, Bent,
Chaffee, Conejos, Costilla, Crowley,
Custer, Fremont, Huerfano, Kiowa, Lake,
Las Animas, Mineral, Otero, Prowers,
Pueblo, Rio Grande and Saguache Counties

South Dakota Development Corp. (The)
Jesse Jensen/Troy Jones
Capital Lake Plaza
Pierre, SD 57501-3369
(605) 773-5032
SBA Office: Sioux Falls
Area of Operation: Statewide

Weber Capital Development Corp.
Robert Richards
2404 Washington Blvd., #1100
Ogden, UT 84401-2316
(801) 627-1333
SBA Office: Salt Lake City
Area of Operation: Weber County

REGION IX (AZ, CA, GUAM, HI & NV)

Amador Economic Development Corp.
Ron Mittelbrunn
P.O. Box 1077
Jackson, CA 95642
(209) 223-0351
SBA Office: Sacramento
Area of Operation: Amador County

Antelope Valley Local Development Corp.
Vern Lawson
104 East Avenue K-4, #A
Lancaster, CA 93534
(805) 945-2741
SBA Office: Los Angeles
Area of Operation: Antelope Valley Area —
Northern Los Angeles County, Communities of
Lancaster and Palmdale

Arcata Economic Development Corp.
Cindy Copple
100 Ericson Court, #100
Arcata, CA 95521
(707) 822-4616
SBA Office: San Francisco
Area of Operation: Humboldt and Del Norte Counties

Arizona Enterprise Development Corp.
Patty Duff
Arizona Department of Commerce
3800 North Central Avenue, #1500
Phoenix, AZ 85012-1908
(602) 280-1341
SBA Office: Phoenix
Area of Operation: Statewide

Arvin Development Corp.
Jack R. Schulze
200 Campus Drive
P. O. Box 546
Arvin, CA 93203
(805) 861-2041
SBA Office: Fresno
Area of Operation: Kern County

REGION IX (continued)

Bay Area Business Development Co.
Robert Hayden
San Francisco, CA 94501
(510) 541-4616
SBA Office: San Francisco
Area of Operation: San Francisco, Marin,
Sonoma, Napa, Solano, Contra Costa,
Alameda, Santa Clara and San Mateo Counties

Bay Area Employment Development Corp.
James R. Baird
1801 Oakland Blvd., #300
Walnut Creek, CA 94595
(510) 926-1020
SBA Office: San Francisco
Area of Operation: San Francisco, San Mateo,
Santa Clara, Alameda, Contra Costa, Solano,
Napa, Sonoma and Marin Counties

Business Development Finance Corp.
Gary Molenda
345 East Toole Street
Tucson, AZ 85701
(602) 623-3377
SBA Office: Phoenix
Area of Operation: Counties of Cochise,
Graham, Greenlee, Pina, Pinal and Santa
Cruz; Cities of Chandler, Mesa and
Tempe in Maricopa County

Butte County Overall Economic Dev. , Inc.
Mark Nemanic
1166 E. Lassen
P.O. Box 6250
Chico, CA 95927
(916) 893-8732
SBA Office: Sacramento
Area of Operation: Butte County

California Statewide Cert. Development Corp.
Barbara Vohryzek
129 "C" Street
Davis, CA 95616
(916) 756-9310
SBA Office: San Francisco
Area of Operation: Statewide

CDC Small Business Finance Corp.
Arthur Goodman
5353 Mission Center Road, #218
San Diego, CA 92108
(619) 291-3594
SBA Office: San Diego
Area of Operation: Imperial, San Diego and
Orange Counties

Central Coast Development Corp.
Tom Martin
100 Civic Center Plaza
Lompoc, CA 93436-8001
(805) 736-1445
SBA Office: Los Angeles
Area of Operation: San Luis Obispo,
Santa Barbara and Ventura Counties

Commercial Industrial Dev. Co., Inc.
Lors C. Cyr
1101 Airport Road, #D
Imperial, CA 92251
(619) 355-1025
SBA Office: San Diego
Area of Operation: Imperial County

Crown Development Corp. of Kings County
Bill Lindsteadt
1222 West Lacy Blvd., #101
Hanford, CA 93230
(209) 582-4326
SBA Office: Fresno
Area of Operation: Kings County

Econ. Dev. Corp. of Monterey County (The)
Virginia Cooper
340 El Camino Real South 22
Salinas, CA 93901
SBA Office: Fresno
Area of Operation: Monterey County

Economic Development Corp. of Shasta County
Bruce Daniels
737 Auditorium Drive, #D
Redding, CA 96001
SBA Office: San Francisco
Area of Operation: Shasta, Trinity, Siskiyou
and Modoc Counties

REGION IX (continued)

Economic Dev. Foundation of Sacramento, Inc.
Frank Dinsmore
7509 Madison Avenue, #1111
Citrus Heights, CA 95610
(916) 962-3669
SBA Office: Sacramento
Area of Operation: Alameda, Contra Costa,
El Dorado, Fresno, Marin, Mendocino, Napa,
Nevada, Placer, Sacramento, San Benito,
San Francisco, San Mateo, San Joaquin,
Santa Clara, Santa Cruz, Sierra, Solano, Sonoma,
Sutter, Yolo and Yuba Counties

Enterprise Funding Corp.
Nick Landis
3350 Shelby Street, #200
Ontario, CA 91761
(714) 989-1485
SBA Office: Los Angeles
Area of Operation: San Bernardino County

Fresno Certified Development Corp.
Robert Garcia
2300 Tulare Street, #235
Fresno, CA 93721
(209) 485-5302
SBA Office: Fresno
Area of Operation: Fresno County

Greater Sacramento Cert. Development Corp.
Ray Sebastian
10301 Placer Lane, #200
Sacramento, CA 95827
(916) 369-1582
SBA Office: Sacramento
Area of Operation: Sacramento, El Dorado,
Placer and Yolo Counties

HEDCO Local Development Corp.
Dexter J. Taniguchi
222 S. Vineyard Street, Penthouse 1
Honolulu, HI 96813-2445
(808) 521-6502
SBA Office: Honolulu
Area of Operation: Statewide and
American Samoa

La Habra Local Development Co., Inc.
A. Edward Evans
Civic Center
P. O. Box 337
La Habra, CA 90631-0337
(213) 905-9741
SBA Office: Los Angeles
Area of Operation: Orange and Los Angeles Counties

Long Beach Area Certified Development Corp.
Regina Grant Peterson
11 Golden Shore, #630
Long Beach, CA 90802
(310) 983-7475
SBA Office: Los Angeles
Area of Operation: Southern Los Angeles County

Los Angeles County Small Business Dev. Corp.
Raymond K. Saikaida
2525 Corporate Place
Monterey Park, CA 91754
(213) 260-2204
SBA Office: Los Angeles
Area of Operation: Los Angeles County

Los Angeles LDC, Inc.
Wilfred Marshall
200 North Spring Street, #2008
Los Angeles, CA 90012
(213) 485-6154
SBA Office: Los Angeles
Area of Operation: Citywide Los Angeles

Los Medanos Fund, A Local Development Co.
Thomas LaFleur
501 Railroad Avenue
Pittsburg, CA 94565
(510) 439-1056
SBA Office: San Francisco
Area of Operation: City of Pittsburg; Alameda,
Contra Costra, Marin, Napa, San Francisco,
San Mateo, Santa Clara, Solano and Sonoma Counties

REGION IX (continued)

Mid State Development Corp.
Jason Binaham
515 Truxtun Avenue
Bakersfield, CA 93301
(805) 322-4241
SBA Office: Fresno
Area of Operation: Kern County

Nevada State Development Corp.
Harry H. Weinberg
350 South Center, #310
Reno, NV 89501
(702) 323-3625
SBA Office: Las Vegas
Area of Operation: Statewide

New Ventures Capital Development Co.
Charles Stevenson
626 South Ninth Street
Las Vegas, NV 89101
(702) 382-9102
SBA Office: Las Vegas
Area of Operation: Clark County

Oakland Certified Development Corp.
Floyd Hicks
Dufwin Towers
519 17th Street, #111
Oakland, CA 94612
(510) 763-4297
SBA Office: San Francisco
Area of Operation: City of Oakland

Phoenix Local Dev. Corp., Phoenix, Arizona
Jill E. Triwush
34 W. Monroe, #901
Phoenix, AZ 85003
(602) 495-6495
SBA Office: Phoenix
Area of Operation: Citywide Phoenix

Riverside County Economic Development Corp.
Brian P. Thiebeux
3499 Tenth Street
P. O. Box 413
Riverside, CA 92501
(714) 788-9811
SBA Office: San Diego
Area of Operation: Riverside County

Santa Ana City Economic Development Corp.
Patricia Nunn
902 Santa Ana Blvd., #106
Santa Ana, CA 92701
(714) 647-1143
SBA Office: Santa Ana
Area of Operation: Orange County

Small Business Development Corp.
Simon Sanchez
Calvo Insurance Building
115 Chalan Santo Papa, #204
Agana, GUAM 96910
(617) 472-8083
SBA Office: Honolulu
Area of Operation: Territory of Guam

Southern Nevada Certified Development Corp.
Thomas J. Gutherie
2770 South Maryland Parkway, #216
Las Vegas, NV 89109
(702) 732-3998
SBA Office: Las Vegas
Area of Operation: Mineral, Esmeralda, Nye, Lincoln, Lyon, Douglas, White Pine and Clark Counties

Stanislaus County Economic Dev. Corp.
William Carney
1012 Eleventh Street, #201
Modesto, CA 95354-0808
(209) 521-9333
SBA Office: Fresno
Area of Operation: Stanislaus County

Tracy/San Joaquin County Certified Dev. Corp.
Roger Birdsall
815 N. Hunter Street
Stockton, CA 95320
(209) 468-2266
SBA Office: Sacramento
Area of Operation: San Joaquin County

REGION IX (continued)

Tulare County Economic Development Corp.
Mary J. Gonsalues
2380 West Whitendale Avenue
P. O. Box 5033
Visalia, CA 93278
(209) 627-0766
SBA Office: Fresno
Area of Operation: Tulare County

REGION X (AK, ID, OR & WA)

C.C.D. Business Development Corp.
Peter Graff
744 SE Rose Street
Roseburg, OR 97470
(503) 672-6728
SBA Office: Portland
Area of Operation: State of Oregon, except for
Wallowa County

Cascades West Financial Services, Inc.
Debbie Wright
105 High Street
Corvallis, OR 97333
(503) 757-6854
SBA Office: Portland
Area of Operation: Benten, Lane, Lincoln, Linn,
Marion, Polk and Yamhill Counties

Clearwater Economic Development Association
Bob Wood
1626 B – 6th Avenue North
Lewiston, ID 83501
(208) 746-0015
SBA Office: Spokane
Area of Operation: Counties of Clearwater,
Latah, Lewis and Nez Pierce in Idaho; Asotin,
Garfield and Whitman in Washington

East Central Idaho Development Company
David Ogden
12 North 2nd E.
P. O. Box 330
Rexburg, ID 83440
(208) 356-4524
SBA Office: Boise
Area of Operation: Bonneville, Butte, Clark, Custer,
Fremont, Jefferson, Lemhi, Madison and Teton
Counties

Eastern Idaho Development Corp.
Paul Cox
1651 Alvin Ricken Drive
Pocatello, ID 83201
(208) 234-7541
SBA Office: Boise
Area of Operation: Bannock, Power, Bear Lake,
Bingham, Caribou, Franklin and Oneida Counties

Evergreen Community Development Association
Robert Wisniewski
2015 Smith Tower
Seattle, WA 98104
(206) 622-3731
SBA Office: Seattle
Area of Operation: State of Washington; Oregon
Counties of Clackamas, Columbia, Clatsop,
Multnomah, Washington, Hood River, Wasco
and Tillamook

Greater Eastern Oregon Development Corp.
Jim Rowan
17 SW Frazer, #20
P.O. Box 1041
Pendleton, OR 97801
(503) 276-6745
SBA Office: Portland
Area of Operation: Gilliam, Grant, Morrow,
Umatilla, Wheeler, Union Baker and
Wallowa Counties

REGION X (continued)

Greater Spokane Business Development Assoc.
Tony Rund
W. 808 Spokane Fall Blvd.
Spokane, WA 99201
(509) 625-6325
SBA Office: Spokane
Area of Operation: State of Washington except
Pacific County

Northwest Small Business Finance Corp.
President
700 NE Multnomah, #400
Portland, OR 97232
(503) 232-7796
SBA Office: Portland
Area of Operation: Multnomah, Clackamas
and Washington Counties

Oregon Certified Business Dev. Corp.
Richard G. Mackay
1135 W. Highland
P. O. Box 575
Redmond, OR 97756
(503) 548-8163
SBA Office: Portland
Area of Operation: Crook, Deschutes, Harney,
Jefferson, Klamath, Lake and Malheur Counties

Panhandle Area Council, Inc.
Deborah Holmberg
11100 Airport Drive
Hayden, ID 83835
(208) 772-0584
SBA Office: Spokane
Area of Operation: Benewah, Bonner, Boundary,
Kootenai and Shoshone Counties

Railbelt Community Development Corp.
Elaine Hollier
619 Warehouse Avenue, #256
Anchorage, AK 99501
(907) 277-5161
SBA Office: Anchorage
Area of Operation: State of Alaska except
First Judical District (Southeast Alaska)

Region IV Development Corp.
Van Petterson
1300 Kimberly Road
P.O. Box 1844
Twin Falls, ID 83303-1844
(208) 736-3065
SBA Office: Boise
Area of Operation: Blaine, Camas, Cassia,
Gooding, Jerome, Lincoln, Minidoka and Twin
Falls Counties

Southeastern Washington Development Assoc.
Conrad Tobin
901 N. Colorado Street
Kennewick, WA 99336
(509) 735-1000
SBA Office: Spokane
Area of Operation: Benton, Franklin, Grant,
Adams, Yakima and Walla Walla Counties

Treasure Valley Certified Development Corp.
Dave Palumbo
10624 W. Executive Drive
Boise, ID 83704-8934
(208) 322-7033
SBA Office: Boise
Area of Operation: Idaho Counties of Ada,
Adams, Boise, Canyon, Elmore, Gem, Owyhee,
Payette, Valley and Washington; Oregon
Counties of Harney and Malheur

Appendix D
SBA Preferred and Certified Lending Institutions

The following is a listing of 198 SBA Preferred Lending Institutions — marked with an asterisk (*), and 830 SBA Certified Lending Institutions. These expert lenders now account for over 60 percent of all SBA Loans. Assuming an SBA loan application is in proper order, the turnaround time can be as little as three days when utilizing the services of one of these institutions. All of these lenders understand the problems of small business financing and most routinely make business loans without SBA participation. They are presented by SBA Region, State and Community location.

REGION I

Connecticut

Hamden	American National Bank
Hartford	* First National Bank of Hartford
Hartford	Mechanics Savings Bank
New Haven	Founders Bank

Maine

Augusta	* Key Bank of Central Maine
Portland	Fleet Bank of Maine

Massachusetts

Boston	Massachusetts Business Development Corp.
Danvers	* Danvers Savings Bank
Fitchburg	First Safety Fund National Bank
Framingham	* Shawmut Bank of Boston
Hyannis	* Cape Cod Bank and Trust Company
Rockland	Rockland Trust Company
Waltham	* Bank of Boston
Worcester	Commerce Bank and Trust Company
Worcester	* Flagship Bank & Trust Company

New Hampshire

Berlin	The Berlin City Bank
Concord	Concord Savings Bank
Dover	Southeast Bank for Savings
Keene	CFX Bank

New Hampshire (continued)

Keene	Granite Bank
Manchester	Bank of New Hampshire
Manchester	* First New Hampshire Bank
Manchester	New Dartmouth Bank
Manchester	New Hampshire Business Development Corp.
Nashua	Fleet Bank — NH
Nashua	N.F.S. Savings Bank
Peterborough	Peterborough Savings Bank

Rhode Island

Providence	The Citizens Trust Company
Providence	Fleet National Bank
Providence	Home Loan and Investment Association
Providence	Rhode Island Hospital Trust National Bank

Vermont

Barre	Granite Savings Bank & Trust
Brattleboro	First Vermont Bank & Trust
Brattleboro	Vermont National Bank
Burlington	* Chittenden Trust Company
Burlington	The Howard Bank
Burlington	* The Merchant's Bank
Charlotte	* The Money Store Investment Corp.
Manchester Center	Factory Point National Bank
Morrisville	* Union Bank
Northfield	Northfield Savings Bank
Rutland	* Green Mountain Bank
St. Albans	* Franklin Lamoille Bank

REGION II

New Jersey

Annandale	First Community Bank
Burlington	First Fidelity Bank, N.A. South Jersey
Chatham	Summit Bank
Flemington	* Prestige State Bank
Hackensack	United Jersey Bank
Hasbrouck	* Bank of New York (National Community Division)
Jackson	* Garden State Bank
Mount Laurel	Midatlantic Bank
North Brunswick	Farrington Bank

New Jersey (continued)

North Plainfield	* Rock Bank
Pennington	CoreStates/New Jersey National Bank
Somerset	New Era Bank
Union	* The Money Store of New York
Wayne	* The Ramapo Bank

New York

Albany	Key Bank, N.A.
Albany	New York Business Development Corp.
Albany	* Fleet Bank of New York
Bath	The Bath National Bank
Buffalo	* Manufacturers and Traders Trust Company
Buffalo	* Marine Midland Bank
Buffalo	* Fleet Bank of New York
Canadaigua	The Canadaigua National Bank & Trust Co.
Cortland	First National Bank of Cortland
Dewitt	Community Bank, N.A.
East Hampton	The Bank of the Hamptons
Elmira	Chemung Canal Trust Company
Geneva	The National Bank of Geneva
Glens Falls	* Glens Falls National Bank and Trust Company
Islandia	Long Island Commercial Bank
Ithaca	Thompkins County Trust Company
Little Falls	Herkimer County Trust Company
Melville	The Bank of New York
Melville	Fleet Bank
Newburgh	Key Bank of New York
New Hyde Park	State Bank of Long Island
New York City	* Chase Manhattan Bank, N.A.
New York City	Chemical Community Development, Inc.
New York City	* Citibank, N.A.
New York City	* National Westminster Bank
New York City/Bronx	New York National Bank
New York City	Republic National Bank
Norwich	The National Bank and Trust Co. of Norwich
Rochester	Chase Lincoln First Bank, N.A.
Roslyn Heights	* The Money Store Investment Corporation
Syracuse	* Marine Midland Bank
Syracuse	OnBank & Trust Company
Uniondale	European American Bank
Warsaw	Wyoming County Bank
Williamsville	ITT Small Business Finance Corporation

Puerto Rico

Hatc Rey	Banco Santander Puerto Rico
San Juan	* Banco Popular de Puerto Rico

REGION III

Delaware

Newark	* Delaware Trust Company
Wilmington	Mellon Bank (DE), N.A.
Wilmington	Wilmington Trust Company

District of Columbia

Washington, D.C.	Adams National Bank
Washington, D.C.	* Allied Lending Corporation

Maryland

Baltimore	* First National Bank of Maryland
Baltimore	* Maryland National Bank
Baltimore	Provident Bank of Maryland
Baltimore	* Signet Bank
Greenbelt	Suburban Bank of Maryland
Owings Mills	Key Federal Savings Bank

Pennsylvania

Bethlehem	Lehigh Valley Bank
Erie	* Integra National Bank North
Erie	Mellon Bank (North)
Erie	* PNC Bank (Northwest)
Ft. Washington	* The Money Store Investment Corporation
Harrisburg	Mellon Bank (Commonwealth Region), N.A.
Harrisburg	Pennsylvania National Bank
Hermitage	* First National Bank of Pennsylvania
Horsham	Frankford Bank
Laceyville	Grange National Bank of Wyoming County
Morrisville	* Bucks County Bank & Trust Company
New Castle	First Western Bank, N.A.
Philadelphia	Corestate Bank, NA
Philadelphia	* Mellon Bank, N.A./Mellon PSFS
Pittsburgh	Integra Bank/Pittsburgh
Pittsburgh	Mellon Bank, N.A.
Pittsburgh	* PNC Bank
Pittston	Commonwealth Bank, a Division of Meridian Bank
Reading	* Meridian Bank

Pennsylvania (continued)

Scranton	PNC Bank, Northeast Pennsylvania
Sharon	First Western Bank, FSB
Souderton	* Union National Bank
State College	Mellon Bank (Central)
Unionville	* Integra National Bank/South
Wilkes-Barre	Mellon Bank

Virginia

Reston	Patriot National Bank of Reston
Richmond	* The Money Store Investment Corporation
Richmond	NationsBank of Virginia, N.A.
Virginia Beach	Commerce Bank

West Virginia

Clarksburg	Bank One, West Virginia
Huntington	* Bank One
Morgantown	One Valley Bank of Morgantown, Inc.
Wheeling	Wheeling National Bank

REGION IV

Alabama

Anniston	SouthTrust Bank of Calhoun County
Birmingham	AmSouth Bank, N.A.
Birmingham	AT&T Small Business Lending Corp.
Birmingham	Compass Bank
Birmingham	First Commercial Bank
Birmingham	SouthTrust Bank of Alabama — Birmingham, N.A.
Dothan	Southland Bancorporation
Dothan	SouthTrust Bank of Dothan
Florence	First National Bank of Florence
Fultondale	Bank of Alabama
Guntersville	The Home Bank
Huntsville	SouthTrust Bank of Huntsville
Montgomery	First Montgomery Bank
Montgomery	SouthTrust Bank, N.A.
Opelika	Farmers National Bank
Opp	SouthTrust Bank of Covington County
Selma	Peoples Bank & Trust Company

Florida

Boca Raton	First United Bank
Clearwater	Citizens Bank of Clearwater
Fernandina Beach	First Coast Community Bank
Ft. Walton Beach	First National Bank and Trust
Jacksonville	Community Savings Bank
Jacksonville	First Guaranty Bank & Trust Company
Longwood	Liberty National Bank
Miami	International Bank of Miami
Miami	Sun Bank/Miami, N.A.
Naples	First Western SBLC, Inc.
Panama City	Emergent Business Capital, Inc.
Panama City	First National Bank
Pensacola	Liberty Bank
Ponte Vedra Beach	Ponte Vedra National Bank
Port Charlotte	Charlotte State Bank
Sarasota	Enterprise National Bank of Sarasota
St. Petersburg	United Bank of Pinellas
Tampa	NationsBank
Tampa	Southern Commerce Bank
West Palm Beach	* Barnett Bank of Palm Beach

Georgia

Atlanta	* Bank South
Atlanta	* The Business Development Corp. of Georgia
Atlanta	* Commercial Bank of Georgia
Atlanta	Fidelity National Bank
Atlanta	* Georgia Bankers Bank
Atlanta	* Metro Bank
Atlanta	* Nations Bank of Georgia
Atlanta	The Summit National Bank
Augusta	Bankers First Savings & Loan Association
Blairsville	Union County Bank
Byron	Middle Georgia Bank
Cordele	First State Bank & Trust
Macon	* First South Bank
Morristown	AT&T Small Business Lending Corporation
Morrow	Southern Crescent Bank
Norcross	* First Capital Bank Norcross
Savannah	* The Coastal Bank
Snellville	Eastside Bank & Trust
Tucker	Mountain National Bank
Woodstock	First National Bank of Cherokee

Kentucky

Florence	The Fifth Third Bank
Lexington	Bank One, Lexington
Louisville	Liberty National Bank
Louisville	PNC Bank — Kentucky
Louisville	National City Bank
Mount Sterling	Exchange Bank of Kentucky
Murray	Peoples Bank of Murray
Pikeville	Pikeville National Bank & Trust Company

Mississippi

Batesville	Batesville Security Bank
Biloxi	The Jefferson Bank
Grenada	Sunburst Bank
Gulfport	Hancock Bank
Jackson	Deposit Guaranty National Bank
Jackson	Trustmark National Bank
McComb	Pike County National Bank
Picayune	First National Bank of Picayune
Starkville	National Bank of Commerce of Mississippi
Tupelo	* Bank of Mississippi

North Carolina

Charlotte	First Union National Bank of North Carolina
Charlotte	NationsBank of North Carolina
Durham	Central Carolina Bank & Trust Company
Lumberton	Southern National Bank of North Carolina
Rocky Mount	Centura Bank
Whiteville	United Carolina Bank
Wilson	Branch Banking & Trust Company
Winston-Salem	* Wachovia Bank & Trust Company, N.A.

South Carolina

Columbia	* Business Development Corp. of South Carolina
Columbia	Emergent Business Capital, Inc.
Columbia	* First Citizens Bank
Columbia	NationsBank
Lexington	The Lexington State Bank

Tennessee

Brentwood	Brentwood National Bank
Chattanooga	American National Bank & Trust Company
Chattanooga	Volunteer Bank and Trust Co.

Tennessee (continued)

Columbia	First Farmers & Merchants National Bank
Elizabethton	Citizens Bank
Knoxville	Third National Bank of East Tennessee
Memphis	Union Planters National Bank
Memphis	United American Bank
Nashville	First American National Bank, N.A.
Nashville	NationsBank of Tennessee
Nashville	Third National Bank

REGION V

Illinois

Aurora	Merchants Bank of Aurora
Aurora	Old Second National Bank of Aurora
Bellwood	The Bank of Bellwood
Blue Island	The First National Bank of Blue Island
Chicago	Albany Bank and Trust Company, N.A.
Chicago	First National Bank of Chicago
Chicago	Foster Bank
Chicago	Harris Trust and Savings Bank
Chicago	* The Money Store
Chicago	* South Central Bank & Trust
Chicago	* The South Shore Bank of Chicago
Danville	Palmer American National Bank
Evergreen Park	* ITT Small Business Finance Corp.
Elgin	* Union National Bank & Trust of Elgin
Fairview Heights	* Central Bank
Homewood	Bank of Homewood
La Grange	Bank One, Chicago
Maywood	Maywood-Proviso State Bank
Naperville	First Colonial Bank of DuPage County
Naperville	Firstar Bank West, N.A.
Park Ridge	First State Bank of Park Ridge
Park Ridge	NBD Park Ridge Bank
Pekin	* First State Bank of Pekin
Rockford	Bank One, Rockford
Springfield	First of American Bank
Springfield	Bank One, Springfield
Urbana	* Busey First National Bank
Urbana	Central Illinois Bank
West Frankfort	Banterra Bank of West Frankfort

Indiana

Covington	Bank of Western Indiana
Evansville	Citizens National Bank of Evansville
Fort Wayne	NBD Summit Bank
Indianapolis	Bank One Indianapolis
Indianapolis	* Huntington National Bank of Indiana
Indianapolis	National City Bank
Indianapolis	NBD Bank, Indiana
South Bend	First Source Bank of South Bend
South Bend	Society National Bank
Whiting	Centier Bank

Michigan

Detroit	Comerica Bank
Flint	The Citizens Commercial Savings Bank
Grand Rapids	* United Bank of Michigan
Kalamazoo	First of America Bank — Michigan, N.A.
Kalamazoo	Old Kent Bank of Kalamazoo
Lansing	Michigan National Bank
Midland	* Chemical Bank & Trust Company
Owosso	Key State Bank
Traverse City	* The Empire National Bank of Traverse City
Traverse City	Old Kent Bank — Traverse City

Minnesota

Bloomington	* Firstar Bank of Minnesota
Edina	* First Bank National Association
Minneapolis	* Norwest Bank, Minnesota, N.A.
St. Cloud	* First American Bank, N.A.
St. Cloud	Zapp National Bank
West St. Paul	Signal Bank, Inc.
Young America	State Bank of Young America

Ohio

Akron	First National Bank of Ohio
Cincinnati	North Side Bank and Trust Co.
Cincinnati	PNC Bank, Cincinnati
Cleveland	American National Bank
Cleveland	Society National Bank
Columbus	Bank One, Columbus, N.A.
Columbus	* The Huntington National Bank
Columbus	National City Bank of Columbus
Columbus	Society Bank

Ohio (continued)

Dayton	Bank One, Dayton, N.A.
Dayton	* National City Bank
Dayton	Society Bank — Dayton area
Dublin	The Money Store Investment Co.
Elyria	PremierBank and Trust
Lorain	* Lorain National Bank
Piqua	The Fifth Third Bank of Western Ohio
Toledo	* Mid American National Bank & Trust Co.
Toledo	National City Bank, Northwest

Wisconsin

Appleton	Firstar Bank, Appleton
Appleton	* Valley Bank
Eau Claire	* Firstar Bank, Eau Claire
Eau Claire	M&I Community State Bank, Eau Claire
Fond du Lac	* Firstar of Fond du Lac
Green Bay	Associated Bank, Green Bay
Green Bay	Firstar Bank, Green Bay
Green Bay	Norwest Bank
Madison	Bank One, Madison
Madison	* Firstar Bank of Madison
Madison	M&I Madison Bank
Madison	Valley Bank Madison
Manitowoc	Associated Bank Lakeshore, N.A.
Manitowoc	First National Bank of Manitowoc
Menomonee Falls	* Associated Bank of Menomonee Falls
Milwaukee	* Bank One, Milwaukee
Milwaukee	* First Bank, Milwaukee
Milwaukee	* Firstar Bank of Milwaukee
Milwaukee	Marshall and Iisley Bank of Milwaukee
Neenah	Associated Bank, N.A.
Oshkosh	Firstar Bank Oshkosh N.A.
Sheboygan	* Firstar Bank Sheboygan
Sturgeon Bay	Baylake Bank
Wausau	* M&I First American National Bank
Wausau	M & I First American National Bank
West Bend	Bank One, West Bend

REGION VI

Arkansas

Arkadelphia	Elk Horn Bank & Trust

Arkansas (continued)

Batesville	Worthen National Bank
Bentonville	Worthen National Bank of Northwest Arkansas/Bentonville
Camden	Worthen National Bank of Camden
Clarksville	Arkansas State Bank
Conway	First National Bank of Conway
El Dorado	First Financial Bank
El Dorado	First National Bank of El Dorado
Fayetteville	McIlroy Bank & Trust
Fayetteville	Worthen National Bank of Northwest Arkansas
Fort Smith	City National Bank of Fort Smith
Fort Smith	Merchants National Bank
Hot Springs	Worthern National Bank of Hot Springs
Jonesboro	Citizens Bank of Jonesboro
Little Rock	Arkansas Capital Corporation
Little Rock	First Commercial Bank, N.A.
Little Rock	Metropolitan National Bank
Little Rock	Worthen National Bank of Arkansas
Mongolia	First National Bank Mongolia
North Little Rock	National Bank of Arkansas
North Little Rock	The Twin City Bank
Pine Bluff	Simmons First National Bank
Pocahontas	Bank of Pocahontas
Rogers	First National Bank
Russellville	Worthen National Bank of Russellville
Searcy	First National Bank of Searcy

Louisiana

Abbeville	Gulf Coast Bank
Baton Rouge	City National Bank
Baton Rouge	Guaranty Bank and Trust Co.
Baton Rouge	Premier Bank, N.A.
Eunice	Tri-Parish Bank
Gonzales	Bank of Gonzales
Harvey	Schwegmann Bank and Trust Co.
Kenner	Metro Bank
Lafayette	First National Bank
Metairie	Hibernia National Bank in Jefferson Parish
Metairie	Jefferson Guaranty Bank
Metairie	Omni Bank
Monroe	Central Bank
Monroe	First American Bank
Morgan City	First National Bank in St. Mary Parish

Louisiana (continued)

New Orleans	First National Bank of Commerce
New Orleans	Gulf Coast Bank and Trust Co.
New Orleans	Whitney National Bank
Plattenville	Bayoulands Bank
Port Allen	Bank of West Baton Rouge
Ruston	Ruston State Bank
Shreveport	Commercial National Bank
Shreveport	Pioneer Bank

New Mexico

Albuquerque	Bank of America Nevada
Albuquerque	* First Security Bank
Albuquerque	Sunwest Bank of Albuquerque
Albuquerque	* United New Mexico Bank of Albuquerque
Belen	First National Bank of Belen
Carlsbad	Western Commerce Bank
Clovis	Sunwest Bank
Clovis	Western Bank of Clovis
Hobbs	Lea County State Bank
Las Cruces	Bank of the Rio Grande, NA
Las Cruces	* Citizens Bank of Las Cruces
Las Cruces	* United New Mexico Bank at Las Cruces
Las Cruces	Western Bank
Santa Fe	Bank of Santa Fe
Taos	First State Bank of Taos
Tucumcari	The First National Bank of Tucumcari

Oklahoma

Broken Arrow	First National Bank and Trust
Midwest City	Community Bank and Trust
Oklahoma City	* BancFirst
Oklahoma City	Bank of Oklahoma, N.A.
Oklahoma City	Boatman's First National Bank
Oklahoma City	First National Bank
Oklahoma City	Liberty Bank & Trust Co. of Oklahoma City
Oklahoma City	Rockwell Bank, N.A.
Ponca City	* Pioneer Bank & Trust
Poteau	Central National Bank
Stillwater	* Stillwater National Bank & Trust Company
Tonkawa	* First National Bank of Tonkawa
Tulsa	Bank IV Oklahoma, N.A. of Tulsa
Tulsa	Boatman's First National Bank
Tulsa	Woodland Bank

Texas

Abilene	Security State Bank
Amarillo	Amarillo National Bank
Amarillo	The First National Bank of Amarillo
Arlington	Bank One, Texas MidCit
Austin	Cattlemen's State Bank
Austin	Hill County Bank
Austin	* Horizon Savings Association
Austin	Liberty National Bank
Austin	Texas Bank
Austin	Texas Commerce Bank
Baytown	Citizens Bank and Trust Co.
Beaumont	Bank One, Texas, N.A.
Bellaire	Park National Bank
Brownsville	International Bank of Commerce, N.A.
Brownsville	Mercantile Bank, N.A.
Brownsville	Texas Commerce Bank, Brownsville
Bryan	Victoria Bank and Trust
College Station	Commerce National Bank
Converse	Converse National Bank
Corpus Christi	American National Bank
Corpus Christi	Bank of Corpus Christi
Corpus Christi	Citizens State Bank
Corpus Christi	First Commerce Bank
Corpus Christi	First National Bank
Dallas	Abrams Centre National Bank
Dallas	* Bank One Texas, N.A.
Dallas	Comerica Bank — Texas
Dallas	* Equitable Bank
Dallas	First Texas Bank
Dallas	* First Western SBLC, Inc.
Dallas	Gateway National Bank
Dallas	* Heller First Capital Corp.
Dallas	* Independence Funding Co., LTD.
Dallas	* The Money Store
Dallas	Texas Commerce Bank
El Paso	The Bank of El Paso
El Paso	The Bank of the West
El Paso	Montwood National Bank
El Paso	State National Bank
El Paso	Sunwest Bank of El Paso
El Paso	Texas Commerce Bank of El Paso, N.A.
Fort Worth	* Bank of North Texas

Texas (continued)

Fort Worth	Citizens National Bank
Galveston	Bank of Galveston
Garland	* Central Bank
Garland	Security Bank
Harlingen	Harlingen National Bank
Harlingen	The Harlingen State Bank
Houston	Allied Lending Corp.
Houston	Bank of America — Nevada
Houston	Bank of North Texas
Houston	Bank One, Texas
Houston	Charter National Bank — Houston
Houston	Commerica Bank — Texas
Houston	Compass Bank
Houston	Enterprise Bank
Houston	First Bank Houston
Houston	First Interstate Bank
Houston	First Western SBLC
Houston	Frost National Bank
Houston	Great Southwest Bank, FBB
Houston	Harrisburg Bank
Houston	Heller First Capital Corp.
Houston	Houston Independent Bank
Houston	Independence Bank
Houston	Klein Bank
Houston	Langham Creek National Bank
Houston	Lockwood National Bank
Houston	Merchants Bank
Houston	Metrobank, N.A.
Houston	The Money Store Investment Corp.
Houston	NationsBank
Houston	Northwest Bank
Houston	* Park National Bank
Houston	* QuestStar Bank
Houston	Southwest Bank of Texas
Houston	Sterling Bank
Houston	Sunbelt National Bank
Houston	Texas Capital Bank, N.A.
Houston	Texas Central Bank
Houston	Texas Commerce Bank
Houston	Texas Guaranty Bank
Hutto	Hutto State Bank
Idalou	Security Bank

Texas (continued)

Irving	Bank of America, Nevada
Irving	* Bank of the West
Irving	Irving National Bank
Katy	Community Bank
Katy	First Bank
Kerrville	First National Bank
Kilgore	Kilgore First National Bank
Lampasas	First National Bank of Lampasas
La Porte	Bayshore National Bank of LaPorte
Laredo	South Texas National Bank
League City	League City Bank and Trust
Los Fresnos	First Bank Los Fresnos
Lubbock	American State Bank
Lubbock	* First National Bank of Lubbock
Lubbock	Lubbock National Bank
Lubbock	Plains National Bank
Mansfield	Overton Bank and Trust, N.A.
McAllen	Inter National Bank of McAllen
McAllen	Texas State Bank
Midland	Midland American Bank
Midland	Texas National Bank of Midland
Missouri City	* First National Bank of Missouri City
Navasoto	First Bank
Odessa	First State Bank of Odessa
Odessa	Texas Bank
Pharr	Lone Star National Bank
Plainview	First National Bank of Plainview
Plano	Plano Bank and Trust
San Angelo	Bank of the West
San Angelo	Texas Commerce Bank
San Antonio	Bank of America — Nevada
San Antonio	Bank One, Texas, N.A.
San Antonio	Broadway National Bank
San Antonio	First Western SBLC
San Antonio	Frost National Bank/Corpus Christi
San Antonio	Heller First Capital Corp.
San Antonio	ITT Small Business Finance Corporation
San Antonio	* The Money Store Investment Corporation
San Antonio	NationsBank of Texas, N.A.
San Antonio	Plaza Bank
San Antonio	Security National Bank
San Antonio	Valley-Hi Bank

Texas (continued)

Schertz	Schertz Bank
Sequin	First Commercial Bank
Sonora	First National Bank of Sonora
Sundown	Sundown State Bank
Tomball	Texas National Bank
Victoria	Citizens National Bank
Weatherford	* Texas Bank, Weatherford
Wolfforth	American Bank of Commerce

REGION VII

Iowa

Ames	Firstar Bank Ames
Cedar Rapids	* Firstar Bank Cedar Rapids
Davenport	* Northwest Bank Iowa, N.A.
Des Moines	Bankers Trust Company
Des Moines	Boatman's Bank Iowa, N.A.
Des Moines	* Brenton National Bank of Des Moines
Des Moines	Firstar Bank of Des Moines
Des Moines	Hawkeye Bank & Trust of Des Moines
Des Moines	* Norwest Bank Des Moines, N.A.
Dubuque	Dubuque Bank & Trust Company
Fort Dodge	Norwest Bank Iowa, N.A.
Iowa City	Iowa State Bank & Trust Company
Maquoketa	Maquoketa State Bank
Marion	Farmers State Bank
Newton	Hawkeye Bank of Jasper County
Oskaloosa	Mahasha State Bank
Sioux Center	American State Bank
Spencer	Boatman's National Bank of Northeast Iowa
Storm Lake	Commercial Trust and Savings Bank
West Des Moines	* West Des Moines State Bank

Kansas

Dodge City	Fidelity State Bank & Trust Company
Dodge City	First National Bank & Trust Co. in Dodge City
Great Bend	Farmers Bank & Trust
Hays	Emprise Bank
Haysville	Intrust Bank, N.A.
Hutchinson	Emprise Bank, N.A.
Kansas City	* Guaranty State Bank & Trust

Kansas (continued)

Lawrence	Mercantile Bank of Lawrence
Liberal	First National Bank of Liberal
Merriam	* United Kansas Bank and Trust
Newton	Midland National Bank
Neodesha	First National Bank of Neodesha
Olathe	Bank IV Olathe
Olathe	First National Bank
Overland Park	Metcalf State Bank
Overland Park	UMB Bank Kansas
Topeka	Commerce Bank and Trust
Ulysses	Grant County State Bank
Wichita	American National Bank
Wichita	* Bank IV Wichita
Wichita	Emergent Business Capital, Inc.
Wichita	Emprise Bank
Wichita	Intrust Bank
Wichita	Union National Bank

Missouri

Brentwood	Magna Bank of Missouri
Carthage	Boatman's Bank of Carthage
Clayton	The Money Store Investment Corp.
Columbia	Capital Bank of Columbia
Independence	Standard Bank and Trust Co.
Jefferson City	The Central Trust Bank
Joplin	Mercantile Bank and Trust Co. of Joplin
Kansas City	Bannister Bank and Trust
Kansas City	Boatman's First National Bank of Kansas City
Kansas City	First National Bank of Platte County
Kansas City	United Missouri Bank of Kansas City, N.A.
Springfield	* The Boatman's National Bank of Southern MO
Springfield	Citizens National Bank of Springfield
Springfield	* Commerce Bank of Springfield
Springfield	* First City National Bank
Springfield	Mercantile Bank of Springfield
St. Louis	* Boatman's Bank of Southern Missouri
St. Louis	ITT Small Business Finance Corporation
St. Louis	Mercantile Bank, St. Louis, N.A.
St. Louis	United Missouri Bank of St. Louis, N.A.
Washington	Bank of Washington

Nebraska

Blair	The Washington County Bank
Lincoln	* FirsTier Bank, Lincoln
Lincoln	National Bank of Commerce
Lincoln	* Union Bank & Trust Company
North Platte	First National Bank of North Platte
Omaha	* Douglas County Bank and Trust
Omaha	* FirsTier Bank, Omaha
Omaha	First National Bank of Omaha
Omaha	Norwest Bank Nebraska

REGION VIII

Colorado

Alamosa	The First National Bank in Alamosa
Aurora	Aurora National Bank
Aurora	* The Money Store Investment Corporation
Breckenridge	The Bank, N.A.
Broomfield	Eagle Bank
Clifton	Alpine Bank, Clifton
Colorado Springs	State Bank and Trust
Denver	Colorado National Bank
Denver	ITT Small Business Finance Corp.
Denver	Key Bank of Colorado
Denver	Norwest Bank Denver
Denver	Vectra Bank
Durango	Durango National Bank
Englewood	AT&T Capital Corp.
Englewood	Emergent Business Capital, Inc.
Englewood	First Commercial Bank, N.A., dba First Commercial Capital Corp.
Estes Park	Park National Bank
Evergreen	The Bank
Fort Collins	Bank One, Fort Collins — Loveland N.A.
Golden	Golden Bank of Colorado
Grand Junction	Bank of Grand Junction
Grand Junction	Grand Valley National Bank
Hotchkiss	The First State Bank of Hotchkiss
Lakewood	Bank One, Denver, N.A.
Montrose	Bank One, Montrose — Main
Montrose	Norwest Bank Montrose, N.A.
Steamboat Springs	First National Bank of Steamboat Springs

Montana

Bigfork	Flathead Bank of Bigfork
Billings	* First Interstate Bank
Billings	* Norwest Bank Billings
Billings	Yellowstone Bank
Bozeman	First Security Bank of Bozeman
Bozeman	* Montana Bank of Bozeman
Great Falls	Norwest Bank of Great Falls
Helena	Mountain West Bank
Helena	Valley Bank of Helena
Kalispell	* Norwest Bank Kalispell, NA
Kalispell	Valley Bank of Kalispell
Livingston	First National Park Bank
Missoula	First Interstate Bank
Missoula	* First Security Bank of Missoula
Missoula	Montana Bank of South Missoula
Polson	First Citizens Bank
Sidney	Richland Bank and Trust
Whitefish	* Mountain Bank

North Dakota

Bismarck	Bank Center First
Bismarck	United Bank of Bismarck
Dickinson	Liberty National Bank and Trust
Fargo	First Community Bank
Fargo	State Bank of Fargo
Grand Forks	Community National Bank
Grand Forks	First American Bank Valley
Grand Forks	First National Bank in Grand Forks
Mandan	First Southwest Bank of Mandan
Minot	First American Bank West
Minot	First Western Bank of Minot
West Fargo	First National Bank North Dakota
Williston	American State Bank and Trust Company

South Dakota

Belle Fourche	* Pioneer Bank and Trust
Brookings	First National Bank in Brookings
Burke	First Fidelity Bank
Custer	First Western Bank
Huron	Farmers & Merchants Bank
Milbank	Dakota State Bank
Philip	First National Bank

South Dakota (continued)

Pierre	American State Bank
Pierre	BankWest, N.A.
Pierre	First National Bank
Rapid City	* Rushmore State Bank
Sioux Falls	First Bank of South Dakota, N.A.
Sioux Falls	First National Bank in Sioux Falls
Sioux Falls	Marquette Bank of South Dakota, N.A.
Sioux Falls	Norwest Bank Sioux Falls, N.A.
Sioux Falls	Western Bank
Yankton	First Dakota National Bank

Utah

Ogden	Bank of Utah
Salt Lake City	Bank One
Salt Lake City	Brighten Bank
Salt Lake City	* First Security Bank
Salt Lake City	* Guardian State Bank
Salt Lake City	* Key Bank
Salt Lake City	* Zions First National Bank, N.A.

Wyoming

Casper	Hilltop National Bank
Casper	Norwest Bank Wyoming
Cheyenne	* Key Bank
Cody	Shoshone First Bank
Gillette	First National Bank of Gillette

REGION IX

Arizona

Phoenix	Bank One, Arizona
Phoenix	* First Interstate Bank of Arizona, N.A.
Phoenix	ITT Small Business Finance Corporation
Phoenix	M & I Thunderbird Bank
Phoenix	National Bank of Arizona
Phoenix	Republic National Bank

California

Anaheim	Landmark Bank
Auburn	* The Bank of Commerce, N.A.
Bakersfield	* San Joaquin Bank

California (continued)

Cameron Park	Western Sierra National Bank
Carlsbad	* Capital Bank of Carlsbad
Chula Vista	Pacific Commerce Bank
Concord	Tracy Federal Bank
Coronado	Bank of Coronado
Cupertino	Cupertino National Bank
El Centro	* Valley Independent Bank
Encinitas	San Diequito National Bank
Escondido	First Pacific National Bank
Escondido	* North County Bank
Eureka	* U. S. Bank of California
Fallbrook	* Fallbrook National Bank
Fresno	Bank of Fresno
Fresno	Regency Bank
Hemet	Valley Merchants Bank
Huntington Beach	Liberty National Bank
Inglewood	Imperial Bank
La Palma	Frontier Bank
Los Angeles	Hanmi Bank
Los Angeles	* National Bank of California
Los Angeles	Wilshire Bank
Modesto	Modesto Banking Company
Modesto	* Pacific Valley National Bank
Monterey	* Monterey County Bank
Ontario	Western Community Bank
Orange	* Orange National Bank
Rancho Cordova	* Bank of America Community Development Bank
Redding	North Valley Bank
Rosemead	General Bank
Sacramento	* The Money Store Investment Corp.
Sacramento	* Sacramento Commercial Bank
Sacramento	Sacramento First National Bank
Salinas	First National Bank of Central CA
San Diego	* Bank of Commerce
San Diego	* Bank of Southern California
San Diego	* ITT Small Business Finance Corporation
San Diego	Rancho Santa Fe National Bank
San Diego	San Diego Trust & Savings Bank
San Diego	Union Bank
San Francisco	* Commercial Bank of San Francisco
San Francisco	* Heller First Capital
San Jose	* California Business Bank

California (continued)

San Jose	Comerica Bank
San Jose	San Jose National Bank
San Leandro	* Bay Bank of Commerce
San Luis Obispo	* First Bank of San Luis Obispo
Santa Cruz	* Coast Commercial Bank
Santa Rosa	* National Bank of Redwoods
Santa Rosa	* Sonoma National Bank
Sherman Oaks	* American Pacific State Bank
Truckee	* Truckee River Bank
Tustin	* Eldorado Bank
Van Nuys	Industrial Bank
West Covina	* California State Bank
Yorba Linda	Bank of Yorba Linda

Hawaii

Honolulu	* Bank of Hawaii
Honolulu	Central Pacific Bank
Honolulu	City Bank
Honolulu	First Hawaiian Bank

Nevada

Las Vegas	* Bank of America
Las Vegas	* First Interstate Bank of Nevada, N.A.
Las Vegas	Nevada State Bank

REGION X

Alaska

Anchorage	First National Bank of Anchorage
Anchorage	Key Bank of Alaska
Anchorage	National Bank of Alaska
Anchorage	Northrim Bank
Fairbanks	Denali State Bank

Idaho

Boise	American Bank of Commerce
Boise	First Interstate Bank of Idaho
Boise	* First Security Bank of Idaho
Boise	* Key Bank of Idaho
Boise	* West One Bank

Oregon

Eugene	Pacific Continental Bank
Medford	* Western Bank
Portland	* First Interstate Bank of Oregon, N.A.
Portland	* Key Bank of Oregon
Portland	* The Money Store Investment Corporation
Portland	* U. S. National Bank of Oregon

Washington

Aberdeen	The Bank of Grays Harbor
Bellevue	* The Money Store Investment Corporation
Chelan	* North Cascades National Bank
Coupeville	Whidbey Island Bank
Duvall	Valley Community Bank
Everett	American First National Bank
Everett	Frontier Bank
Ferndale	Whatcom State Bank
Kennewick	American National Bank
Lacey	* First Community Bank of Washington
Lynnwood	* City Bank
Olympia	* Centennial Bank
Seattle	First Interstate Bank of Washington, N.A.
Seattle	* Key Bank of Puget Sound
Seattle	Pacific Northwest Bank
Seattle	Puget Sound National Bank
Seattle	* Seattle — First National Bank
Seattle	* U. S. Bank of Washington
Seattle	West One Bank Washington
Snohomish	* First Heritage Bank
Spokane	* Washington Trust Bank
Tacoma	North Pacific Bank
Tukwila	National Bank of Tukwila
Yakima	* Pioneer National Bank

Appendix E
Small Business Investment Companies
(SBICs and SSBICs)

How To Seek SBIC Financing

Small business investment companies (SBICs) exist to supply equity capital, long-term loans and management assistance to qualifying small businesses.

The privately owned and operated SBICs use their own capital and funds borrowed from the U. S. Small Business Administration (SBA) to provide financing to small businesses in the form of equity securities and long-term loans. SBICs are profit-seeking organizations that select small businesses to be financed within the rules and regulations set by the SBA. Specialized SBICs (SSBICs) are a particular type of SBIC that provides assistance solely to small businesses owned by socially or economically disadvantaged persons.

SBICs invest in a broad range of industries. Some SBICs seek out small businesses with new products or services because of the strong growth potential of such firms. Some specialize in the fields in which their management has special competency. Most SBICs however, consider a wide variety of investment opportunities.

Only firms defined by the SBA as "small" are eligible for SBIC financing. The SBA defines a company as small when its net worth is $18 million or less, and its average net (after tax) income for the preceding two years does not exceed $6 million. For businesses in industries for which the above standards are too low, alternative size standards are available. In determining whether a business qualifies, all of the business's parents, subsidiaries and affiliates are considered.

Approaching an SBIC

If you own or operate a small business and would like to obtain SBIC financing, you should first identify and investigate the existing SBICs listed herein that may be interested in financing your company. Use this Appendix as a first step in learning as much as possible about the SBICs in your state, or in other areas important to your company's needs. In choosing an SBIC, consider the types of investments it makes, how much money is available for investment and how much might be available in the future. You should also consider whether the SBICs selected can offer you management services appropriate to your company's needs.

Plan in Advance

You should determine your company's financing needs and research the potential SBICs who may have an interest long before you will actually require the funds. Your research will take time, as will the SBIC's research of your business.

Prepare a Proposal, Prospectus or Business Plan

When you have identified the SBICs you think are best suited for your company, you'll need to prepare a formal presentation. Your initial presentation will play a major role in your success toward obtaining financing. It is up to you to demonstrate that such an investment in your firm is worthwhile. And, the best way to achieve this is to present a detailed and comprehensive proposal, prospectus or plan that includes, at a minimum, the following information.

Identification

- The name of the business as it appears on the official records of the state or community in which it operates.
- The city, county and state of the principal location and any branch offices or facilities.
- The form of business organization and, if a corporation, the date and state of incorporation.

Product or Service

- A description of the business performed, including the principal products sold or services rendered.
- A history of the general development of the products and/or services during the past five years (or since inception).
- Information about the relative importance of each principal product or service to the sales volume of the business and to its profits.

Production Facilities and Property

- Description of real and physical property and adaptability to other business ventures.
- Description of the technical attributes of the company's production facilities.

Marketing

- Detailed information about your business's customer-base, including potential customers. Indicate the percentage of gross revenue generated by your five largest customers.

- A marketing survey and/or economic feasibility study.
- A description of the distribution system by which you provide products or services.

Competition

- A descriptive summary of the competitive conditions in the industry in which your business is engaged, including your position relative to its largest and smallest competitors.
- A full explanation and summary of your business's pricing policies.

Management

- Brief resumes of the business's management personnel and principal owners including their ages, education, and business experience.
- Banking, business and personal references for each member of management and for the principal owners.

Financial Statements

- Balance sheets, and profit and loss statements for the last three fiscal years or from your business's inception.
- Detailed projections of revenues, expenses, and net earnings for the coming year.
- A statement of the amount of funding you are requesting and the time requirement for the funds.
- The reasons for your request for funds and a description of the proposed use of the proceeds upon receipt.

Who To Contact

The following SBA licensed firms are actively engaged in making loans and/or equity investments. **When known**, each listing includes the name of the company, the contact person, address, telephone number, fax number, loan or investment range, investment policy, the types of investment preferred, industry preference and the geographical area served.

Since these businesses frequently move and change their policies, the details presented cannot be guaranteed 100% accurate, but are the most current available. The author recommends calling the SBIC selected to confirm the information provided before mailing a financing request and business plan.

ALABAMA

Alabama Capital Corporation (SSBIC)
David C. Delaney, President
16 Midtown Park East
Mobile, AL 36606
(205) 476-0700
Fax: (205) 476-0026

Contact For Further Information
Investment Policy: Diversified

**Alabama Small Business
Investment Company (SSBIC)**
Harold Gilchrist, Manager
1732 5th Avenue North
Birmingham, AL 35203
(205) 324-5231
Fax: (205) 324-5234

Contact For Further Information
Investment Policy: Diversified

FJC Growth Capital Corp. (SSBIC)
William B. Noojin, Vice Pres. & Gen. Mgr.
200 West Ct. Square, #750
Huntsville, AL 35801
(205) 922-2918
Fax: (205) 922-2909

Loan/Investment Range: Up to $500,000
Will make loans and/or equity investments
Prefers Expansion Stage or Seasoned Companies
Industry Peference: Diversified
Geographical Area: Southern States

First SBIC of Alabama
David C. DeLaney, President
16 Midtown Park East
Mobile, AL 36606
(205) 476-0700
Fax: (205) 476-0026

Loan/Investment Range: Up to $500,000
Will make loans and/or equity investments
Industry Preference: Diversified
Geographical Area: Southern States

Hickory Venture Capital Corporation
J. Thomas Noojin, President
200 W. Court Square, Suite 100
Huntsville, AL 35801
(205) 539-5130
Fax: (205) 539-5130

Contact For Further Information
Investment Policy: Diversified

ARIZONA

First Commerce and Loan LP
Ross M. Horowitz, General Partner
5620 N. Kolb, #260
Tucson, AZ 85715
(602) 298-2500
Fax: (602) 745-6112

Contact For Further Information
Investment Policy: Diversified

First Interstate Equity Corporation
Edmund G. Zito, President
100 West Washington Street
Phoenix, AZ 85003
(602) 528-6647
Fax: (602) 440-1320

Contact For Further Information
Investment Policy: Diversified

ARIZONA (continued)

Sundance Venture Partners, LP
(Main Office in CA)
Gregory S. Anderson, Vice President
400 East Van Buren, #650
Phoenix, AZ 85004
(602) 252-5373
Fax: (408) 252-1450

Loan/Investment Range: Up to $1 million
Will make loans and/or equity investments
Prefers Early Stage, Expansion Stage, Seasoned
Companies and Management Buyouts
Industry Preference: Diversified
Geographical Area: California and Western States

ARKANSAS

Small Business Stores Investment Capital, Inc.
Charles E. Toland, President
10003 New Benton Highway
P. O. Box 3627
Little Rock, AR 72203
(501) 455-6599
Fax: (501) 455-6556

Contact For Further Information
Investment Policy: Grocery Stores

CALIFORNIA

Allied Business Investors, Inc. (SSBIC)
Jack Hong, President
428 S. Atlantic Blvd., #201
Monterey Park, CA 91754
(818) 289-0186
Fax: (818) 289-2369

Contact For Further Information
Investment Policy: Diversified

Ally Finance Corporation (SSBIC)
Percy P. Lin, President
9100 Wilshire Blvd., #408
Beverly Hills, CA 90212
(213) 550-8100
Fax: (310) 550-6236

Contact For Further Information
Investment Policy: Diversified

Asian American Capital Corp. (SSBIC)
Jennie Chien, President
1251 West Tennyson Road, #4
Hayward, CA 94544
(510) 887-6888
Fax: (510) 782-6432

Contact For Further Information
Investment Policy: Diversified

Astar Capital Corporation (SSBIC)
George Hsu, President
429 S. Euclid Avenue, #B
Anaheim, CA 92802
(714) 490-1149
Fax: (714) 597-5950

Contact For Further Information
Investment Policy: Diversified

CALIFORNIA (continued)

Bentley Capital (SSBIC)
John Hung, President
592 Vallejo Street, #2
San Francisco, CA 94133
(415) 362-2868
Fax: (415) 398-8209

Loan/Investment Range: Up to $500,000
Will make loans and/or equity investments
Prefers Early Stage Companies
Industry Preference: Diversified
Geographical Area: Western States

Best Finance Corporation (SSBIC)
Vincent Lee, General Manager
4929 W. Wilshire Blvd., #407
Los Angeles, CA 90010
(213) 731-2268
Fax: (213) 937-6393

Contact For Further Information
Investment Policy: Diversified

Calsafe Capital Corporation (SSBIC)
Ming-Min Su, President
245 East Main Street, #107
Alhambra, CA 91801
(818) 289-3400
Fax: (818) 300-8025

Contact For Further Information
Investment Policy: Diversified

Charterway Investment Corp. (SSBIC)
Tien Chen, President
One Wilshire Blvd.
624 South Grand Avenue, #1600
Los Angeles, CA 90017
(213) 689-9107
Fax: (213) 689-9108

Contact For Further Information
Investment Policy: Diversified

Citicorp Venture Capital, Ltd.
(Main Office in New York, NY)
2 Embarcadero Place
2200 Geny Road, #203
Palo Alto, CA 94303
(415) 424-8000
Fax: None

Contact For Further Information
Investment Policy: Diversified

Developers Equity Capital Corp.
Larry Sade, Chairman
1880 Century Park East, #211
Los Angeles, CA 90067
(213) 277-0330
Fax: (310) 277-4271

Contact For Further Information
Investment Preference: Real Estate

Draper Associates, A California LP
Timothy C. Draper, President
400 Seaport Court, #250
Redwood City, CA 94063
(415) 599-9000
Fax: (415) 599-9726

Contact For Further Information
Investment Policy: Diversified

CALIFORNIA (continued)

Far East Capital Corp. (SSBIC)
Tom Wang, President
350 S. Grand Avenue
Los Angeles, CA 90071
(213) 253-0599
Fax: (213) 253-0806

Loan/Investment Range: Up to $300,000
Will make loans and/or equity investments
Prefers Expansion Stage Companies
Industry Preference: Diversified
Geographical Area: California

First American Capital Funding, Inc. (SSBIC)
Chuoc Vota, President
10840 Warner Avenue, #202
Fountain Valley, CA 92708
(714) 965-7190
Fax: (714) 965-7193

Loan/Investment Range: Over $2 Million
Prefers to make loans
Prefers Startup Companies
Industry Preference: Medical and Health
Geographical Area: California

First SBIC of California
Robert L. Boswell, Senior Vice President
650 Town Center, 17th Floor
Costa Mesa, CA 92626
(714) 556-1964
Fax: (714) 546-8021

Loan/Investment Range: $1 - $2 Million
Prefers equity investments
Will consider Startups, Early Stage, Expansion
Stage, Seasoned Companies and Management
Buyouts
Industry Preference: Diversified
Geographical Area: National

First SBIC of California
(Main Office in Costa Mesa, CA)
Manager
5 Palo Alto Square, #938
Palo Alto, CA 94306
(415) 424-8011
Fax: (415) 424-6830

Loan/Investment Range: $1 - $2 Million
Prefers equity investments
Will consider Startups, Early Stage, Expansion
Stage, Seasoned Companies and Management
Buyouts
Industry Preference: Diversified
Geographical Area: National

First SBIC of California
(Main Office in Costa Mesa, CA)
Manager
155 North Lake Street, #1010
Pasadena, CA 91109
(818) 304-3451
Fax: (818) 440-9931

Loan/Investment Range: $1 - $2 Million
Prefers equity investments
Will consider Startups, Early Stage, Expansion
Stage, Seasoned Companies and Management
Buyouts
Industry Preference: Diversified
Geographical Area: National

Fulcrum Venture Capital Corp. (SSBIC)
Brian Argrett, President
3683 Crenshaw Blvd., 4th Floor
Los Angeles, CA 90016'
(213) 299-8016
Fax: (213) 299-8059

Contact For Further Information
Investment Policy: Diversified

G C & H Partners
Edwin Huddleston, General Partner
One Maritime Plaza, 20th Floor
San Francisco, CA 94110
(415) 981-5252
Fax: (415) 951-3699

Contact For Further Information
Investment Policy: Diversified

CALIFORNIA (continued)

Hall, Morris & Drufva II, L. P.
Ronald J. Hall, Managing Director
25401 Cabbott Road, #116
Newport Beach, CA 92653
(714) 707-5096
Fax: (714) 707-5121

Contact For Further Information
Investment Policy: Diversified

Imperial Ventures, Inc.
Ray Vadalma, Manager
9920 South La Cienega Blvd.,
Inglewood, CA 90301
Mail: P. O. Box 92991
Los Angeles, CA 90009
(213) 417-5710
Fax: (213) 417-5874

Contact For Further Information
Investment Policy: Diversified

Jupiter Partners
John M. Bryan, President
600 Montgomery Street, 35th Floor
San Francisco, CA 94111
(415) 421-9990
Fax: (415) 421-0471

Contact For Further Information
Investment Policy: Diversified but 50% in
Electronic Manufacturing

Lailai Capital Corporation (SSBIC)
Danny Ku, President
223 E. Garvey Avenue, #228
Monterey, CA 91754
(818) 288-0704
Fax: (818) 288-4101

Contact For Further Information
Investment Policy: Diversified

Magna Pacific Investments (SSBIC)
David Wong, President
330 North Brand Blvd., #670
Glendale, CA 91203
(818) 547-0809
Fax: (818) 547-9303

Contact For Further Information
Investment Policy: Diversified

Marwit Capital Corporation
Martin W. Witte, President
180 Newport Center Drive, #200
Newport Beach, CA 92660
(714) 640-6234
Fax: (714) 759-1363

Contact For Further Information
Investment Policy: Diversified

Merrill Pickard, Anderson & Eyre I
Steven L. Merrill, President
2840 Sand Hill Road, #200
Menlo Park, CA 94025
(415) 854-8600
Fax: (415) 854-0345

Contact For Further Information
Investment Policy: Diversified

CALIFORNIA (continued)

Myriad Capital, Inc. (SSBIC)
Chuang-I Lin, President
701 S. Atlantic Blvd., #302
Monterey Park, CA 91754
(818) 570-4548
Fax: (818) 570-9570

Contact For Further Information
Investment Policy: Diversified

New West Partners II
Timothy P. Haidinger, Manager
4350 Executive Drive, #206
San Diego, CA 92121
(619) 457-0723
Fax: (619) 457-0829

Contact For Further Information
Investment Policy: Diversified

Northwest Venture Partners
(Main Office in Minneapolis, MN)
3000 Sand Hill Road, Bldg. #3, #245
Menlo Park, CA 94025
(415) 854-6366
Fax: (415) 854-6652

Loan/Investment Range: Over $2 Million
Prefers equity investments
Prefers Startups, Early and Expansion Stage,
Seasoned Companies and Management Buyouts
Industry Preference: Diversified
Geographical Area: National

Norwest Equity Partners IV
(Main Office in Minneapolis, MN)
3000 Sand Hill Road, Bldg. #3, #245
Menlo Park, CA 94025
(415) 854-6366
Fax: (415) 854-6652

Contact For Further Information
Investment Policy: Diversified

Norwest Growth Fund, Inc.
(Main Office in Minneapolis, MN)
3000 Sand Hill Road, Bldg. #3, #245
Menlo Park, CA 94025
(415) 854-6366
Fax: (415) 854-6652

Contact For Further Information
Investment Policy: Diversified

Opportunity Capital Corp. (SSBIC)
J. Peter Thompson, President
39650 Liberty Street, #425
Fremont, CA 94538
(510) 651-4412
Fax: (510) 651-0128

Loan/Investment Range: Up to $250,000
Will make loans and/or equity investments
Prefers Expansion Stage, Seasoned Companies
and Management Buyouts
Industry Preference: Communications, Industrial
Products and Transportation
Geographical Area: Western States

Opportunity Capital Partners II, L.P.
J. Peter Thompson, General Partner
39650 Liberty Street, #425
Fremont, CA 94538
(510) 651-4412
Fax: (510) 651-0128

Contact For Further Information
Investment Policy: Diversified

CALIFORNIA (continued)

Pacific Mezzanine Fund, L.P.
David C. Woodward, General Partner
88 Kearney Street, #1850
San Francisco, CA 94108
(415) 362-6776

Loan/Investment Range: Over $2 Million
Will make loans and/or equity investments
Prefers Expansion Stage, Seasoned Companies
and Management Buyouts
Industry Preference: Diversified
Geographical Area: Southwestern and Western States

Positive Enterprises, Inc. (SSBIC)
Kwok Szeto, President
1489 Webster Street, #228
San Francisco, CA 94115
(415) 885-6600
Fax: (415) 928-6363

Contact For Further Information
Investment Policy: Diversified

Ritter Partners
William C. Edwards, President
150 Isabella Avenue
Atherton, CA 94025
(415) 854-1555
Fax: (415) 854-5015

Contact For Further Information
Investment Policy: Diversified but 50% in
Electronic Manufacturing

**San Joaquin Business Investment
Group (SSBIC)**
Roger Palomino, President
1900 Mariposa Mall, #100
Fresno, CA 93721
(209) 233-3580
Fax: (209) 233-3709

Loan/Investment Range: Up to $250,000
Prefers to make loans
Prefers Expansion Stage and Seasoned Companies
Industry Preference: Diversified
Geographical Area: California

South Bay Capital Corportion (SSBIC)
Charles C. Chiang, President
18039 Crenshaw Blvd., #203
Torrance, CA 90504
(213) 515-1033
Fax: (213) 324-9273

Contact For Further Information
Investment Policy: Diversified

Sundance Venture Partners, LP
Larry J. Wells, General Partner
10600 N. De Anza Blvd., #215
Cupertino, CA 95014
(408) 257-8100
Fax: (408) 257-8111

Loan/Investment Range: Up to $1 Million
Will make loans and/or equity investments
Prefers Early Stage, Expansion Stage, Seasoned
Companies and Management Buyouts
Industry Preference: Diversified
Geographical Area: California and Western States

Union Venture Corporation
Kathleen Burns, President
445 South Figueroa Street
Los Angeles, CA 90071
(213) 236-4092
Fax: (213) 688-0101

Loan/Investment Range: $1 - $2 Million
Will make loans and/or equity investments
Prefers Expansion Stage, Seasoned Companies
and Management Buyouts
Industry Preference: Diversified
Geographical Area: California

CALIFORNIA (continued)

VK Capital Company
Franklin Van Kasper, General Partner
600 California Street, #1700
San Francisco, CA 94108
(415) 391-5600
Fax: (415) 397-2744

Loan/Investment Range: Up to $250,000
Will make loans and/or equity investments
Prefers Early Stage and Expansion Companies
Industry Preference: Diversified
Geographical Area: Midwest, Southwest
and Western States

Western General Capital Corp. (SSBIC)
Alan Thian, President
13701 Riverside Drive, #610
Sherman Oaks, CA 91423
(818) 986-5038
Fax: (818) 905-9220

Contact For Further Information
Investment Policy: Diversified

CONNECTICUT

AB SBIC, Inc.
Adam J. Bozzuto, President
275 School House Road
Cheshire, CT 06410
(203) 272-0203
Fax: (203) 272-9978

Contact For Further Information
Investment Policy: Grocery Stores

All State Venture Capital Corporation
Ceasar N. Anquillare, President
The Bishop House
32 Elm Street
P. O. Box 1629
New Haven, CT 06506
(203) 787-5029
Fax: (203) 785-0018

Contact For Further Information
Investment Policy: Diversified

Capital Resource Co. of Connecticut, LP
Morris Morgenstein, General Partner
2558 Albany Avenue
West Hartford, CT 06117
(203) 236-4336
Fax: (203) 232-8161

Loan/Investment Range: Up to $250,000
Will make loans and/or equity investments
Prefers Expansion Stage Companies
Industry Preference: Diversified
Geographical Area: Northeastern States

Financial Opportunities, Inc.
Frank Colaccino, President
One Vision Drive
Enfield, CT 06082
(203) 741-4444
Fax: (203) 741-4487

Loan/Investment Range: Up to $100,000
Prefers to make loans
Prefers Seasoned Companies
Industry Preference: Consumer Products/Services
Geographical Area: Northeastern, Southern
and Midwestern States

CONNECTICUT (continued)

First New England Capital, LP
Richard C. Kaffky, President
100 Pearl Street
Hartford, CT 06103
(203) 293-3333
Fax: (203) 293-4131

Loan/Investment Range: Up to $1 Million
Will make loans and/or equity investments
Prefers Expansion Stage, Seasoned Companies
and Management Buyouts
Industry Preference: Diversified
Geographical Area: Northeastern States

Marcon Capital Corporation
Martin A. Cohen, President
10 John Street
Southport, CT 06490
(203) 259-7233
Fax: (203) 259-9428

Contact For Further Information
Investment Policy: Diversified

RFE Capital Partners, LP
Robert M. Williams, Managing Partner
36 Grove Street
New Canaan, CT 06840
(203) 966-2800
Fax: (203) 966-3109

Loan/Investment Range: $1 - $2 Million
Prefers equity investments
Prefers Seasoned Companies and Management
Buyouts
Industry Preference: Diversified
Geographical Area: Northeastern, Southern and
Midwestern States

TSG Ventures, Inc.
Duane Hill, President
1055 Washington Blvd., 10th Floor
Stamford, CT 06901
(203) 363-5344
Fax: (203) 363-5340

Loan/Investment Range: Up to $1 Million
Will make loand and/or investments
Prefers Early, Expansion Stage, SeasonedCompanies
and Management Buyouts
Industry Preference: Diversified
Geographical Area: National

DISTRICT OF COLUMBIA

Allied Financial Services Corp. (SBIC/SSBIC)
Cable Williams, President
1666 K Street, NW, #901
Washington, DC 20006
(202) 331-1112
Fax: (202) 659-2053

Contact For Further Information
Investment Policy: Communications Media

Allied Capital Advisors, Inc.
Cable Williams, President
1666 K Street, NW, 9th Floor
Washington, DC 20006
(202) 331-1112
Fax: (202) 659-2053

Loan/Investment Range: Up to $8 Million
Will make loans and/or equity investments
Will Consider All Stages of Company Development
From Startup to Seasoned Firms
Industry Preference: Diversified
Geographical Area: National

Allied Investment Corp. II
William F. Dunbar, President
1666 K Street, NW, #901
Washington, DC 20006
(202) 331-1112
Fax: (202) 659-2053

Contact For Further Information
Investment Policy: Diversified

DISTRICT OF COLUMBIA (continued)

Broadcast Capital, Inc. (SSBIC)
John E. Oxendine, President
1771 N Street, NW, #421
Washington, DC 20036
(202) 429-5393
Fax: (202) 775-2991

Contact For Further Informtion
Investment Policy: Communications Media

Legacy Fund Limited Partnership
Jonathan L. Ledecky, General Partner
1400 34th Street, NW, #800
Washington, DC 20007
(202) 659-1100
Fax: (202) 342-7474

Loan/Investment Range: $1 - $2 Million
Will make loans and/or equity investments
Prefers Expansion Stage, Seasoned Companies
and Management Buyouts
Industry Preference: Diversified
Geographical Area: National

Minority Broadcast Investment Corp. (SSBIC)
Walter L. Threadgill, President
1001 Connecticut Ave., NW, #622
Washington, DC 20036
(202) 293-1166
Fax: (202) 293-1181

Contact For Further Information
Investment Policy: Communications Media

FLORIDA

Allied Financial Services Corp. (SBIC/SSBIC)
Main Office in Washington, D.C.)
Manager
Executive Office Center
2770 N. Indian River Blvd., #305
Vero Beach, FL 32960
(407) 778-5556
Fax: (407) 569-9303

Contact For Further Information
Investment Policy: Diversified

BAC Investment Corp. (SSBIC)
Gregory Hobbs, Manager
6600 N. W. 27th Avenue
Miami, FL 33247
(305) 693-5919
Fax: (305) 693-7450

Contact For Further Information
Investment Policy: Diversified

Florida Capital Ventures, Ltd.
Warren Miller, President
880 Riverside Plaza
100 W. Kennedy Blvd.
Tampa, FL 33602
(813) 229-2294
Fax: (813) 229-2028

Loan/Investment Range: Up to $1 Million
Prefers equity investments
Prefers Early Stage, Expansion Stage, Seasoned
Companies and Management Buyouts
Industry Preference: Diversified
Geographical Area: Florida and Southern States

FLORIDA (continued)

J & D Financial Corporation
Jack Carmel, President
12747 Biscayne Blvd.,
N. Miami, FL 33181
(305) 893-0303
Fax: (305) 891-2338

Loan/Investment Range: Up to $500,000
Prefers to make loans
Will consider Startups, Expansion and Seasoned
Companies
Industry Preference: Diversified
Geographical Area: Southern States

Market Capital Corporation
Donald Kolvenbach, President
1102 North 28th Street
P. O. Box 31667
Tampa, FL 33631
(813) 247-1357
Fax: (813) 248-5531

Contact For Further Information
Investment Policy: Grocery Stores

Pro-Med Investment Corporation (SSBIC)
(Main Office in Dallas, TX)
AmeriFirst Bank Bldg., 2nd Floor S
18301 Biscayne Blvd.,
N. Miami Beach, FL 33160
(305) 933-5858
Fax: (305) 931-3054

Contact For Further Information
Investment Policy: Diversified

Quantum Capital Partners, Ltd.
Michael E. Chaney, General Partner
4400 Northeast 25th Avenue
Ft. Lauderdale, FL 33308
(305) 776-1113
Fax: (305) 938-9406

Loan/Investment Range: Up to $250,000
Will make loans and/or equity investments
Prefers Expansion Stage Companies
Industry Preference: Diversified
Geographical Area: National

Western Financial Capital Corporation
(Main Office in Dallas, TX)
AmeriFirst Bank Bldg., 2nd Floor S
18301 Biscayne Blvd.
N. Miami Beach, FL 33160
(305) 933-5858
Fax: (305) 931-3054

Contact For Further Information
Investment Policy: Medical

GEORGIA

Cordova Capital Partners, L.P.
Paul DiBella & Ralph Wright, Managers
3350 Cumberland Circle, #970
Atlanta, GA 30339
(404) 951-1542
Fax: (494) 955-7610

Contact For Further Information
Investment Policy: Grocery Stores

GEORGIA (continued)

First Growth Capital, Inc. (SSBIC)
Vijay K. Patel, President
I-75 & GA 42, Best Western Plaza
P.O. Box 815
Macon, GA 31029
(912) 994-9260
Fax: (912) 994-1280

Contact For Further Information
Investment Policy: Diversified

Investor's Equity, Inc.
I. Walter Fisher, President
945 E. Paces Ferry Road, #1735
Atlanta, GA 30326
(404) 266-8300
Fax: None

Contact For Further Information
Investment Policy: Diversified

North Riverside Capital Corporation
Thomas R. Barry, President
50 Technology Park/Atlanta
Norcross, GA 30092
(404) 446-5556
Fax: (404) 446-8627

Loan/Investment Range: Up to $500,000
Prefers equity investments
Prefers Expansion Stage and Seasoned Companies
Industry Preference: Diversified
Geographical Area: Southern States

Renaissance Capital Corporation
Anita P. Stephens, President
34 Peachtree Street, #2230
Atlanta, GA 30303
(404) 658-9061
Fax: (404) 658-9064

Loan/Investment Range: Up to $250,000
Will make loans and/or equity investments
Prefers Early and Expansion Stage Companies
Industry Preference: Diversified
Geographical Area: Southern States

HAWAII

Bancorp Hawaii SBIC, Inc.
Robert W. Paris, President
111 South King Street, #1060
P.O. Box 2900
Honolulu, HI 96846
(808) 537-8012
Fax: (808) 521-5701

Loan/Investment Range: Up to $500,000
Will make loans and/or equity investments
Prefers Expansion Stage, Seasoned Companies
and Management Buyouts
Industry Preference: Diversified
Geographical Area: Hawaii and Western States

Pacific Venture Capital, Inc. (SSBIC)
Dexter J. Taniguchi, President
222 South Vineyard Street, PH.1
Honolulu, HI 96813
(808) 521-6502
Fax: (808) 521-6541

Loan/Investment Range: Up to $250,000
Will make loan and/or equity investments
Prefers Early and Expansion State, Seasoned
Companies
and Management Buyouts
Industry Preference: Diversified
Geographical area: Hawaii

ILLINOIS

Chicago Community Ventures, Inc. (SSBIC)
Phyllis E. George, President
25 E. Washington Street, #2015
Chicago, IL 60602
(312) 726-6084
Fax: (312) 726-0167

Loan/Investment Range: Up to $250,000
Will make loans and/or equity investments
Prefers Early and Expansion Stage Companies
Industry Preference: Diversified
Geographical Area: Midwestern States

Combined Fund, Inc. (The) (SSBIC)
Manager
915 East Hyde Park Blvd.
Chicago, IL 60615
(312) 363-0300
Fax: (312) 363-6816

Contact For Further Information
Investment Policy: Diversified

Continental Illinois Venture Corp.
John R. Willis, President
209 S. LaSalle Street
Mail: 213 S. LaSalle Street
Chicago, IL 60697
(312) 828-8021
Fax: (312) 987-0763

Loan/Investment Range: Over $2 Million
Prefers equity investments
Prefers and Seasoned Companies and Management Buyouts
Industry Preference: Diversified
Geographical Area: National

First Capital Corp. of Chicago
J. Mikesell Thomas, President
Three First National Plaza, #1330
Chicago, IL 60670
(312) 732-5400
Fax: (312) 732-4098

Loan/Investment Range: Over $2 Million
Prefers equity investments
Prefers Expansion Stage and Seasoned Companies
Industry Preference: Diversified
Geographical Area: National

Heller Equity Capital Corporation
John M. Goense, President
500 West Monroe Street
Chicago, IL 60661
(312) 441-7200
Fax: (312) 441-7378

Loan/Investment Range: Over $2 Million
Will make loans and/or equity investments
Prefers Expansion Stage, Seasoned Companies and Management Buyouts
Industry Preference: Diversified
Geographical Area: National

Neighborhood Fund, Inc. (The) (SSBIC)
James Fletcher, President
1950 East 71st Street
Chicago, IL 60649
(312) 753-5670
Fax: (312) 493-6609

Contact For Further Information
Investment Policy: Diversified

Peterson Finance and Investment Co. (SSBIC)
James S. Rhee, President
3300 W. Peterson Avenue, #A
Chicago, IL 60659
(312) 539-0502
Fax: (312) 583-6714

Contact For Further Information
Investment Policy: Diversified

ILLINOIS (continued)

Polestar Capital, Inc. (SSBIC)
Wallace Lennox, President
180 N. Michigan Ave., #1905
Chicago, IL 60601
(312) 984-9875
Fax: (312) 984-9877

Loan/Investment Range: Up to $500,000
Will make loans and/or equity investments
Prefers Early and Expansion Stage Companies
and Management Buyouts
Industry Preference: Diversified
Geographical Area: National

Tower Ventures, Inc. (SSBIC)
Manager
3330 Beverly Road
Hoffman Estates, IL 60179
(312) 875-0571
Fax: (312) 906-0164

Loan/Investment Range: Up to $250,000
Will make loans and/or equity investments
Prefers Expansion Stage Companies
Industry Preference: Diversified
Geographical Area: National

Walnut Capital Corporation
Burton W. Kanter, President
Two N. LaSalle Street, #2410
Chicago, IL 60602
(312) 346-2033
Fax: (312) 346-2231

Loan/Investment Range: Up to $1 Million
Prefers equity investments
Prefers Startup, Early, Expansion Stage and
Seasoned Companies and Management Buyouts
Industry Preference: Diversified
Geographical Area: National

INDIANA

1st Source Capital Corp.
Eugene L. Cavanaugh, Jr., Vice President
100 North Michigan Street
Mail: P.O. Box 1602
South Bend, IN 46634
(219) 235-2180
Fax: (219) 235-2719

Loan/Investment Range: Up to $500,000
Prefers equity investments
Prefers Expansion Stage, Seasoned Companies
and Management Buyouts
Industry Preference: Diversified
Geographical Area: Midwestern States

Cambridge Ventures, LP
Jean Wojtowicz, President
8440 Woodfield Crossing Blvd., #315
Indianapolis, IN 46240
(317) 469-3927
Fax: (317) 469-3926

Loan/Investment Range: Up to $600,000
Will make loans and/or equity investments
Will Consider All Stages of Development
Industry Preference: Diversified
Geographical Area: Midwestern States (within 200
miles of Indianapolis)

Circle Ventures, Inc.
Carrie Walkup, V. President
26 N. Arsenal Avenue
Indianapolis, IN 46201
(317) 636-7242
Fax: (317) 637-7581

Loan/Investment Range: Up to $250,000
Will make loans and/or equity investments
Prefers Expansion Stage, Seasoned Companies
and Management Buyouts
Industry Preference: Diversified
Geographical Area: Indiana

IOWA

InvestAmerica Venture Group, Inc.
MorAmerica Capital Corp.
David R. Schroder, Vice President
101 2nd Street, S.E., #800
Cedar Rapids, IA 52401
(319) 363-8249
Fax: (319) 363-9683

Loan/Investment Range: Up to $1.4 Million
Prefers equity investments
Prefers Expansion Stage, Seasoned Companies
and Management Buyouts
Industry Preference: Communications,Computer,
Medical, Health, Light & Heavy Industrial
Geographical Area: National

KANSAS

Kansas Venture Capital, Inc.
Rex E. Wiggins, President
6700 Antioch Plaza, #460
Overland Park, KS 66204
(913) 262-7117
Fax: (913) 262-3509

Loan/Investment Range: Up to $1 Million
Will make loans and/or equity investments
Prefers Startups, Early Stage, Expansion Stage,
Seasoned Companies and Management Buyouts
Industry Preference: Diversified
Geographical Area: Kansas/Midwestern States

Kansas Venture Capital, Inc.
(Main Office in Overland Park, KS)
Thomas C. Blackburn, Vice President
One Main Place #806
Wichita, KS 67202
(316) 262-1221
Fax: (316) 262-0780

Loan/Investment Range: Up to $500,000
Will make loans and/or equity investments
Prefers Early Stage, Expansion Stage Companies,
and Management Buyouts
Industry Preference: Diversified
Geographical Area: Kansas

KENTUCKY

Equal Opportunity Finance, Inc. (SSBIC)
David A. Sattich, President
420 S. Hurstbourne Parkway, #201
Louisville, KY 40222
(502) 423-1943
Fax: (502) 423-1945

Loan/Investment Range: Up to $500,000
Will make loans and/or equity investments
Prefers Early Stage, Expansion Stage Companies,
and Management Buyouts
Industry Preference: Diversified
Geographical Area: Indiana, Ohio and West
Virginia

Mountain Ventures, Inc.
L. Ray Moncrief, President
362 Old Whitley Road
P.O. Box 1738
London, KY 40743
(606) 864-5175
Fax: (606) 864-5194

Contact For Further Information
Investment Policy: Diversified

LOUISIANA

Premier Venture Capital Corporation
G. Lee Griffin, President
451 Florida Street
Mail: P.O. Box 1511
Baton Rouge, LA 70801
(504) 332-4421
Fax: (504) 332-7929

Loan/Investment Range: Up to $1 - $2 Million
Prefers equity investments
Prefers Early Stage, Expansion Stage, Seasoned
Companies and Management Buyouts
Industry Preference: Diversified
Geographical Area: National

MARYLAND

Greater Washington Investments, Inc.
Haywood Miller, Manager
5454 Wisconsin Avenue
Chevy Chase, MD 20815
(301) 656-0626
Fax: (301) 656-4053

Contact For Further Information
Investment Policy: Diversified

**Security Financial & Investment Corp.
(SSBIC)**
Gus Levathes, Exec. Vice President
7720 Wisconsin Avenue, #207
Bethesda, MD 20814
(301) 951-4288
Fax: None

Contact For Further Information
Investment Policy: Diversified

Syncom Capital Corp. (SSBIC)
Terry L. Jones, President
8401 Colesville Road, #300
Silver Springs, MD 20910
(301) 608-3207
Fax: None

Contact For Further Information
Investment Policy: Communications Media

MASSACHUSETTS

Advent Atlantic Capital Company, LP
David D. Croll, Managing Partner
75 State Street, #2500
Boston, MA 02109
(617) 345-7200
Fax: (617) 7201

Contact For Further Information
Investment Policy: Diversified

Advent Industrial Capital Company, LP
David D. Croll, Managing Partner
75 State Street, #2500
Boston, MA 02109
(617) 345-7200
Fax: (617) 345-7201

Contact For Further Information
Investment Policy: Diversified

MASSACHUSETTS (continued)

Advent V Capital Company, LP
David D. Croll, Managing Partner
75 State Street, #2500
Boston, MA 02109
(617) 345-7200
Fax: (617) 345-7201

Contact For Further Information
Investment Policy: Diversified

Argonauts MESBIC Corp. (The) (SSBIC)
Kevin Chen, General Manager
929 Worcester Road
Framingham, MA 01701
(508) 820-3430
Fax: (508) 872-3741

Contact For Further Information
Investment Policy: Diversified

BancBoston Ventures, Inc.
BancBoston Capital
Frederick M. Fritz, President
100 Federal Street, 31st Floor
Boston, MA 02110
(617) 434-2509
Fax: (617) 434-1153

Loan/Investment Range: $20 Million
Will make loans and/or equity investments
Prefers Expansion Stage, Seasoned Companies
and Management Buyouts
Industry Preference: Communications, Computer,
Medical, Health and Light Industrial
Geographical Area: National

Business Achievement Corporation
Michael L. Katzeff, President
1172 Beacon Street, #202
Newton, MA 02161
(617) 965-0550
Fax: (617) 345-7201

Contact For Further Information
Investment Policy: Diversified

Chestnut Capital International II LP
David D. Croll, Managing Partner
75 State Street, #2500
Boston, MA 02109
(617) 345-7200
Fax: (617) 345-7201

Contact For Further Information
Investment Policy: Diversified

Chestnut Street Partners, Inc.
David D. Croll, President
75 State Street, #2500
Boston, MA 02109
(617) 345-7220
Fax: (617) 345-7201

Contact For Further Information
Investment Policy: Diversified

Commonwealth Enterprise Fund, Inc. (SSBIC)
Gabrielle Greene, Manager
10 Post Office Square, #1090
Boston, MA 02109
(617) 482-1881
Fax: (617) 482-7129

Contact For Further Information
Investment Policy: Diversified

MASSACHUSETTS (continued)

First Capital Corp. of Chicago
(Main Office in Chicago, IL)
One Financial Center, 27th Floor
Boston, MA 02111
(617) 457-2500
Fax: (617) 457-2506

Contact For Further Information
Investment Policy: Diversified

LRF Capital LP
Joseph J. Freeman, President
189 Wells Avenue, #4
Newton, MA 02159
(617) 965-4100
Fax: (617) 964-5318

Loan/Investment Range: Up to $500,000
Will make loans and/or equity investments
Prefers Expansion Stage Companies
Industry Preference: Diversified
Geographical Area: Northeastern States

Mezzanine Capital Corporation
David D. Croll, President
75 State Street, #2500
Boston, MA 02109
(617) 345-7200
Fax: (617) 345-7201

Loan/Investment Range: Over $2 Million
Will make loan and/or equity investments
Prefers Early and Expansion Stage Companies
and Management Buyouts
Industry Preference: Communications Equipment
Products and Services
Geographical Area: Nationwide

Northeast SBI Corp.
Joseph Mindick, Treasurer
16 Cumberland Street
Boston, MA 02115
(617) 267-3983
Fax: (617) 267-3983

Contact For Further Information
Investment Policy: Diversified

Pioneer Ventures LP
Frank M. Polestra, President
60 State Street
Boston, MA 02109
(617) 422-4751
Fax: (617) 742-7315

Loan/Investment Range: Up to $1 - $2 Million
Prefers equity investments
Will consider Startups, Early Stage, Expansion
Stage Companies and Management Buyouts
Industry Preference: Diversified
Geographical Area: Northeastern States

Transportation Capital Corp. (SSBIC)
(Main Office in New York, NY)
Manager
45 Newbury Street, #207
Boston, MA 02116
(617) 536-0344
Fax: (212) 949-9836

Contact For Further Information
Investment Policy: Diversified

UST Capital Corporation
Arthur F. F. Snyder, President
40 Court Street
Boston, MA 02108
(617) 726-7000
Fax: (617) 723-9414

Contact For Further Information
Investment Policy: Diversified

MICHIGAN

Capital Fund, The
Barry Wilson, President
6412 Centurion Drive, #150
Lansing, MI 48917
(517) 323-7772
Fax: (517) 323-1999

Contact For Further Information
Investment Policy: Expanding Businesses

Dearborn Capital Corp. (SSBIC)
Gary L. Ferguson, President
c/o Ford Motor Credit Corporation
The American Road
Dearborn, MI 48121
(313) 337-8577
Fax: (313) 390-4051

Contact For Further Information
Investment Policy: Diversified

Metro-Detroit Investment Co. (SSBIC)
William J. Fowler, President
30777 Northwestern Highway, #300
Farmington Hill, MI 48018
(313) 851-6300
Fax: (313) 851-9551

Contact For Further Information
Investment Policy: Grocery Stores

Motor Enterprises, Inc. (SSBIC)
James Kobus, Manager
General Motors Bldg., Room 13-147
3044 W. Grand Blvd.,
Detroit, MI 48202
(313) 556-4273
Fax: (313) 974-4499

Contact For Further Information
Investment Policy: Diversified

White Pines Corporation
Ian Bund, President
2929 Plymouth Road, #210
Ann Arbor, MI 48105
(313) 747-9401
Fax: (313) 747-9704

Loan/Investment Range: Up to $1 Million
Will make loans and/or equity investments
Prefers Expansion Stage, Seasoned Companies
and Management Buyouts
Industry Preference: Manufacturing & Services
Geographical Area: Midwestern States

MINNESOTA

Capital Dimensions Ventures Fund
Inc. (SSBIC)
Dean R. Pickerell, President
Two Appletree Square, #335
Minneapolis, MN 55425
(612) 854-3007
Fax: (612) 854-6657

Contact For Further Information
Investment Policy: Diversified

MINNESOTA (continued)

FBS SBIC, Limited Partnership
John M. Murphy, Jr., Managing Agent
600 Second Avenue South
Minneapolis, MN 55402
(612) 973-0988
Fax: (612) 973-0203

Contact For Further Information
Investment Policy: Diversified

Milestone Growth Fund, Inc. (SSBIC)
Esperanza Guerrero, President
45 South 7th Avenue South
Minneapolis, MN 55402
(612) 338-0090
Fax: (612) 338-1172

Loan/Investment Range: Up to $250,000
Will make loans and/or equity investments
Prefers Expansion Stage Companies and
Management Buyouts
Industry Preference: Diversified
Geographical Area: National

Northland Capital Venture Partnership
George G. Barnum, Jr., President
623 Missabe Building
277 W. First Street
Duluth, MN 55802
(218) 722-0545
Fax: (218) 722-7241

Loan/Investment Range: Up to $250,000
Prefers equity investments
Prefers Early Stage, Expansion Stage, Seasoned
Companies and Management Buyouts
Industry Preference: Diversified
Geographical Area: National

Norwest Venture Partners
Daniel J. Haggerty, President & CEO
2800 Piper Jaffray Tower
222 South Ninth Street
Minneapolis, MN 55402
(612) 667-1650
Fax: (612) 667-1660

Loan/Investment Range: Over $2 Million
Prefers equity investments
Will consider Startups, Early Stage, Expansion
Stage, Seasoned Companies and Management
Buyouts
Industry Preference: Diversified
Geographical Area: National

Norwest Equity Partners IV
Robert Zicarelli, General Partner
2800 Piper Jaffray Tower
222 South Ninth Street
Minneapolis, MN 55402
(612) 667-1650
Fax: (612) 667-1660

Contact For Further Information
Investment Policy: Diversified

Norwest Growth Fund, Inc.
Daniel J. Haggerty, President
2800 Piper Jaffray Tower
222 South Ninth Street
Minneapolis, MN 55402
(612) 667-1650
Fax: (612) 667-1660

Contact For Further Information
Investment Policy: Diversified

MISSISSIPPI

Sun Delta Capital Access Center, Inc. (SSBIC)
Howard Boutte, Jr., Vice President
819 Main Street
Greenville, MS 38701
(601) 335-5291
Fax: (601) 335-5295

Loan/Investment Range: $200,000
Will make loans and/or/equity investments
Prefers Startup Companies
Industry Preference: Diversified
Geographical Area: National

MISSOURI

Bankers Capital Corporation
Raymond E. Glasnapp, President
3100 Gillham Road
Kansas City, MO 64109
(816) 531-1600
Fax: (816) 531-1334

Loan/Investment Range: Up to $100,000
Will make loans and/or equity investments
Prefers Expansion Stage, Seasoned Companies and
Management Buyouts
Industry Preference: Diversified
Geographical Area: Midwestern States

CFB Venture Fund I, Inc.
James F. O'Donnell, Chairman
11 S. Meramec, #800
St. Louis, MO 63105
(314) 746-7427
Fax: (314) 746-8739

Loan/Investment Range: $1 - $2 Million
Prefers equity investments
Prefers Expansion Stage, Seasoned Companies and
Management Buyouts
Industry Preference: Diversified
Geographical Area: Midwestern States

CFB Venture Fund II, Inc.
Bart S. Bergman, President
1000 Walnut Street, 18th Floor
Kansas City, MO 64106
(816) 234-2357
Fax: (816) 234-2333

Contact For Further Information
Investment Policy: Diversified

MorAmerica Capital Corp.
(Main Office: InvestAmerica, Cedar Rapids, IA)
Commerce Tower Building
911 Main Street, #2724A
Kansas City, MO 64105
(816) 842-0114
Fax: (816) 471-7339

Loan/Investment Range: Up to $1 Million
Prefers equity investments
Prefers Early and Expansion Stage Companies
and Management Buyouts
Industry Preference: Diversified
Geographical Area: National

United Missouri Capital Corporation
Noel J. Shull, Manager
1010 Grand Avenue
P. O. Box 419226
Kansas City, MO 64141
(816) 860,7914
Fax: (816) 860-7413

Loan/Investment Range: Up to $500,000
Will make loans and/or equity investments
Prefers Expansion Stage Companies
Industry Preference: Diversified
Geographical Area: Midwest/Southwestern States

NEBRASKA

United Financial Resources Corp.
Joan Boulay, Manager
7401 "F" Street
P. O. Box 1131
Omaha, NE 68101
(402) 339-7300
Fax: (402) 734-0650

Contact For Further Information
Investment Policy: Grocery Stores

NEW JERSEY

Bishop Capital, LP
Charles J. Irish, General Partner
500 Morris Avenue
Springfield, NJ 07081
(201) 376-1595
Fax: (201) 376-6527

Loan/Investment Range: Up to $500,000
Prefers equity investments
Prefers Seasoned Companies
and Management Buyouts
Industry Preference: Diversified
Geographical Area: Northeastern and
Midwestern States

Capital Circulation Corp. (SSBIC)
Judy M. Kao, General Partner
2035 Lemoine Avenue, 2nd Floor
Fort Lee, NJ 07024
(201) 947-8637
Fax: (201) 585-1965

Loan/Investment Range: Up to $250,000
Prefers to make straight loans
Prefers Expansion Stage Companies
Industry Preference: Diversified
Geographical Area: Northeastern States

The CIT Group/Venture Capital, Inc.
Colby W. Collier, Vice President
650 CIT Drive
Livingston, NJ 07039
(201) 740-5429
Fax: (201) 740-5555

Loan/Investment Range: $1 - $2 Million
Will make loans and/or equity investments
Prefers Early and Expansion Stage Companies
and Management Buyouts
Industry Preference: Diversified
Geographical Area: National

ESLO Capital Corporation
Leo Katz, President
212 Wright Street
Newark, NJ 07114
(201) 242-4488
Fax: (201) 643-6062

Loan/Investment Range: Up to $100,000
Prefers to make loans
Prefers Startup Companies
Industry Preference: Diversified
Geographical Area: Northeastern States

Fortis Capital Corporation
Martin S. Orland, President
333 Thornall Street, 2nd Floor
Edison, NJ 08837
(908) 603-8500
Fax: (908) 603-8250

Loan/Investment Range: Up to $1 Million
Prefers equity investments
Prefers Expansion Stage Companies and
Management Buyouts
Industry Preference: Diversified
Geographical Area: National

NEW JERSEY (continued)

Rutgers Minority Investment Co. (SSBIC)
Oscar Figueroa, President
1180 University Avenue, 3rd Floor
Newark, NJ 07102
(201) 648-5627
Fax: (201) 648-1110

Loan/Investment Range: Up to $250,000
Will make loans and/or equity investments
Prefers Early Stage and Expansion Stage
Companies
Industry Preference: Diversified
Geographical Area: Northeastern States

Tappan Zee Capital Corporation
Jeffrey Birnberg, President
201 Lower Notch Road
P.O. Box 416
Little Falls, NJ 07424
(201) 256-8280
Fax: (201) 256-2841

Loan/Investment Range: Up to $1 Million
Will make loans and/or equity investments
Prefers Expansion Stage and Seasoned Companies
Industry Preference: Diversifed
Geographical Area: New Jersey, New York,
Connecticut and Pennsylvania

Transpac Capital Corporation (SSBIC)
Tsuey Tang Wang, President
1037 Route 46 East
Clifton, NJ 07013
(201) 470-8855
Fax: (201) 470-8827

Contact For Further Information
Investment Policy: Diversified

NEW YORK

399 Venture Partners
William Comfort, Chairman
399 Park Ave., 14th Floor/Zone 4
New York, NY 10043
(212) 559-1127
Fax: (212) 888-2940

Contact For Further Information
Investment Policy: Diversified

American Asian Capital Corp. (SSBIC)
Howard H. Lin, President
130 Water Street, #6-L
New York, NY 10005
(212) 422-6880
Fax: None

Contact For Further Information
Investment Policy: Diversified

ASEA Harvest Partners II
Harvey Wertheim, General Partner
767 Third Avenue
New York, NY 10017
(212) 838-7776
Fax: (212) 593-0734

Loan/Investment Range: Over $2 Million
Will make loans and/or equity investments
Prefers Expansion Stage, Seasoned Companies
and Management Buyouts
Industry Preference: Diversified
Geographical Area: National

Argentum Capital Partners, LP
Daniel Raynor, Chairman
405 Lexington Avenue, 54th Floor
New York, NY 10174
(212) 949-8272
Fax: (212) 949-8294

Contact For Further Information
Investment Policy: Diversified

NEW YORK (continued)

Atalanta Investment Company, Inc.
L. Mark Newman, Chairman
650 5th Avenue, 15th Floor
New York, NY 10019
(212) 956-9100
Fax: (212) 956-9103

Contact For Further Information
Investment Policy: Diversified

BT Capital Corp.
Noel E. Urben, President
280 Park Avenue, 32 West
New York, NY 10017
(212) 454-1903
Fax: (212) 454-2121

Loan/Investment Range: Over $2 Million
Will make loans and/or equity investments
Prefers Expansion Stage, Seasoned Companies
and Management Buyouts
Industry Preference: Diversified
Geographical Area: National

Barclays Capital Investors Corp.
Graham McGahen, President
222 Broadway, 12th Floor
New York, NY 10038
(212) 412-6796
Fax: (212) 412-6780

Loan/Investment Range: $1 - $2 Million
Will make loans and/or equity investments
Prefers Seasoned Companies and Management
Buyouts
Industry Preference: Business and Consumer Products
and Services, Industrial Equipment and Products
Geographical Area: National

BT Capital Corporation
Noel E. Urben, President
280 Park Avenue, 10 West
New York, NY 10017
(212) 454-1916
Fax: (212) 454-2421

Loan/Investment Range: Over $2 Million
Will make loans and/or equity investments
Prefers Expansion Stage Companies and
Management Buyouts
Industry Preference: Diversified
Geographical Area: National

**Capital Investors & Management
Corp. (SSBIC)**
Rose Chao, Manager
210 Canal Street, #611
New York, NY 10013
(212) 964-2480
Fax: (212) 349-9160

Contact For Further Information
Investment Policy: Diversified

CB Investors, Inc.
Edward L. Kock III, President
270 Park Avenue
New York, NY 10017
(212) 286-3222
Fax: (212) 983-0626

Contact For Further Information
Investment Policy: Diversified

CIBC Wood Gundy Ventures
Gordon H. Muessel, Senior V. President
425 Lexington Avenue, 9th Floor
New York, NY 10017
(212) 856-4013
Fax: (212) 697-1554

Loan/Investment Range: Over $2 Million
Prefers equity investments
Prefers Expansion Stage Companies and
Management Buyouts
Industry Preference: Consumer Products, Medical and
Health, Communications, Computer, Electronic
Geographical Area: National

NEW YORK (continued)

CMNY Capital II, LP
Howard G. Davidoff, Managing Director
135 East 57th Street, 26th Floor
New York, NY 10022
(212) 909-8428
Fax: (212) 980-2630

Loan/Investment Range: Up to $1 Million
Prefers equity investments
Prefers Startups, Early, Expansion Stage, Seasoned
Companies and Management Buyouts
Industry Preference: Diversified
Geographical Area: National

Chase Manhattan Capital Corp.
Maria Willetts, President
One Chase Manhattan Plaza, 8th Floor
New York, NY 10081
(212) 552-5083
Fax: (212) 552-1159

Loan/Investment Range: Over $2 Million
Prefers equity investments
Prefers Expansion Stage, Seasoned Companies and
Management Buyouts
Industry Preference: Consumer Products, Energy,
Natural Resources, Industrial Products, Medical,
Health and Diversified
Geographical Area: National

Chemical Venture Capital Associates
Jeffrey C. Walker, Managing Gen. Partner
270 Park Avenue, 5th Floor
New York, NY 10017
(212) 270-3220
Fax: (212) 270-2327

Loan/Investment Range: Over $2 Million
Prefers equity investments
Prefers Expansion Stage, Seasoned Companies
and Management Buyouts
Industry Preference: Diversified
Geographical Area: National

Citicorp Venture Capital, Ltd.
William T. Comfort, Chairman
399 Park Avenue, 14th Floor, Zone 4
New York, NY 10043
(212) 559-2565
Fax: (212) 888-2940

Loan/Investment Range: Over $2 Million
Will make loans and/or equity investments
Prefers Expansion Stage Companies and
Management Buyouts
Industry Preference: Diversified
Geographical Area: National

East Coast Venture Capital, Inc. (SSBIC)
Zindel Zelmanovitch, President
313 West 53rd Street, 3rd Floor
New York, NY 10019
(212) 245-6460
Fax: (212) 265-2962

Contact For Further Information
Investment Policy: Diversified

Edwards Capital Company
Edward H. Teitlebaum, President
Two Park Avenue, 20th Floor
New York, NY 10016
(212) 686-5449
Fax: (212) 213-6234

Contact For Further Information
Investment Policy: Transportation Industry

ELK Associates Funding Corp. (SSBIC)
Gary C. Granoff, President
747 Third Avenue, 4th Floor
New York, NY 10017
(212) 421-2111
Fax: (212) 983-0571

Loan/Investment Range: Up to $250,000
Prefers to make straight loans
Prefers Expansion Stage Companies
Industry Preference: Diversified
Geographical Area: Northeastern States

NEW YORK (continued)

Empire State Capital Corp. (SSBIC)
Dr. Joseph Wu, President
170 Broadway, #1200
New York, NY 10038
(212) 513-1799
Fax: (212) 513-1892

Contact For Further Information
Investment Policy: Diversified

Esquire State Capital Corp. (SSBIC)
Wen-Chan Chin, President
69 Veterans Memorial Highway
Commack, NY 11725
(516) 462-6946
Fax: (516) 462-6945

Contact For Further Information
Investment Policy: Diversified

Exim Capital Corp. (SSBIC)
Victor K. Chun, President
241 5th Avenue, 3rd Floor
New York, NY 10016
(212) 683-3375
Fax: (212) 689-4118

Contact For Further Information
Investment Policy: Diversified

Exeter Venture Lenders, L.P.
Keith Fox, Manager
10 East 53rd Street, 32nd Floor
New York, NY 10022
(212) 872-1172
Fax: (212) 872-1198

Loan/Investment Range: Over $2 Million
Will make loans and/or equity investments
Prefers Expansion Stage, Seasoned Companies
and Management Buyouts
Industry Preference: Diversified
Geographical Area: National

Fair Capital Corporation (SSBIC)
Rose Chao, Manager
210 Canal Street, #611
New York, NY 10013
(212) 964-2480
Fax: (212) 349-9160

Contact For Further Information
Investment Policy: Diversified

Fifty-Third Street Ventures, L.P.
Patricia Cloherty & Dan Tessler, G. P.
155 Main Street
Cold Spring, NY 10516
(914) 265-4244
Fax: (914) 265-4158

Contact For Further Information
Investment Policy: Diversified

First County Capital, Inc. (SSBIC)
Zenia Yuan, President
135-14 Northern Blvd., 2nd Floor
Flushing, NY 11354
(718) 461-1778
Fax: (718) 461-1835

Loan/Investment Range: Up to $250,000
Will make loans and/or equity investments
Prefers Startups, Early and Expansion Stage
Companies
Industry Preference: Diversified
Geographical Area: New York and Northeastern States

NEW YORK (continued)

First Pacific Capital Corp. (SSBIC)
Michael Cipriani, Manager
273 Wyckoff Avenue
Brooklyn, NY 11378
(718) 381-5095
Fax: (718) 381-5192

Contact For Further Information
Investment Policy: Diversified

First Wall Street SBIC, LP
Alan L. Farkas, President
26 Broadway, #1320
New York, NY 10004
(212) 742-3770
Fax: (212) 742-3776

Loan/Investment Range: Up to $1 Million
Will make loans and/or equity investments
Prefers Expansion Stage, Seasoned Companies
and Management Buyouts
Industry Preference: Diversified
Geographical Area: Northeastern States

Flushing Capital Corp. (SSBIC)
Frank J. Mitchell, President
137-80 Northern Blvd.
Flushing, NY 11354
(718) 886-5866
Fax: (718) 939-7761

Contact For Further Information
Investment Policy: Diversified

Freshstart Venture Capital Corp. (SSBIC)
Zindel Zelmanovich, President
313 West 53rd Street, 3rd Floor
New York, NY 10019
(212) 265-2249
Fax: (212) 265-2962

Contact For Further Information
Investment Policy: Diversified

Fundex Capital Corporation
Howard Sommer, President
525 Northern Blvd., #210
Great Neck, NY 11021
(516) 466-8550
Fax: (516) 466-0180

Loan/Investment Range: Up to $1,000,000
Will make loans and/or equity investments
Prefers Early Stage, Expansion Stage, Seasoned
Companies and Management Buyouts
Industry Preference: Diversified
Geographical Area: Northeastern States

Genesee Funding, Inc.
Stuart Marsh, President
70 Linden Oaks, 3rd Floor
Rochester, NY 14625
(716) 383-5550
Fax: (716) 383-5305

Loan/Investment Range: Up to $250,000
Will make loans and/or equity investments
Prefers Expansion Stage, Seasoned Companies
and Management Buyouts
Industry Preference: Diversified
Geographical Area: Northeastern States

Hanam Capital Corp. (SSBIC)
Robert Schairer, President
208 West 30th Street, #1205
New York, NY 10001
(212) 564-5225
Fax: (212) 564-5307

Contact For Further Information
Investment Policy: Diversified

NEW YORK (continued)

Ibero American Investors Corp. (SSBIC)
Emilio Serrano, President
104 Scio Street
Rochester, NY 14604
(716) 262-3440
Fax: (716) 262-3441

Contact For Further Information
Investment Policy: Diversified

IBJS Capital Corporation
Peter A. Handy, President
One State Street, 9th Floor
New York, NY 10004
(212) 858-2827
Fax: (212) 858-2768

Loan/Investment Range: Up to $1 Million
Will make loans and/or equity investments
Prefers Expansion Stage, Seasoned Companies
and Management Buyouts
Industry Preference: Diversified (No Real Estate)
Geographical Area: Northeastern and
Midwestern States

InterEquity Capital Partners, L.P.
Irwin Schlass, President
220 Fifth Avenue, 10th Floor
New York, NY 10001
(212) 779-2022
Fax: (212) 779-2103

Loan/Investment Range: $1 - $2 Million
Will make loans and/or equity investments
Prefers Early Stage, Expansion Stage, Seasoned
Companies and Management Buyouts
Industry Preference: Diversified
Geographical Area: National

International Paper Capital Foundation, Inc.
(Main Office in Memphis, TN)
Frank Polney, Manager
Two Manhattanville Road
Purchase, NY 10577
(914) 397-1578
Fax: (914) 397-1090

Contact For Further Information
Investment Policy: Transportation

J. P. Morgan Investment Corporation
David M. Cromwell, Managing Director
60 Wall Street, 14th Floor
New York, NY 10260
(212) 648-9781
Fax: (212) 648-5032

Loan/Investment Range: Over $2 Million
Prefers equity investments
Prefers Expansion Stage, Seasoned Companies and
Management Buyouts
Industry Preference: Diversified
Geographical Area: National

KOCO Capital Company, L.P.
Walter Farley, CFO
111 Radio Circle
New York, NY 10260
(914) 241-7430
Fax: (914) 241-7476

Contact For Further Information
Investment Policy: Diversified

Kwiat Capital Corporation
Sheldon F. Kwait, President
579 Fifth Avenue
New York, NY 10017
(212) 223-1111
Fax: (212) 223-2796

Contact For Further Information
Investment Policy: Diversified

NEW YORK (continued)

M & T Capital Corporation
Phillip A. McNeill, Vice President
One Fountain Plaza, 9th Floor
Buffalo, NY 14203
(716) 848-3800
Fax: (716) 848-3424

Loan/Investment Range: $1 - $2 Million
Will make loans and/or equity investments
Prefers Expansion Stage, Seasoned Companies
and Management Buyouts
Industry Preference: Diversified
Geographical Area: Northeastern and
Midwestern States

Medallion Funding Corp. (SSBIC)
Alvin Murstein, President
205 E. 42nd Street, #2020
New York, NY 10017
(212) 682-3300
Fax: (212) 983-0351

Loan/Investment Range: Up to $250,000
Will make straight loans
Prefers Seasoned Companies
Industry Preference: Diversified
Geographical Area: New York State

NYBDC Capital Corporation
Robert W. Lazar, President
41 State Street
P. O. Box 738
Albany, NY 12201
(518) 463-2268
Fax: (518) 463-0240

Contact For Further Information
Investment Policy: Diversified

NatWest USA Capital Corporation
Phillip Krall, General Manager
175 Water Street, 25th Floor
New York, NY 10038
(212) 602-1200
Fax: (212) 602-2149

Loan/Investment Range: $1 - $2 Million
Will make loans and/or equity investments
Prefers Seasoned Companies and Management
Buyouts
Industry Preference: Diversified
Geographical Area: National

Norwood Venture Corporation
Mark R. Littell, President
1430 Broadway, #1607
New York, NY 10018
(212) 869-5075
Fax: (212) 869-5331

Loan/Investment Range: Up to $1 Million
Prefers equity investments
Prefers Seasoned Companies and Management
Buyouts
Industry Preference: Diversified
Geographical Area: National

Pan Pac Capital Corporation (SSBIC)
Dr. In Ping Jack Lee, President
121 East Industry Court
Deer Park, NY 11729
(516) 586-7653
Fax: (516) 586-7505

Loan/Investment Range: Up to $500,000
Will make loans and/or equity investments
Prefers Expansion Stage Companies
Industry Preference: Diversified
Geographical Area: National

Paribas Principal Incorporated
Steven Alexander, President
787 Seventh Avenue, 33rd Floor
New York, NY 10019
(212) 841-2115
Fax: (212) 841-3558

Loan/Investment Range: Over $1 Million
Prefers to make equity investments
Prefers Management Buyouts
Industry Preference: Diversified
Geographical Range: National

NEW YORK (continued)

Pierre Funding Corp. (SSBIC)
Elias Debbas, President
805 Third Avenue, 6th Floor
New York, NY 10022
(212) 888-1515
Fax: (212) 688-4252

Contact For Further Information
Investment Policy: Transportation

Pyramid Ventures, Inc.
Brian Talbot, Vice President
130 Liberty Street, 31st Floor
New York, NY 10017
(212) 250-9571
Fax: (212) 250-7651

Contact For Further Information
Investment Policy: Diversified

R & R Financial Corporation
Martin Eisenstadt, Vice President
1370 Broadway, 2nd Floor
New York, NY 10018
(212) 356-1468
Fax: (212) 356-0900

Loan/Investment Range: Up to $250,000
Prefers to make straight loans
Prefers Expansion Stage and Seasoned Companies
Industry Preference: Diversified
Geographical Area: Northeastern States

Rand SBIC, Inc.
Donald A. Ross, President
1300 Rand Building
Buffalo, NY 14203
(716) 853-0802
Fax: (716) 854-8480

Loan/Investment Range: Up to $500,000
Will make loans and/or equity investments
Prefers Startups and Early Stage Companies
Industry Preference: Diversified
Geographical Area: Northeastern States

Situation Ventures Corp. (SSBIC)
Sam Hollander, President
56-20 59th Street
Maspeth, NY 11378
(718) 894-2000
Fax: (718) 326-4642

Contact For Further Information
Investment Policy: Diversified

Square Deal Venture Capital Corp. (SSBIC)
Gloria Feilbusch, Manager
766 N. Main Street
New Square, NY 10977
(914) 354-7917
Fax: None

Contact For Further Information
Investment Policy: Diversified

Sterling Commercial Capital, Inc.
Harvey L. Granat, President
175 Great Neck Road, #408
Great Neck, NY 11021
(516) 482-7374
Fax: (516) 487-0781

Loan/Investment Range: Up to $1 Million
Will make loans and/or equity investments
Prefers Seasoned Companies
Industry Preference: Diversified
Geographical Area: Northeastern States

NEW YORK (continued)

TLC Funding Corporation
Philip G. Kass, President
660 White Plains Road
Tarrytown, NY 10591
(914) 332-5200
Fax: (914) 332-5660

Loan/Investment Range: Up to $500,000
Will make loans and/or equity investments
Prefers Early Stage, Expansion Stage Companies
Industry Preference: Diversified
Geographical Area: Northeastern States

Tappan Zee Capital Corporation
(Main Office in Little Falls, NJ)
Manager
120 North Main Street
New City, NY 10956
(914) 634-8890
Fax: None

Contact For Further Information
Investment Policy: Diversified

Transportation Capital Corp. (SSBIC)
Paul J. Borden, President
60 E. 42nd Street, #3115
New York, NY 10165
(212) 697-4885
Fax: (212) 883-0885

Loan/Investment Range: Up to $1 Million
Prefers to make loans
Prefers Startups, Expansion Stage and Seasoned
Companies
Industry Preference: Diversified
Geographical Area: Northeastern States

Triad Capital Corp. of New York (SSBIC)
Marciel E. Robiou, President
15 West 39th Street, 9th Floor
New York, NY 10018
(212) 764-5590
Fax: (212) 719-9611

Contact For Further Information
Investment Policy: Diversified

Trusty Capital Inc. (SSBIC)
Yungduk Hahn, President
350 Fifth Avenue, #2026
New York, NY 10118
(212) 736-7653
Fax: (212) 629-3019

Contact For Further Information
Investment Policy: Diversified

United Capital Investment Corp. (SSBIC)
Paul Lee, President
60 East 42nd Street, #1515
New York, NY 10165
(212) 682-7210
Fax: (212) 573-6352

Contact For Further Information
Investment Policy: Diversified

Vega Capital Corporation
Ronald A. Linden, President
80 Business Park Drive, #201
Armonk, NY 10504
(914) 273-1025
Fax: (914) 273-1028

Loan/Investment Range: Up to $1 Million
Will make loans and/or equity investments
Prefers Expansion Stage, Seasoned Companies
and Management Buyouts
Industry Preference: Diversified
Geographical Area: Northeastern and
Southeastern States

NEW YORK (continued)

Venture Opportunities Corp. (SSBIC)
A. Fred March, President
110 E. 58th Street, 16th Floor
New York, NY 10155
(212) 832-3737
Fax: (212) 223-4912

Loan/Investment Range: Up to $750,000
Will make loans and/or equity investments
Prefers Expansion Stage Companies and
Management Buyouts
Industry Preference: Diversified
Geographical Area: New York/Mid-Atlantic States

Winfield Capital Corporation
Stanley Pechman, President
237 Mamaroneck Avenue
White Plains, NY 10605
(914) 949-2600
Fax: (914) 949-7195

Loan/Investment Range: Up to $1 Million
Will make loans and/or equity investments
Prefers Expansion Stage, Seasoned Companies
and Management Buyouts
Industry Preference: Diversified
Geographical Area: Northeastern States

NORTH CAROLINA

First Union Capital Partners, Inc.
Kevin J. Roche, Senior Vice President
One First Union Center, 18th Floor
301 South College Street
Charlotte, NC 28288
(704) 374-4768
Fax: (704) 374-6711

Loan/Investment Range: Over $2 Million
Will make loans and/or equity investments
Prefers Early, Expansion Stage, Seasoned
Companies and Management Buyouts
Industry Preference: Diversified
Geographical Area: National

NationsBanc SBIC Corporation
(Main Office in Dallas, TX)
Manager
100 N. Tyron, 7th Floor
Charlotte, NC 28255
(704) 386-8063
Fax: (704) 386-6432

Contact For Further Information
Investment Policy: Diversified

NationsBanc SBIC Corporation
George W. Campbell, Jr., President
901 West Trade Street, #1020
Charlotte, NC 28202
(704) 386-7720
Fax: (704) 386-6662

Contact For Further Information
Investment Policy: Diversified

Springdale Venture Partners, LP
S. Epes Robinson, General Partner
2039 Queens Road, East
Charlotte, NC 28207
(704) 344-8290
Fax: (704) 386-6695

Contact For Further Information
Investment Policy: Diversified

OHIO

Banc One Capital Partners Corp.
(Main Office in Dallas, TX)
William P. Leahy, Director
10 West Broad Street, #400
Columbus, OH 43215
(216) 227-4209
Fax: None

Loan/Investment Range: Over $2 Million
Will make loans and/or equity investments
Prefers Expansion Stage and Seasoned Companies
Industry Preference: Diversified
Geographical Area: Midwestern and
Southwestern States

Cactus Capital Company (SSBIC)
Edward C. Liu, President
870 High Street, #216
Worthington, OH 43085
(614) 436-4060
Fax: (614) 436-4060

Contact For Further Information
Investment Policy: Diversified

Center City MESBIC, Inc. (SSBIC)
Steven Budd, President
8 North Main Street
Dayton, OH 45402
(513) 226-0457
Fax: (513) 222-7035

Loan/Investment Range: Up to $100,000
Will make loans and/or equity investments
Prefers Early Stage and Expansion Stage
Companies
Industry Preference: Diversified
Geographical Area: Southwest Ohio

Clarion Capital Corporation
Morton A. Cohen, Chairman & CEO
1801 E. 9th Street, #1520
Cleveland, OH 44114
(216) 687-1096
Fax: (216) 694-3545

Loan/Investment Range: Up to $1 Million
Prefers to make equity investments
Prefers Early Stage and Expansion Stage Companies
Industry Preference: Chemical, Comunications,
Electronics, Computer, Health, Energy,
Natural Resources
Geographical Area: Midwestern and Western States

Key Equity Capital Corporation
Raymond Lancaster, President
127 Public Square, 6th Floor
Cleveland, OH 44114
(216) 689-4890
Fax: (216) 689-3204

Loan/Investment Range: Over $2 Million
Prefers to make equity investments
Prefers Expansion Stage, Seasoned Companies
and Management Companies
Industry Preference: Diversified
Geographical Area: National

National City Capital Corporation
William H. Schecter, President
1965 East 6th Street, #400
Cleveland, OH 44114
(216) 575-2491
Fax: (216) 575-3355

Loan/Investment Range: Over $2 Million
Will make loans and/or equity investments
Prefers Expansion Stage, Seasoned Companies
and Management Buyouts
Industry Preference: Diversified
Geographical Area: Midwest and Northeastern States

OKLAHOMA

Alliance Business Investment Co.
Barry M. Davis, President
One Williams Center, #2000
17 East Second Street
Tulsa, OK 74172
(918) 584-3581
Fax: (918) 582-3403

Loan/Investment Range: Up to $500,000
Prefers equity investments
Prefers Early Stage, Expansion Stage Companies
and Management Buyouts
Industry Preference: Diversified
Geographical Area: Southwestern States

BancFirst Investment Corp.
T. Kent Faison, Manager
101 North Broadway
Mail: P.O. Box 26788
Oklahoma City, OK 73126]
(405) 270-1000
Fax: (405) 270-1089

Contact For Further Information
Investment Policy: Diversified

OREGON

Northern Pacific Capital Corporation
Joseph P. Tennant, Jr., President
937 SW 14th Street, #200
P. O. Box 1658
Portland, OR 97207
(503) 241-1255
Fax: (503) 299-6653

Loan/Investment Range: Up to $250,000
Will make loans and/or equity investments
Prefers Expansion Stage Companies and
Management Buyouts
Industry Preference: Industrial Equipment and
Services
Geographical Area: Northwestern States

U. S. Bancorp Capital Corporation
Gary Patterson, President
111 SW Fifth Ave., #T-10
Portland, OR 97204
(503) 275-5710
Fax: (503) 275-7565

Loan/Investment Range: $1 - $2 Million
Prefers equity investments
Prefers Expansion Stage, Seasoned Companies
and Management Buyouts
Industry Preference: Diversified
Geographical Area: Pacific Northwestern States

PENNSYLVANIA

CIP Capital, Inc.
Winston J. Churchill, Jr., Manager
20 Valley Stream Parkway, #265
Malvern, PA 19355
(215) 695-8380
Fax: (215) 695-8388

Loan/Investment Range: $1 - $2 Million
Prefers to make equity investments
Prefers Startups, Early, Expansion Stage Companies
and Management Buyouts
Industry Preference: Business Products & Services,
Communications, Electronic and Medical
Geographical Area: National

Enterprise Venture Capital Corp. of PA
Don Cowle, CEO
111 Main Street,
Johnstown, PA 15901
(814) 535-7597
Fax: (814) 535-8677

Loan/Investment Range: Up to $100,000
Will make loans and/or equity investments
Will consider Startups, Early Stage, Expansion
Stage, Seasoned Companies and Management
Buyouts
Industry Preference: Diversified
Geographical Area: Pennsylvania

PENNSYLVANIA (continued)

Fidelcor Capital Corporation
Elizabeth T. Crawford, President
123 S. Broad Street, 11th Floor
Philadelphia, PA 19109
(215) 985-3722
Fax: (215) 985-7282

Loan/Investment Range: Up to $1 Million
Will make loans and/or equity investments
Prefers Expansion Stage and Seasoned Companies
Industry Preference: Diversified
Geographical Area: Northeastern States

First SBIC of California
(Main Office in Costa Mesa, CA)
Daniel A. Dye, Manager
P. O. Box 512
Washington, PA 15301
(412) 223-0707
Fax: (714) 546-8021

Contact For Further Information
Investment Policy: Diversified

**Greater Philadelphia Venture
Capital Corp. (SSBIC)**
Fred S. Choate, Manager
351 East Conestoga Road, #203
Philadelphia, PA 19087
(215) 688-6829
Fax: (215) 254-2996

Loan/Investment Range: Up to $250,000
Will make loans and/or equity investments
Prefers Expansion Stage, Seasoned Companies
and Management Buyouts
Industry Preference: Diversified
Geographical Area: Within 150 Miles of
Philadelphia

Meridian Capital Corporation
Pamela E. Davis, President
601 Penn Street
Reading, PA 19603
(215) 655-2924
Fax: (215) 655-1908

Loan/Investment Range: Up to $500,000
Prefers equity investments
Prefers Expansion Stage, Seasoned Companies
and Management Buyouts
Industry Preference: Diversified
Geographical Area: Northeastern States

Meridian Venture Partners
Raymond R. Rafferty, General Partner
The Fidelity Court Building
259 Radnor-Chester Road, #140
Radnor, PA 19087
(215) 254-2999
Fax: (215) 254-2996

Loan/Investment Range: $1 - $2 Million
Prefers equity investments
Prefers Expansion Stage, Seasoned Companies
and Management Buyouts
Industry Preference: Diversified
Geographical Area: Northeast States

PNC Capital Corporation
Gary J. Zentner, President
PNB Building, 19th Floor
5th Avenue & Wood Street
Pittsburgh, PA 15222
(412) 762-2238
Fax: (412) 762-6233

Loan/Investment Range: Over $2 Million
Will make loans and/or equity investments
Prefers Expansion Stage, Seasoned Companies
and Management Buyouts
Industry Preference: Diversified
Geographical Area: Northeastern States

PUERTO RICO

North American Investment Corp. (SSBIC)
Rita V. de Fajardo, Chairwoman
P. O. Box 191831
Hato Rey Station
San Juan, PR 00919
(809) 754-6178
Fax: (809) 754-6181

Loan/Investment Range: Up to $250,000
Will make loans and/or equity investments
Prefers Expansion Stage Companies
Industry Preference: Diversified
Geographical Area: Puerto Rico

RHODE ISLAND

Domestic Capital Corporation
Nathaniel B. Baker, President
815 Reservoir Avenue
Cranston, RI 02910
(401) 946-3310
Fax: (401) 943-6708

Loan/Investment Range: Up to $250,000
Prefers to make straight loans
Prefers Expansion Stage, Seasoned Companies
Industry Preference: Diversified
Geographical Area: Northeastern States

Fleet Venture Resources, Inc.
Robert M. Van Degna, President
111 Westminster Street, 4th Floor
Providence, RI 02903
(401) 278-6770
Fax: (401) 251-1274

Loan/Investment Range: Over $2 Million
Prefers equity investments
Prefers Expansion Stage, Seasoned Companies
and Management Buyouts
Industry Preference: Communications, Consumer,
Industrial Products, Medical, Health and Service
Companies
Geographical Area: National

Moneta Capital Corporation
Arnold Kilberg, President
99 Wayland Avenue
Mail: 285 Governor Street
Providence, RI 02906
(401) 454-7500
Fax: (401) 455-3636

Contact For Further Information
Investment Policy: Diversified

NYSTRS/NV Capital Limited Partnership
Robert M. Van Degna, Managing Partner
111 Westminster Street
Providence, RI 02903
(401) 276-5597
Fax: (401) 278-6387

Contact For Further Information
Investment Policy: Diversified

Richmond Square Capital Corp.
Harold I. Schein, President
One Richmond Square
Providence, RI 02906
(401) 521-3000
Fax: (401) 751-3940

Loan/Investment Range: Up to $1 Million
Will make loans and/or equity investments
Prefers Expansion Stage Companies
and Management Buyouts
Industry Preference: Diversified
Geographical Area: Northeastern States

RHODE ISLAND (continued)

Wallace Capital Corporation
Lloyd W. Granoff, President
170 Westminister Street, #300
Providence, RI 02903
(401) 273-9191
Fax: (401) 273-9648

Loan/Investment Range: $500,000
Primarily makes straight loans
Will Consider All Stages of Development
Industry Preference: Diversified
Grographical Area: Northeastern States

SOUTH CAROLINA

Charleston Capital Corporation
Thomas M. Ervin, President
111 Church Street
P. O. Box 328
Charleston, SC 29402
(803) 723-6464
Fax: (803) 723-1228

Loan/Investment Range: $400,000
Prefers to make straight loans
Will Consider All Stages of Development
Industry Preference: Diversified
Geographical Area: South Carolina, North Carolina and Georgia

Floco Investment Company, Inc. (The)
William H. Johnson Sr., President
Highway 52 North
P. O. Box 919
Lake City, SC 29560
(803) 389-2731
Fax: (803) 389-4199

Contact For Further Information
Investment Policy: Food Retailers

Lowcountry Investment Corporation
Joseph T. Newton, Jr., President
4444 Daley Street
P. O. Box 10447
Charleston, SC 29411
(803) 554-9880
Fax: (803) 745-2730

Contact For Further Information
Investment Policy: Grocery Stores

TENNESSEE

Byrd Business Investment, L.P.
Damon W. Byrd, General Partner
2000 Echo Glen Road, #100
P.O. Box 158838
Nashville, TN 37215
(615) 383-8673
Fax: (615) 383-8693

Loan/Investment Range: Up to $1 Million
Will make loans and/or equity investments
Prefers Expansion Stage, Seasoned Companies
and Management Buyouts
Industry Preference: Diversified
Geographical Area: Southern and Midwest States

Chickasaw Capital Corp. (SSBIC)
Greg Hadaway, President
6200 Poplar Avenue
Memphis, TN 38119
(901) 383-6404
Fax: (901) 383-6191

Loan/Investment Range: Up to $100,000
Will make loans and/or equity investments
Prefers Seasoned Companies
Industry Preference: Diversified
Geographical Area: Tennessee

TENNESSEE (continued)

Int'l Paper Capital Formation, Inc. (SSBIC)
Bob J. Higgins, Vice President
International Place II
6400 Poplar Avenue
Memphis, TN 38197
(901) 763-6282
Fax: (901) 763-7278

Contact For Further Information
Investment Policy: Diversified

Sirrom Capital, L.P.
George M. Miller, II, Manager
511 Union Street, #2310
Nashville, TN 37219
(615) 256-0701
Fax: (615) 726-1208

Loan/Investment Range: Up to $3 Million
Prefers to make straight loans
Prefers Expansion Stage, Seasoned Companies
and Management Buyouts
Industry Preference: Diversified
Geographical Area: South and Southwestern States

Tennessee Venture Capital Corp. (SSBIC)
Wendell P. Knox, President
511 Union Street, #900
Nashville, TN 37219
(615) 244-6935
Fax: (615) 254-0947

Contact For Further Information
Investment Policy: Diversified

Valley Capital Corp. (SSBIC)
Lamar J. Partridge, President
Krystal Building, #212
100 W. Martin Luther King Blvd.,
Chattanooga, TN 37402
(615) 265-1557
Fax: (615) 265-1588

Loan/Investment Range: Up to $300,000
Will make loans and/or equity investments
Prefers Expansion Stage, Seasoned Companies
and Management Buyouts
Industry Preference: Diversified
Geographical Area: Southern States

West Tennessee Venture Capital Corp. (SSBIC)
Frank Banks, President
5 North Third Street
Memphis, TN 38103
(901) 522-9237
Fax: (901) 527-6091

Contact For Further Information
Investment Policy: Diversified

TEXAS

AMT Capital, Ltd.
Tom H. Delimitros, President
8204 Elmbrook, #101
Dallas, TX 75247
(214) 905-9760
Fax: (214) 905-9761

Loan/Investment Range: Up to $500,000
Will make loans and/or equity investments
Prefers Early Stage and Expansion Stage
Companies
Industry Preference: Chemical/Industrial Products
Geographical Area: National

TEXAS (continued)

Alliance Business Investment Co.
(Main Office in Tulsa, OK)
911 Louisiana
One Shell Plaza, #3990
Houston, TX 77002
(713) 224-8224
Fax: (713) 659-8070

Contact For Further Information
Investment Policy: Diversified

Alliance Enterprise Corp. (SSBIC)
Donald R. Lawthorne, President
North Central Plaza 1, #710
12655 North Central Expressway
Dallas, TX 75243
(214) 991-1597
Fax: (214) 991-1647

Contact For Further Information
Investment Policy: Diversified

Banc One Capital Partners
Suzanne B. Kriscunas, President
300 Crescent Court, #1600
Dallas, TX 75201
(214) 979-4364
Fax: (214) 979-4355

Loan/Investment Range: Over $2 Million
Prefers equity investments/Will make loans
Prefers Expansion Stage, Seasoned Companies
and Management Buyouts
Industry Preference: Business Services,
Communications, Industrial, Medical Companies
Geographical Area: Midwestern and Southwestern
States

Capital Southwest Venture Corp.
William R. Thomas, President
12900 Preston Road, #700
Dallas, TX 75230
(214) 233-8242
Fax: (214) 233-7362

Loan/Investment Range: $1 - $2 Million
Prefers equity investments
Will consider Startups, Early Stage, Expansion
Stage, Seasoned Companies and Management
Buyouts
Industry Preference: Diversified
Geographical Area: National

Catalyst Fund, Ltd. (The)
Richard L. Herrman, President
3 Riverway, #770
Houston, TX 77056
(713) 623-8133
Fax: (713) 623-0473

Loan/Investment Range: Up to $1 Million
Prefers to make loans
Prefers Expansion Stage, Seasoned Companies
and Management Buyouts
Industry Preference: Diversified
Geographical Area: Southwestern States

Central Texas SBI Corporation
Robert H. Korman II, President
1401 Elm Street, #4764
Dallas, TX 75202
(214) 508-0900
Fax: (214) 508-0604

Contact For Further Information
Investment Policy: Diversified

TEXAS (continued)

Charter Venture Group, Inc.
Winston C. Davis, President
2600 Citadel Plaza Drive, #600
P. O. Box 4525
Houston, TX 77008
(713) 622-7500
Fax: (713) 552-8446

Contact For Further Information
Investment Policy: Diversified

Chen's Financial Group, Inc.
Samuel S. C. Chen, President
10101 Southwest Freeway, #370
Houston, TX 77074
(713) 772-8868
Fax: (713) 772-2168

Contact For Further Information
Investment Policy: Diversified

Citicorp Venture Capital, Ltd.
(Main Office in New York, NY)
717 North Hollywood, #2920-LB87
Dallas, TX 75201
(214) 880-9670
Fax: (214) 953-1495

Contact For Further Information
Investment Policy: Diversified

Ford Capital, Ltd.
C. Jeff Pan, President
200 Crescent Court, #1350
P. O. Box 2140
Dallas, TX 75221
(214) 871-5177
Fax: (214) 871-5199

Contact For Further Information
Investment Policy: Diversified

HCT Capital Corporation
V.W. Young, Jr., President
4916 Camp Bowie Blvd., #200
Fort Worth, TX 76107
(817) 763-8706
Fax: (817) 377-8049

Loan/Investment Range: Up to $250,000
Will make loans and/or equity investments
Will consider Startups, Early Stage, Expansion Stage,
Seasoned Companies and Management Buyouts
Industry Preference: Medical and Health
Geographical Area: Southwestern States

Houston Partners SBIC, Ltd.
Harvard Hill, President
Capital Center Penthouse, 8th Floor
401 Louisiana
Houston, TX 77002
(713) 222-8600
Fax: (713) 222-8932

Loan/Investment Range: Up to $500,000
Will make loans and/or equity investments
Prefers Expansion Stage Companies
Industry Preference: Consumer Products,
Industrial Products, Medical, Health and Service
Companies
Geographical Area: Southwestern States

Jiffy Lube Capital Corporation
Mark Youngs, Manager
700 Milam Street
P. O. Box 2967
Houston, TX 77252
(713) 546-8910
Fax: (713) 546-4154

Loan/Investment Range: Up to $100,000
Prefers to make loans
Prefers Startups, Early Stage and Expansion
Stage Companies
Industry Preference: Diversified
Geographical Area: National

TEXAS (continued)

Mapleleaf Capital Ltd.
Patrick A. Rivelli, Manager
Three Forest Plaza, #1300
Dallas, TX 77251
(214) 239-5650
Fax: (214) 701-0024

Loan/Investment Range: Up to $1 Million
Prefers to make equity investments
Prefers Expansion Stage, Seasoned Companies
and Management Buyouts
Industry Preference: Communications, Computer
and Electronic Equipment Products & Services
Geographical Area: Southwest & Western States

MESBIC Financial Corp. of Houston (SSBIC)
Atillio Galli, President
401 Studewood, #200
Houston, TX 77007
(713) 869-4061
Fax: (713) 869-4462

Contact For Further Information
Investment Policy: Diversified

MESBIC Ventures, Inc. (SSBIC)
Donald R. Lawhorne, President
12655 N. Central Expressway, #710
Dallas, TX 75243
(214) 991-1597
Fax: (214) 991-1647

Loan/Investment Range: Up to $500,000
Will make loans and/or equity investments
Prefers Expansion Stage Companies
Industry Preference: Diversified
Geographical Area: Southwestern States

NationsBanc Capital Corporation
Chet Walker, V. Chairman and President
901 Main Street, 66th Floor
Dallas, TX 75202
(214) 508-0900
Fax: (214) 508-0604

Loan/Investment Range: Over $2 Million
Prefers equity investments
Prefers Early, Expansion Stage, Seasoned Companies
and Management Buyouts
Industry Preference: Diversified
Geographical Area: National   Geographical Area:

North Texas MESBIC, Inc. (SSBIC)
Allan Lee, President
12770 Colt Road, #525, Dallas, TX 75151
Mail: P. O. Box 832673, Richardson, TX 75083
(214) 991-8060
Fax: (214) 991-8061

Loan/Investment Range: Up to $250,000
Will make loans and/or equity investments
Prefers expansion stage companies
Industry Preference: Diversified
Geographical Area: Texas

Pro-Med Investment Corp. (SSBIC)
Mrs. Marion Rosemore, President
17290 Preston Road, #300
Dallas, TX 75252
(214) 380-0044
Fax: (214) 380-1371

Contact For Further Information
Investment Policy: Diversified

SBI Capital Corp.
William E. Wright, President   .
6305 Beverly Hill Lane
P. O. Box 570368
Houston, TX 77257
(713) 975-1188
Fax: (713) 975-1302

Loan/Investment Range: Up to $1,000,000
Prefers equity investments
Prefers Expansion Stage Companies and
Management Buyouts
Industry Preference: Diversified
Geographical Area: Texas

TEXAS (continued)

Stratford Capital Group, Inc.
Michael D. Brown, President
200 Crescent Court, #1650
Dallas, TX 75201
(214) 740-7377
Fax: (214) 740-7340

Contact For Further Information
Investment Policy: Diversified

UNCO Ventures, Ltd.
Walter Cunningham, Managing Partner
520 Post Oak Blvd., #130
Houston, TX 77027
(713) 622-9595
Fax: (713) 622-9007

Loan/Investment Range: Up to $500,000
Will make loans and/or equity investments
Prefers Early Stage or Expansion Stage Companies
Industry Preference: Diversified
Geographical Area: National

United Oriental Capital Corp. (SSBIC)
Jai Min Tai, President
908 Town & Country Blvd., #310
Houston, TX 77024
(713) 461-3909
Fax: (713) 465-7559

Contact For Further Information
Investment Policy: Diversified

Ventex Partners, Ltd.
Richard S. Smith, President
1000 Louisiana, #1110
Houston, TX 77002
(713) 659-7860
Fax: (713) 659-7855

Contact For Further Information
Investment Policy: Diversified

Victoria Capital Corp.
David Jones, President
One O'Connor Plaza
Victoria, TX 77902
(512) 573-5151
Fax: (512) 574-5236

Contact For Further Information
Investment Policy: Diversified

Victoria Capital Corp.
(Main Office in Victoria, TX)
Jeffrey P. Blanchard, Vice President
750 E. Mulberry, #305
Mail: Box 15616
San Antonio, TX 78212
(210) 736-4233
Fax: (210) 736-5449

Contact For Further Information
Investment Policy: Diversified

Western Financial Capital Corp.
Andrew S. Rosemore, President
17290 Preston Road, #300
Dallas, TX 75252
(214) 380-0044
Fax: (214) 380-1371

Contact For Further Information
Investment Policy: Medical

UTAH

First Security Business Investment Corp.
Mark Howell, President
79 South Main Street, #800
Salt Lake City, UT 84111
(801) 246-5735

Loan/Investment Range: Up to $1 Million
Will make loans and/or equity investments
Prefers Expansion Stage, Seasoned Companies
and Management Buyouts

Wasatch Venture Corp.
Todd J. Steven, Secretary/Treasurer
1 South Main Street, 10th Floor
Salt Lake City 84133
(801) 524-8939
Fax: (801) 524-8941

Loan/Investment Range: Up to $1 Million
Prefers to make equity investments
Prefers Early and Expansion Stage Companies
Industry Preference: Diversified
Geographical Area: Arizona, California, Nevada

VERMONT

Green Mountain Capital, L.P.
Michael Sweatman, General Manager
RD 1, Box 1503
Waterbury, VT 05676
(802) 244-8981
Fax: (802) 244-8890

Loan/Investment Range: Up to $500,000
Prefers to make straight loans
Prefers Expansion Stage Companies
Industry Preference: Diversified
Geographical Area: Northeastern States

Queneska Capital Corporation
Ethan A. Allen, Jr., President
123 Church Street
P.O. Box 1009
Burlington, VT 05401
(802) 865-1806
Fax: (802) 865-1891

Loan/Investment Range: Up to $250,000
Will make loans and/or equity investments
Will Consider All Stages of Development
Industry Preference: Diversified
Geographical Area: Vermont

VIRGINIA

Continental SBIC
Arthur L. Walters, President
4141 N. Henderson Road, #8
Arlington, VA 22203
(703) 527-5200
Fax: (703) 527-3700

Loan/Investment Range: Up to $500,000
Will make loans and/or equity investments
Will Consider All Stages of Development
Industry Preference: Diversified/Real Estate
Geographical Area: Virginia, Maryland, North
Carolina, Delaware, Germany, England

East West United Financial Co. (SSBIC)
Dung Bui, President
1568 Spring Hill Rd., #100
McLean, VA 22102
(703) 442-0150
Fax: (703) 442-0156

Contact For Further Information
Investment Policy: Diversified

VIRGINIA (continued)

Rural America Fund, Inc.
Federick L. Russell, Jr., President
2201 Cooperative Way
Herndon, VA 22071
(703) 709-6750
Fax: (703) 709-6779

Loan/Investment Range: Up to $500,000
Will make loans and/or equity investments
Prefers Startups, Early Stage and Expansion
Stage Companies
Industry Preference: Diversified
Geographical Area: National

Walnut Capital Corporation
Plaza Street Holdings, Inc.
(Main Office in Chicago, IL)
Michael Faber, Vice President
8300 Towers Crescent Drive, #1070
Vienna, VA 22182
(703) 448-3771
Fax: (703) 448-7751

Loan/Investment Range: Up to $2.5 Million
Will make loans and/or equity investments
Prefers Early Stage, Expansion Stage
and Seasoned Companies
Industry Preference: Diversified
Geographical Area: National

WEST VIRGINIA

Anker Capital Corporation
Thomas Loehr, Manager
208 Capitol Street, #300
Charleston, WV 25301
(304) 344-1794
Fax: (304) 344-1798

Contact For Further Information
Investment Policy: Diversified

WestVen Limited Partnership
Thomas Loehr, Manager
208 Capitol Street, #300
Charleston, WV 25301
(304) 344-1794
Fax: (304) 344-1798

Loan/Investment Range: Up to $500,000
Will make loans and/or equity investments
Prefers Early and Expansion Stage Companies
Industry Preference: Diversified
Geographical Area: Northeastern and Southern States

WISCONSIN

Banc One Venture Corporation
H. Wayne Foreman, President
111 E. Wisconsin Avenue
Milwaukee, WI 53202
(414) 765-2274
Fax: (414) 765-2235

Loan/Investment Range: $1 - $2 Million
Prefers equity investments
Prefers Expansion Stage Companies
Industry Preference: Diversified
Geographical Area: National

Bando McGlocklin Capital Corp.
George R. Schonath, CEO
13555 Bishops Court, #205
Brookfield, WI 53005
(414) 784-9010
Fax: (414) 784-3426

Loan/Investment Range: Up to $1 Million
Prefers to make loans
Prefers Expansion Stage Companies
Industry Preference: Diversified
Geographical Area: Midwestern States

WISCONSIN (continued)

Capital Investments, Inc.
Steven C. Rippl, Exec. Vice President
744 N. 4th Street, #540
Milwaukee, WI 53203
(414) 273-6560
Fax: (414) 273-0530

Loan/Investment Range: Up to $1 Million
Will make loans and/or equity investments
Prefers Expansion Stage, Seasoned Companies
and Management Buyouts
Industry Preference: Diversified
Geographical Area: Will Consider National —
Generally Midwestern and Southwestern States

Future Value Ventures, Inc. (SSBIC)
William P. Beckett, President
Plaza East Office Center, #711
Milwaukee, WI 53202
(414) 278-0377
Fax: (414) 278-7321

Loan/Investment Range: Up to $250,000
Will make loans and/or equity investments
Prefers Early, Expansion Stage, Seasoned
Companies and Management Buyouts
Industry Preference: Diversified
Geographical Area: National

M & I Ventures Corporation
John T. Byrnes, President
770 N. Water Street
Milwaukee, WI 53202
(414) 765-7800
Fax: (414) 765-7850

Loan/Investment Range: Over $2 Million
Prefers equity investments
Prefers Expansion Stage, Seasoned Companies
and Management Buyouts
Industry Preference: Diversified
Geographical Area: National

MorAmerica Capital Corporation
(Main Office: InvestAmerica, Cedar Rapids, IA)
600 East Mason Street
Milwaukee, WI 53202
(414) 276-3839
Fax: (414) 276-1885

Loan/Investment Range: Up to $1 Million
Prefers equity investments
Prefers Early, Expansion Stage Companies and
Management Buyouts
Industry Preference: Diversified
Geographical Area: National

Polaris Capital Corporation
Richard Laabs, President
11270 W. Park Place, #320
Milwaukee, WI 53224
(414) 359-3040
Fax: (414) 359-3059

Loan/Investment Range: Up to $500,000
Prefers equity investments
Prefers Expansion Stage, Seasoned Companies
and Management Buyouts
Industry Preference: Diversified
Geographical Area: Midwestern States

Appendix F
Venture Capital Companies

The following alphabetically listed venture capital firms are actively engaged in making loans and/or equity investments. When known, each listing includes the name of the company, the contact person, address, telephone number, fax number, loan or investment range, investment policy, the types of investment preferred, industry preference and the geographical area served.

Since these businesses frequently move and change their policies, the details presented cannot be guaranteed 100% accurate, but are the most current available. The author recommends calling your selection(s) first to confirm the information provided before mailing a financing request and business plan.

Acumen Venture Partners, Inc.
Eliot Jacobsen, Managing General Partner
15901 Ranchita Drive
Dallas, TX 75248
(214) 233-4376
Fax: (214) 869-7915

Contact For Further Information

Alimansky Capital Group, Inc.
Burt Alimansky, Managing Director
605 Madison Avenue, #300
New York, NY 10022-1091
(212) 832-7300
Fax: (212) 832-7338

Loan/Investment Range: Over $2 Million
Will make loans and/or equity investments
Prefers Early Stage, Expansion Stage, Seasoned
Companies and Management Buyouts
Industry Preference: Diversified
Geographical Area: National

Allsop Venture Partners
Robert W. Allsop, General Partner
2750 lst Avenue, NE, #210
Cedar Rapids, IA 52402
(319) 363-8971
Fax: (319) 363-9519

Loan/Investment Range: $1 - $2 Million
Prefers equity investments
Prefers Expansion Stage, Seasoned Companies
and Management Buyouts
Industry Preference: Diversified
Geographical Area: National

Allsop Venture Partners
(Main Office in IA)
Robert L. Kuk, General Partner
55 West Port Plaza, #575
St. Louis, MO 63146
(314) 434-1688
Fax: (314) 434-6560

Loan/Investment Range: $1 - $2 Million
Prefers equity investments
Prefers Expansion Stage, Seasoned Companies
and Management Buyouts
Industry Preference: Diversified
Geographical Area: National

Allsop Venture Partners
(Main Office in IA)
Larry C. Maddox, General Partner
7400 College Blvd., #302
Overland Park, KS 66210
(913) 338-0820
Fax: (913) 338-1019

Loan/Investment Range: $1 - $2 Million
Prefers equity investments
Prefers Expansion Stage, Seasoned Companies
and Management Buyouts
Industry Preference: Diversified
Geographical Area: National

Allstate Venture Capital
Michael E. Cahr
3075 Sanders Road — G5D
Northbrook, IL 60062
(708) 402-5681
Fax: (708) 402-0880

Loan/Investment Range: Over $2 Million
Prefers equity investments
Will consider Startups, Early Stage, Expansion
Stage, Seasoned Companies and Management
Buyouts
Industry Preference: Diversified
Geographical Area: National

Alpha Capital Partners, Inc.
Andrew H. Kalnow, President
Three First National Plaza, #1400
Chicago, IL 60602
(312) 214-3440
Fax: (312) 214-3776

Loan/Investment Range: Up to $1 Million
Prefers equity investments
Prefers Early, Expansion Stage, Seasoned
Companies and Management Buyouts
Industry Preference: Diversified
Geographical Area: Midwestern States

American Securities Venture Partners, LP
Michael G. Fisch, President
122 East 42nd Street
New York, NY 10168
(212) 476-8051
Fax: (212) 697-5524

Loan/Investment Range: Over $2 Million
Prefers to make equity investments
Prefers Expansion Stage, Seasoned Companies
and Management Buyouts
Industry Preference: Diversified
Geographical Area: National

Amerimark Capital Corporation
Mark W. Stanley, Principal
1111 W. Mockingbird, Suite 1111
Dallas, TX 75247
(214) 638-7878
Fax: (214) 638-7612

Loan/Investment Range: Over $5 Million
Prefers to make equity investments
Prefers Seasoned Companies and Management
Buyouts
Industry Preference: Diversified
Geographical Area: National

**APA/Fostin Pennsylvania Venture
Capital Funds I & II**
Peter A. Weinbach, Associate
100 Matsonford Road, Bldg. 5, #470
Radnor, PA 19087
(610) 687-3030
Fax: (610) 687-8520

Loan/Investment Range: Up to $5 Million
Prefers to make equity investments
Prefers Early, Expansion Stage and Seasoned
Companies
Industry Preference: Diversified
Geographical Area: National

Arizona Growth Partners, L. P.
John M. Holliman III, General Partner
2525 E. Arizona Biltmore Circle, #240
Phoenix, AZ 85016
(602) 224-0808
Fax: 602) 224-6119

Loan/Investment Range: $1 - $2 Million
Prefers equity investments
Prefers Startups and Management Buyouts
Industry Preference: Chemical, Biological
Communications, Medical & Health
Geographical Area: Southwest & Western States

Atlantic Capital Exchange, Inc.
Vern Landeck, President
11 South LaSalle Street, #2401
Chicago, IL 60603
(312) 857-2200
Fax: (312) 857-2229

Loan/Investment Range: Up to $50 Million
Prefers debt financing, equipment related
loans and leases
Will Consider All Stages of Business
Industry Preferences: Diversified
Geographical Area: National & Mexico

Atlantic Venture Company, Inc.
Edward K. Crawford, President
380 Knollwood Street, #600
Winston-Salem, NC 27103
(910) 725-2961
Fax: (910) 725-4356

Loan/Investment Range: $1 - $2 Million
Prefers to make equity investments
Prefers Seasoned Companies and
Management Buyouts
Industry Preference: Diversified
Geographical Area: Southern States

Ballantree Capital Partners, LP
Ethan Alpert, Managing Partner
415 E. 85th St., #2D
New York, NY 10028
(212) 737-8134
Fax: (212) 972-0225

Contact For Further Information

Bariston Associates
David Barry, President
One International Place
Boston, MA 02110
(617) 330-8950
Fax: (617) 330-8951

Loan/Investment Range: $1 - $2 Million
Prefers to make equity investments
Prefers Expansion Stage, Seasoned Companies
and Management Buyouts
Industry Preference: Communications,
Medical and Environmental
Geographical Area: National

Battelle Venture Partners
(aka Scientific Advances, Inc.)
Paul F. Purcell, Vice President
601 West Fifth Avenue
Columbus, OH 43201
(614) 424-7005
Fax: (614) 424-4874

Loan/Investment Range: Up to $1 Million
Prefers equity investments
Prefers Startups, Early & Expansion Stage
Companies
Industry Preference: Energy & Natural Resources
Geographical Area: National

Ben Franklin Technology Center of
Southeastern Pennsylvania
Phillip A. Singerman, President
3624 Market Street
Philadelphia, PA 19104
(610) 382-0380
Fax: (610) 387-6050

Loan/Investment Range: Up to $500,000
Prefers to make equity investments
Prefers Startups and Early Stage Companies
Industry Preference: Chemical, Biological,
Communications, Computer, Electronic and
Medical Equipment, Products and Services
Geographical Area: Pennsylvania

Business Finance Corporation
James E. Trevino, President
P. O. Box 1140
Bellevue, WA 98009
(206) 649-0258
Fax: (206) 649-0533

Loan/Investment Range: Up to $500,000
Will make loans and/or equity investments
Prefers Expansion Stage and Seasoned
Companies
Industry Preference: Computer, Medical &
Health, Light & Heavy Industrial, Commercial
Construction and Electronics
Geographical Area: Northwestern States

CAPEX Financial Group, Inc.
Kenneth J. Kuczka, President
301 West Indian School Road, #B110
Phoenix, AZ 85013
(602) 265-4366
Fax: (602) 265-1959

Loan/Investment Range: Up to $1 Million
Prefers straight loans
Prefers Seasoned Companies
Industry Preference: Diversified, Light and
Heavy Industries
Geographical Area: National

Capital For Business, Inc.
James F. O'Donnell, Chairman
Eleven South Meramec, #1430
St. Louis, MO 63105
(314) 746-7427
Fax: (314) 746-8739

Loan/Investment Range: Up to $2 Million
Will make loans and/or equity investments
Prefers Expansion Stage, Seasoned Companies,
and Management and 3rd Party Buyouts
Industry Preference: Light & Heavy Industrial,
Electronics, Manufacturing & Distribution
Geographical Area: National

Capital Resource Partners
Robert C. Ammerman, Managing Partner
170 Portland Street, #300
Boston, MA 02114
(617) 723-9000
Fax: (617) 723-9819

Loan/Investment Range: Over $2 Million
Will make loans and/or equity investments
Prefers Expansion Stage, Seasoned Companies
and Management Buyouts
Industry Preference: Diversified
Geographical Area: National

Capital Resources, Inc.
Rene H. Martinez, President
3850 N. Causeway Blvd., #200
Metairie, LA 70002
(504) 835-5622
Fax: (504) 835-5824

Loan/Investment Range: Up to $1 Million
Will make loans and/or equity investments
 Prefers Startups, Early Stage and Expansion
Stage Companies
Industry Preference: Business Products and
Services; Communications and Medical
Industries
Geographical Area: National

Cariad Capital, Inc.
Roger A. Vandenberg, President
One Turks Head Place, #1550
Providence, RI 02903-2215
(401) 751-8111
Fax: (401) 751-8222

Loan/Investment Range: Up to $500,000
Prefers equity investments
Prefers Management Buyouts
Industry Preference: Communications and
Industrial Equipment, Products and Services
Geographical Area: National

Carolinas Capital Investment Corp.
Edward S. Goode, President
6337 Morrison Blvd.,
Charlotte, NC 28211
(704) 362-8222
Fax: (704) 362-8221

Loan/Investment Range: Up to $1 Million
Prefers equity investments
Prefers Early Stage, Expansion Stage, Seasoned
Companies and Management Buyouts
Industry Preference: Diversified
Geographical Area: Southeastern States

Cascade Funding, Inc.
Thomas C. Brophy, President
124 110th Place SE
Bellevue, WA 98004
(206) 453-1352
Fax: (206) 453-1352

Loan/Investment Range: Open
Purchases privately held real estate, secured
notes, deeds of trust and real estate contracts
Prefers Real Estate
Geographical Area: National

Centennial Funds (The)
Sharon R. Hebert, Controller
1999 Broadway, #2100
Denver, CO 80202
(303) 298-9066
Fax: (303) 292-3512

Loan/Investment Range: Up to $8 Million
Will make loans and/or equity investments
Prefers Startups, Early and Expansion stage
Companies
Industry Preference: Chemical and Biological
Products, Communications, Computer, Electronic,
Medical & Health
Geographical Area: Colorado, Texas, Rocky
Mountain States

Cherry Tree Investment Company
Gordon F. Stofer, Managing General Partner
3800 W. 80th Street, #1400
Minneapolis, MN 55431
(612) 893-9012
Fax: (612) 893-9036

Loan/Investment Range: $1 - $2 Million
Prefers equity investments
Prefers Early Stage, Expansion Stage Companies
and Management Buyouts
Industry Preference: Business Products and
Services, Consumer Products and Services,
Computer and Medical Equipment, Products
and Services
Geographical Area: Midwestern States

Chesapeake Capital Fund, LP
Charles E. Coudriet, President
P. O. Box 344
Richmond, VA 23202
(804) 649-2300
Fax: (804) 649-2207

Contact For Further Information

Civic Business Capital, Inc.
Truman R. Tally, President
P. O. Box 39177
Phoenix, AZ 85069
(602) 864-9000
Fax: (602) 864-9742

Loans/Investment Range: Up to $25 Million
Revolving lines of credit for working capital
based on accounts receivable and inventory
in combination with term loans secured by
fixed assets. Also refinancing, seasonal loans,
leverage transactions, turnaround loans and
acquisitions
Prefers Expansion Stage, Seasoned Companies
and Management Buyouts
Industry Preference: Communications, Computer,
Medical & Health, Light & Heavy Industrial,
Commercial Construction, Electronics,
Manufacturing, Wholesaling & Distributing
Geographical Area: National

Davis Venture Partners, LP
Barry M. Davis, Managing Gen. Partner
One Williams Center, #2000
Tulsa, OK 74172-0120
(918) 584-7272
Fax: (918) 582-3403

Loan/Investment Range: $1 - $2 Million
Prefers equity investments
Prefers Early Stage, Expansion Stage Companies
and Management Buyouts
Industry Preference: Diversified
Geographical Area: Southwestern States

Davis Venture Partners, LP
Branch Office - Main Office in OK
Michael A. Stone, General Partner
2121 San Jacinto Street, #975
Dallas, TX 75201
(214) 954-1822
Fax: (214) 969-0256

Loan/Investment Range: Over $2 Million
Prefers equity investments
Prefers Early Stage, Expansion Stage Companies
and Management Buyouts
Industry Preference: Diversified
Geographical Area: Southwestern States

Davis Venture Partners, LP
Branch Office - Main Office in OK
Philip A. Tuttle, General Partner
515 Post Oak Blvd., #250
Houston, TX 77027
(713) 993-0440
Fax: (713) 621-2297

Loan/Investment Range: Over $2 Million
Prefers equity investments
Prefers Early Stage, Expansion Stage Companies
and Management Buyouts
Industry Preference: Diversified
Geographical Area: Southwestern States

Denslow, Shaffer & Company
William R. Denslow, Jr., President
767 Fifth Avenue
New York, NY 10153
(212) 980-4292
Fax: (212) 319-6046

Loan/Investment Range: $1 - $2 Million
Prefers equity investments
Prefers Expansion Stage, Seasoned Companies
and Management Buyouts
Industry Preference: Diversified
Geographical Area: National

Dexxon Capital Corporation
Chris Duncan, Vice President
6133 Blue Circle Drive
Minnetonka, MN 55343
(612) 933-7611
Fax: (612) 933-9032

Loan/Investment Range: Up to $5 Million
Prefers straight loans
Will consider Startups, Early and Expansion
Stage, Seasoned Companies and Management
Buyouts
Industry Preference: Communications,
Computer, Medical & Health, Light & Heavy
Industrial and Biotechnology
Geographical Area: National

E. A. Moos Capital Corp.
Donald V. Scuilli, Managing Director
47 Maple Street
Summit, NJ 07901
(908) 273-6010
Fax: (908) 273-8865

Contact For Further Information

EGL Holdings, Inc.
David O. Ellis, President
Building 300
6600 Peachtree Dunwoody Road, #630
Atlanta, GA 30328
(404) 399-5633
Fax: (404) 393-4825

Loan/Investment Range: $1 - $2 Million
Prefers to make equity investments
Prefers Seasoned Companies and Management
Buyouts
Industry Preference: Diversified
Geographical Area: Southern States

El Dorado Ventures
Brent T. Rider, General Partner
800 East Colorado Blvd., #530
Pasadena, CA 91101
(818) 793-1936
Fax: (818) 793-2613

Loan/Investment Range: $1 - $2 Million
Will make loans and/or equity investments
Prefers Startups and Early Stage Companies
Industry Preference: Communications,
Computer, Electronic and Medical Equipment,
Products and Services
Geographical Area: Western States

El Dorado Ventures
Branch Office - Main Office in Pasadena
Shanda Bahles, General Partner
20300 Stevens Creek Blvd., #395
Cupertino, CA 95014
(408) 725-2472
Fax: (408) 252-2762

Loan/Investment Range: $1 - $2 Million
Will make loans and/or equity investments
Prefers Startups and Early Stage Companies
Industry Preference: Communications,
Computer. Electronic and Medical Equipment,
Products and Services
Geographical Area: Western States

Enterprise Development Fund, L.P.
Mary L. Campbell, General Partner
425 N. Main Street
Ann Arbor, MI 48104-1133
(313) 663-3213
Fax: (313) 663-7358

Loan/Investment Range: Up to $500,000
Prefers equity investments
Prefers Startups
Industry Preference: Computer, Medical &
Health and Electronics
Geographical Area: Michigan

Enterprise Management, Inc.
Hayden H. Harris, Partner
425 North Main Street
Ann Arbor, MI 48104
(313) 633-3213
Fax: (313) 633-7358

Loan/Investment Range: Up to $500,000
Prefers to make equity investments
Will consider all viable opportunities
Industry Preference: Diversified
Geographical Area: Michigan

Epigen, Inc.
J. Steven Barnard, President
1630 30th Street, #312
Boulder, CO 80301
(303) 530-2333
Fax: (303) 530-2366

Loan/Investment Range: Up to $250,000
Will make loans and/or equity investments
Prefers Startups and Early Stage Companies
Industry Preference: Chemical, Biological,
Communications, Electronic & Diversified
Geographical Area: Midwestern, Southwestern
and Western States

First Century Partners
David S. Lobel, General Partner
1270 Avenue of the Americas, #2720
New York, NY 10020
(212) 397-0177
Fax: (212) 397-0877

Loan/Investment Range: Over $2 Million
Prefers equity Investments
Prefers Early Stage, Expansion State, Seasoned
Companies and Management Buyouts
Industry Preference: Business and Consumer
Products and Services
Geographical Area: National

Forsyth Management Company
O. Roane Cross, Jr., President
4265 Brownsboro Road, #200
Winston-Salem, NC 27106
(919) 759-3005
Fax: (919) 759-2382

Loan/Investment Range: Up to $500,000
Prefers equity investments
Prefers Early Stage and Expansion Stage
Companies
Industry Preference: Diversified
Geographical Area: Southern States

Gage Investments
Kenneth F. Gudorf, President
10000 Highway 55
Minneapolis, MN 55441
(612) 595-3845
Fax: (612) 595-3904

Loan/Investment Range: $1 - $2 Million
Prefers to make equity investments
Prefers Expansion Stage Companies and
Management Buyouts
Industry Preference: Business Products and
Services, and Diversified
Geographical Area: Midwestern States

GE Capital
John Hatherly, Managing Director
190 S. LaSalle Street, #1200
Chicago, IL 60603
(312) 419-5901
Fax: (312) 419-5992

Loan/Investment Range: Over $2 Million
Prefers to make equity investments
Prefers Early, Expansion Stage, Seasoned
Companies and Management Buyouts
Industry Preference: Business Products/Services,
Consumer, Industrial, Medical & Diversified
Geographical Area: Midwestern States

Gildea Management Company
John W. Gildea
90 Ferris Hill Road
New Canaan, CT 06840
(203) 966-3401
Fax: None

Loan/Investment Range: Over $2 Million
Prefers equity investments
Prefers Seasoned Companies and
Management Buyouts
Industry Preference: Diversified
Geographical Area: National

GMM Investors
James J. Goodman, President
460 Totten Pond Road, #600
Waltham, MA 02154
(617) 290-5990
Fax: (617) 290-5987

Contact For Further Information

Heartland Capital Fund, Ltd.
Bradley K. Edwards, General Partner
660 NBC Center
1248 "O" Street
Lincoln, NE 68508-1424
(402) 475-5109
Fax: (402) 475-5170

Loan/Investment Range: Up to $1 Million
Will make loans and/or equity investments
Prefers Startups, Early and Expansion Stage
Companies
Industry Preference: Diversified
Geographical Area: Midwestern and
Southwestern States

Heizer Capital
Edgar F. Heizer, President
215 Maple Court
Lake Forest, IL 60045
(708) 234-1677
Fax: (708) 615-0464

Contact For Further Information

Horizon Partners
Robert M. Feerick, Chairman
225 E. Mason Street, #600
Milwaukee, WI 53102
(414) 271-2200
Fax: (414) 271-4016

Loan/Investment Range: Over $2 Million
Will make loans and/or equity investments
Prefers Expansion Stage, Seasoned Companies
and Management Buyouts
Industry Preference: Diversified
Geographical Area: Midwestern States

Indiana Community Business Credit Corp.
Marc J. DeLong, Manager
8440 Woodfield Crossing Blvd., #315
Indianapolis, IN 46240
(317) 469-9704
Fax: (317) 469-3926

Loan/Investment Range: Up to $750,000
Will make loans and/or equity investments
Prefers Startups, Early, Expansion Stage,
Seasoned Companies and Management Buyouts
Industry Preference: Communications, Computer,
Electronics, Medical, Health, Light and Heavy
Industrial
Geographical Area: Indiana

Indiana Statewide Certified Development Corp.
Maureen E. Foy, Manager
8440 Woodfield Crossing Blvd., #315
Indianapolis, IN 46240
(317) 469-6166
Fax: (317) 469-3926

Loan/Investment Range: Up to $750,000
Prefers to make straight loans
Will Consider All Stages Of Development
Industry Preference: Communications, Computer,
Medical, Health, Light & Heavy Industrial,
Commercial Construction and Electronics
Geographical Area: Indiana

Industrial Valleys Investment Corp.
Joseph Bute, Jr., President
120 East 9th Avenue
Homestead, PA 15120
(412) 462-8408
Fax: (412) 462-8407

Loan/Investment Range: Up to $1 Million
Will make loans and/or equity investments
Prefers Expansion State, Seasoned Companies,
Employee and Management Buyouts
Industry Preference: Energy, Natural Resources,
Industrial Equipment and Products
Geographical Area: Ohio & Pennsylvania

International Radiographic, Inc.
Philip Young, Vice President
1840 W. 49th Street, #305A
Hialeah, FL 33012
(305) 821-2225
Fax: (305) 825-7778

Loan/Investment Range: $1 Million & Over
Will make loans and/or equity investments
Prefers Expansion Stage, Seasoned Companies
and Management Buyouts
Industry Preference: Diversified
Geographical Area: National. Will Consider
All International Countries

InterVen Partners
David B. Jones, Partner
301 Arizona Ave., #306
Santa Monica, CA 90401
(310) 587-3550
Fax: (310) 587-3440

Loan/Investment Range: Over $2 Million
Prefers equity investments
Prefers Startups, Early Stage, Expansion Stage,
Seasoned Companies and Management Buyouts
Industry Preference: Diversified
Geographical Area: Western States

InterVen Partners - Branch Office
Wayne B. Kingsley, Partner
227 S. W. Pine Street, #200
Portland, OR 97204
(503) 223-4334
Fax: (503) 223-3213

Loan/Investment Range: Over $2 Million
Prefers equity investments
Prefers Startups, Early Stage, Expansion Stage,
Seasoned Companies and Management Buyouts
Industry Preference: Diversified
Geographical Area: Western States

Japan Associated Finance Co., Ltd. (JAFCO)
Masaki Yoshida, President
Toshiba Bldg. 1OF, 1-1-1 Shibaura
Minato-Ku, Tokyo, Japan 105
(03) 3456-5101
Fax: (03) 3456-4767

Loan/Investment Range: Up to $2 Million
Will make loans and/or equity investments
Will consider all viable opportunities
Industry Preference: Diversified
Geographical Area: National - USA

John Hancock Mutual Life Insurance Co.
D. Dana Donovan, Senior Investment Officer
200 Clarendon Street, 57th Floor
Boston, MA 02117
(617) 572-9626
Fax: (617) 572-1606

Contact For Further Information

Jupiter National, Inc.
Haywood Miller, General Counsel
39 W. Montgomery Avenue
Rockville, MD 20850
(301) 738-3939
Fax: (301) 738-7949

Loan/Investment Range: Up to $2 Million
Will make loans and/or equity investments
Prefers Expansion Stage, Seasoned Companies
and Management Buyouts
Industry Preference: Diversified
Geographical Area: National

Kansas City Equity Partners
Paul H. Henson, President
4200 Somerset, #101
Prairie Village, KS 66208
(913) 649-1771
Fax: (913) 649-2125

Loan/Investment Range: Up to $1 Million
Prefers equity investments
Prefers Early Stage Companies
Industry Preference: Diversified
Geographical Area: Kansas, Missouri and
Midwestern States

Kinship Venture Management, Inc.
Michael I. Block, Managing Director
400 Skokie Blvd., #670
Northbrook, IL 60062
(708) 291-1890
Fax: (708) 291-1890

Contact For Further Information

Kitty Hawk Capital, Ltd.
Walter H. Wilkinson, Jr., General Partner
101 North Tryon Street, #1640
Charlotte, NC 28246
(704) 333-3777
Fax: (704) 333-0603

Loan/Investment Range: Up to $2 Million
Prefers equity investments
Prefers Startups, Early Stage, Expansion
Stage, Seasoned Companies
Industry Preference: Diversified
Geographical Area: Southeastern States

Landmark Ventures, Inc.
Thomas K. Sweeny, Managing Director
920 Hopmeadow Street
Simsbury, CT 06070-0188
(203) 651-5681
Fax: (203) 651-8890

Loan/Investment Range: $1 - $2 Million
Prefers equity investments
Prefers Early Stage, Expansion Stage, Seasoned
Companies and Management Buyouts
Industry Preference: Diversified
Geographical Area: National

Louisiana Seed Capital Corporation
Kevin Couhig, President
P. O. Box 3435
Baton Rouge, LA 70821
(504) 383-1508
Fax: (504) 883-1513

Loan/Investment Range: Up to $500,000
Will make loans and/or equity investments
Prefers Startups, Early Stage and Expansion
Stage Companies
Industry Preference: Diversified
Geographical Area: Southern States

Lynx Capital Corp.
Marc J. DeLong, Manager
8440 Woodfield Crossing Blvd., #315
Indianapolis, IN 46240
(317) 469-3925
Fax: (317) 469-3926

Loan/Investment Range: Up to $250,000
Will make loans and/or equity investments
Prefers Expansion Stage, Seasoned Companies
and Management Buyouts
Industry Preference: Diversified
Geographical Area: City of Indianapolis and
State of Indiana

Manchester Humphreys Group, Inc.
Ernest D. Humphreys, Chairman
101 Dyer Street, #300
Providence, RI 02903
(401) 454-0400
Fax: (401) 454-0403

Loan/Investment Range: Over $2 Million
Will make loans and/or equity investments
Prefers Expansion Stage, Seasoned Companies
and Management Buyouts
Industry Preference: Diversified
Geographical Area: Northeastern, Southern and
Midwestern States

Marwitt Capital Corporation
Matthew L. Witte, President
180 Newport Center Drive, #200
Newport Beach, CA 92660
(714) 640-6234
Fax: (714) 720-8077

Loan/Investment Range: Up to $5 Million
Subordinated debt with equity participation
Prefers Expansion Stage, Seasoned Companies
and Management Buyouts
Industry Preference: Communications,
Computer, Medical & Health, Light Industrial,
Residential Construction, Electronics and Real
Estate
Geographical Area: National

Markwood Capital Alliance
Bill Weaver, Director
56 Hutton Centre Drive, #1110
Santa Ana, CA 92707
(714) 540-8020 Ext: 106
Fax: (714) 957-2799

Loan/Investment Range: Up to $5 Million
Will make loans and/or equity investments
Prefers Expansion Stage, Seasoned Companies
and Management Buyouts
Industry Preference: Communications,
Computer, Medical & Health and Electronics
Geographical Area: Western States

Massachusetts Growth Ventures
Lawrence J. Smith, Jr., President
75 Federal Street, 2nd Floor
Boston, MA 02110
(617) 451-9444
Fax: (617) 451-3429

Loan/Investment Range: Up to $250,000
Will make loans and/or equity investments
Prefers Early and Expansion State Companies
Industry Preference: Communications,
Electronic, Medical Equipment, Products and
Services
Geographical Area: Massachusetts

McCullough Capital
Rod McCullough, President
11511 Katy Freeway, #375
Houston, TX 77079
(713) 497-8183
Fax: (713) 497-8273

Loan/Investment Range: Up to $20 Million
Will make loans and/or equity investments
Prefers Oil & Gas Production and Related
Businesses
Geographical Area: Southwestern States
and All Oil & Gas Producing Areas

Medco, Inc.
Elliott Rabone, Regional Manager
1840 W. 49th Street, #234
Hialeah, FL 33012
(305) 823-2440
Fax: (305) 823-8054

Loan/Investment Range: $50,000 Minimum
Will make loans and/or equity investments
Will Consider All Stages of Development
Industry Preference: Diversified
Geographical Area: National

Mercury Capital
David Elenowitz, President
650 Madison Avenue, 26th Floor
New York, NY 10022
(212) 838-7456
Fax: (212) 838-7598

Loan/Investment Range: Over $2 Million
Prefers to make equity investments
Prefers Expansion Stage, Seasoned Companies
and Management Buyouts
Industry Preference: Business Products and
Services, Construction (Real Estate), Consumer,
Industrial & Diversified
Geographical Area: National

Mesirow Private Equity Investments
James C. Tyree, President
350 N. Clark Street
Chicago, IL 60610
(312) 670-6099
Fax: (312) 670-6211

Loan/Investment Range: Over $2 Million
Prefers equity investments
Prefers Expansion Stage, Seasoned Companies
and Management Buyouts
Industry Preference: Diversified
Geographical Area: National

Metro Equity Fund
Barry Levien, President
521 Fifth Avenue, #1901
New York, NY 10175
(212) 697-3780
Fax: (212) 697-3885

Loan/Investment Range: Over $2 Million
Prefers equity investments
Prefers Expansion Stage, Seasoned Companies
and Management Buyouts
Industry Preference: Diversified
Geographical Area: Northeastern States

Michigan Dept. of Treasury
Alternative Investments Division
Paul E. Rice, Administrator
P. O. Box 15128
Lansing, MI 48901
(517) 373-4330
Fax: (517) 335-3668

Loan/Investment Range: Over $2 Million
Will make loans and/or equity investments
Prefers Expansion Stage, Seasoned Companies
and Management Buyouts
Industry Preference: Diversified
Geographical Area: National

NEPA Venture Fund, LP
Frederick J. Beste, III, President
125 Goodman Drive
Bethlehem, PA 18015
(215) 865-6550
Fax: (215) 861-6427

Loan/Investment Range: Up to $1 Million
Prefers equity investments
Prefers Startups, Early Stage, Expansion Stage
Companies and Management Buyouts
Industry Preference: Diversified
Geographical Area: Mid-Atlantic States

Nippon Investment and Finance Co., Ltd.
Takuro Isoda, President
2/F, 1-9 Kayaba-cho, 1-chome
Tokyo 103 Japan
(03) 5695-8252
Fax: (03) 5695-8289

Loan/Investment Range: Open
Prefers equity investments
Prefers Expansion Stage Companies
Industry Preference: Diversified
Geographical Area: National - USA and
Asia-Pacific Region

Noble Ventures International, Inc.
John J. Huntz, Jr., General Partner
1201 West Peachtree Street, NW, #5000
Atlanta, GA 30309
(404) 815-2000
Fax: (404) 815-4529

Contact For Further Information

North American Capital Corporation
Stanley P. Roth, Chairman
510 Broad Hollow Road, #205
Melville, NY 11747
(516) 752-9600
Fax: (516) 752-9618

Loan/Investment Range: Over $ 2 Million
Will make loans and/or equity investments
Prefers Early Stage, Expansion Stage, Seasoned
Companies and Management Buyouts
Industry Preference: Diversified
Geographical Area: National

North Dakota Small Business Investment Co.
Kermit Bye, Chairman
700 East Main Avenue
P. O. Box 5509
Bismarck, ND 58502
(701) 224-5681
Fax: (701) 224-5632

Loan/Investment Range: Up to $500,000
Prefers equity investments
Prefers Expansion State Companies
Industry Preference: Diversified
Geographical Area: North Dakota and
Midwestern States

Northeast Venture Development Fund, Inc.
Nick Smith, CEO & Chairman
802 Alworth Building
Duluth, MN 55802
(218) 722-9915
Fax: (218) 722-9871

Loan/Investment Range: Up to $250,000
Prefers equity investments
Prefers Startups, Early Stage, Expansion Stage,
Seasoned Companies and Management Buyouts
Industry Preference: Diversified
Geographical Area: Minnesota

Obsidian Equity, Inc.
Charles A. McLaughlin, President
P. O. Box 290
Ronan, MT 59864
(406) 676-2822
Fax: (406) 676-2822

Contact For Further Information

Oxford Capital Corp. - Regional Office
Peter Aransky, Regional Vice President
170 Tremont Street, #1503
Boston, MA 02111
(617) 350-0075
Fax: (617) 350-7233

Loans/Investment Range: Up to $2.5 Million
Purchases accounts receivable
Will Consider All Businesses
Industry Preference: Diversified
Geographical Area: Northeastern States and
National

Oxford Partners
Kenneth W. Rind, Partner
1266 Main Street
Stamford, CT 06902
(203) 964-0592
Fax: (203) 964-3192

Loan/Investment Range: Up to $1 Million
Prefers equity investments
Prefers Startups, Early Stage, Expansion Stage
Companies and Management Buyouts
Industry Preference: Diversified
Geographical Area: National

Palmetto Seed Capital Corporation
Jack Sterling, President
P. O. Box 17526
Greenville, SC 29606
(803) 232-6198
Fax: (803) 271-8374

Loan/Investment Range: Up to $1.5 Million
Prefers equity investments
Prefers Startups, Early Stage and Expansion
Stage Companies
Industry Preference: Diversified
Geographical Area: South Carolina and
Southern States

Pathfinder Ventures Capital Funds
Andrew J. Greenshields, President
7300 Metro Blvd., #585
Minneapolis, MN 55439
(612) 835-1121
Fax: (612) 835-8389

Loan/Investment Range: Up to $1 Million
Prefers equity investments
Will consider Startups, Early Stage, Expansion
Stage, Seasoned Companies and Management
Buyouts
Industry Preference: Diversified
Geographical Area: National

Phoenix Growth Capital Corporation
Norm Nelson, Senior Vice President
2401 Kerner Blvd.,
San Rafael, CA 94901
(415) 485-4560
Fax: (415) 485-4663

Loan/Investment Range: $1 - $2 Million
Prefers straight loans
Industry Preference: Diversified
Geographical Area: National

Phoenix Growth Capital Corp. - Branch
Michael Weeks, Vice President
3000 Sand Hill Road, Bldg. 4, #165
Menlo Park, CA 94025
(415) 854-8404
Fax: (415) 854-5732

Loan/Investment Range: $1 - $2 Million
Prefers straight loans
Industry Preference: Diversified
Geographical Area: National

Phoenix Growth Capital Corp. - Branch
Ron Demer, Vice President
641 E. Morningside Drive, NE
Atlanta, GA 30324-5218
(404) 872-2406
Fax: (404) 876-1729

Loan/Investment Range: $1 - $2 Million
Prefers straight loans
Industry Preference: Diversified
Geographical Area: National

Piedmont Venture Partners, L.L.C.
Stacy E. Anderson, Fund Manager
1901 Roxborough Road, #120
Charlotte, NC 28211
(704) 364-5800
Fax: (704) 364-6700

Loan/Investment Range: Up to $1 Million
Prefers equity investments
Prefers Startups and Early Stage Companies
Industry Preference: Diversified
Geographical Area: North Carolina

PMC Capital, Inc.
F. M. Rosemore, Manager
Presidential Circle
4000 Hollywood Blvd., #435S
Hollywood, FL 33021
(305) 966-8868
Fax: None

Loan/Investment Range: Up to $4 Million
Will make loans and/or equity investments
Will Consider All Stages of Development
Industry Preference: Diversified
Geographical Area: National

Primus Venture Partners
Loyal W. Wilson, Partner
1375 East Ninth Street, #2700
Cleveland, OH 44114
(216) 621-2185
Fax: (216) 621-4543

Loan/Investment Range: Over $2 Million
Prefers equity investments
Prefers Expansion Stage Companies
Industry Preference: Diversified
Geographical Area: Midwestern States

Renaissance Capital Corp.
Anita Stephens, President
34 Peachtree Street NW, #2230
Atlanta, GA 30303
(404) 658-9061
Fax: (404) 658-9064

Loan/Investment Range: Up to $300,000
**Prefers Expansion Stage and Seasoned
Companies
Prefers Communications, Medical & Health,
Light Industrial and Fast Food
Geographical Area: Georgia**

River Cities Capital Fund, LP
R. Glen Mayfield
221 East Fourth Street, #2250
Cincinnati, OH 45202
(513) 621-9700
Fax: (513) 579-8939

Loan/Investment Range: $1 - $2 Million
**Prefers equity investments
Prefers Startups, Early, Expansion Stage,
Seasoned Companies and Management Buyouts
Industry Preference: Diversified
Geographical Area: Indiana, Kentucky, Ohio,
and Midwestern States**

Shared Ventures, Inc.
Howard Weiner, President
6550 York Avenue South, #419
Minneapolis, MN 55435
(612) 925-3411
Fax: (612) 925-4054

Loan/Investment Range: Up to $250,000
**Prefers equity investments
Prefers Early Stage, Expansion Stage Companies
and Management Buyouts
Industry Preference: Diversified
Geographical Area: Midwestern States**

Small Business Funding Group, Inc.
M. Jane Schwartz, President
13 Summit Square, #224
Langhorne, PA 19047
(215) 579-1334
Fax: (215) 579-1208

Loan/Investment Range: Depends on Project
**Prefers straight loans
Will consider Startups, Early, Expansion Stage,
Seasoned Companies and Management Buyouts
Industry Preference: Diversified
Geographical Area: Northeastern and
Southeastern States**

Smith, Miller Partners II, LP
Richard S. Smith, Partner
1000 Louisiana, #1095
Houston, TX 77002
(713) 659-7870
Fax: (713) 659-7855

Loan/Investment Range: $1 - $2 Million
**Prefers equity investments
Prefers Expansion Stage Companies
Industry Preference: Diversified
Geographical Area: National**

State Street Bank and Trust Company
Kent Mitchell, Vice President
3414 Peachtree Road, NE, #736
Atlanta, GA 30326
(404) 364-9500
Fax: (404) 261-4469

Loan/Investment Range: Over $2 Million
**Prefers straight loans
Prefers Expansion Stage, Seasoned Companies
and Management Buyouts
Industry Preference: Diversified
Geographical Area: National**

Stevens Capital Corporation
Arnold Kilberg, Manager
285 Governor Street
Providence, RI 02906
(401) 861-4600
Fax: (401) 331-5226

Loan/Investment Range: Up to $500,000
**Prefers straight loans
Prefers Seasoned Companies
Industry Preference: Diversified
Geographical Area: Northeastern States**

TA Associates
Richard D. Tadler, General Partner
125 High Street, #2500
Boston, MA 02110
(617) 574-6700
Fax: (617) 574-6728

Loan/Investment Range: Over $2 Million
Prefers equity investments
Prefers Expansion Stage, Seasoned Companies
and Management Buyouts
Industry Preference: Diversified
Geographical Area: National

Triad Investors Corporation
Barbara Plantholt, President
1122 Kenilworth Drive
Baltimore, MD 21204
(410) 828-6497
Fax: (410) 337-7312

Loan/Investment Range: Up to $250,000
Will make loans and/or equity investments
Prefers Startups and Early Stage Companies
Industry Preference: Chemical, Biological,
Medical and Communications
Geographical Area: Northeastern and
Mid-Atlantic States

VEDCORP, Inc.
Patrick K. Donnelly, Vice President
951 E. Byrd Street, #940
Richmond, VA 23219
(804) 648-4802
Fax: (804) 648-4809

Loan/Investment Range: Up to $1 Million
Prefers equity investments
Prefers Expansion Stage, Seasoned Companies
and Management Buyouts
Industry Preference: Diversified
Geographical Area: Virginia

Vencap Equities Alberta, Ltd.
R. A. Slator, President
1980 Manulife Pl., 10180 — 101st
Edmonton, Alberta, Canada T5J 3S4
(403) 420-1171
Fax: (403) 429-2451

Loan/Investment Range: Over $2 Million
Prefers equity investments
Will consider Startups, Early Stage, Expansion
Stage and Seasoned Companies
Industry Preference: Diversified
Geographical Area: Western States - USA

Venture Capital Fund of
New England (The)
Richard A. Farrell, General Partner
160 Federal Street, 23rd Floor
Boston, MA 02110
(617) 439-4646
Fax: (617) 439-4652

Loan/Investment Range: Up to $1 Million
Prefers equity investments
Prefers Early Stage Companies
Industry Preference: Chemical, Biological,
Communications, Computer and Medical
Geographical Area: Northeastern States

Venture Investors of Wisconsin, Inc.
Roger H. Ganser, President
565 Science Drive, #A
Madison, WI 53711
(608) 233-3070
Fax: (608) 238-5120

Loan/Investment Range: Up to $500,000
Will make loans and/or equity investments
Prefers Startups, Early Stage and Expansion
Stage Companies
Industry Preference: Diversified
Geographical Area: Wisconsin

West Virginia Capital Corp.
Andrew Zulauf, Manager
1230 Commerce Square
Charleston, WV 25301
(304) 346-0437
Fax: (304) 343-9749

Loan/Investment Range: Up to $750,000
Will make loans and/or equity investments
Will Consider All Stages Of Development
Industry Preference: Diversified
Geographical Area: West Virginia

William Blair Venture Partners
Samuel B. Guren, Partner
135 S. LaSalle Street, 29th Floor
Chicago, IL 60603
(312) 853-8250
Fax: (312) 236-1042

Loan/Investment Range: Over $2 Million
Prefers equity investments
Prefers Early Stage, Expansion Stage, Seasoned
Companies and Management Buyouts
Industry Preference: Diversified
Geographical Area: National

In addition to several Small Business Investment Companies who also provide equity financing (see Appendix E), Chapters 5 & 6 explain how to find more venture capital sources in your state.

Appendix G
U. S. Small Business Administration
Approved Microloan Lenders

The following SBA approved Microloan participants are actively making business loans up to $25,000. Each listing includes the name of the organization, address, contact person, telephone number and the geographical area served.

Since these organizations move from time to time, the information presented is the most current available. The author recommends calling their offices to confirm the information provided before requesting an appointment or submitting a loan request.

STATE:	LENDER:
Alabama	**Elmore Community Action Committee, Inc.** 1011 West Tallassee P. O. Drawer H Wetumpka, AL 36092 Contact: Marian D. Dunlap (205) 567-4361 **Service Area:** Autauga, Elmore and Montgomery Counties
Alaska	**Community Enterprise Development Corp. of Alaska** 1577 C Street Plaza, Suite 304 Anchorage, AK 99501 Contact: Perry R. Eaton (907) 274-5400 **Service Area:** Statewide
Arizona	**Chicanos Por La Causa, Inc.** 1112 E. Buckeye Road Phoenix, AZ 85034 Contact: Pete Garcia (602) 257-0700 **Service Area:** Urban areas of Maricopa and Pima Counties
	PPEP Housing Development Corp./Micro Industry Credit Rural Organization 802 East 46th Street Tucson, AZ 85713 Contact: John D. Arnold (602) 622-3553 **Service Area:** Cochise, Santa Cruz, rural Maricopa, rural Pinal and rural Yuma Counties

Arkansas

Arkansas Enterprise Group
605 Main Street, Suite 203
Arkadelphia, AR 71923
Contact: Brian Kelley
(501) 246-9739
Service Area: Southern portion of the state including Arkansas, Ashley, Bradley, Calhoun, Chicot, Clark, Cleveland, Columbia, Dallas, Desha, Drew, Garland, Grant, Hempstead, Hot Spring, Howard, Jefferson, Lafayette, Lincoln, Little River, Miller, Monroe, Montgomery, Nevasa, Ouachita, Phillips, Pike, Polk, Pulaski, Saline, Sevier and Union Counties

Delta Community Development Corp.
675 Eaton Road
P. O. Box 852
Forrest City, AR 72335
Contact: Michael Jackson
(501) 633-9113
Service Area: Cross, Crittenden, Monroe, Lee and St. Francis Counties

White River Planning and Development District, Inc.
1652 White Drive
P. O. Box 2396
Batesville, AR 72503
Contact: Van C. Thomas
(501) 793-5233
Service Area: Cleburne, Fulton, Independence, Izard, Jackson, Sharp, Stone, Van Buren, White and Woodruff Counties

California

Arcata Economic Development Corp.
100 Ericson Court, Suite 100
Arcata, CA 95521
Contact: Kathleen E. Moxon
(707) 822-4616
Service Area: Del Norte, Humboldt, Mendocino, Siskiyou and Trinity Counties

Center for Southeast Asian Refugee Resettlement
875 O'Farrell Street
San Francisco, CA 94109
Contact: Vu-Duc Vuong
(415) 885-2743
Service Area: Alameda, Contra Costa, Marin, Merced, Sacramento, San Francisco, San Jaoquin, San Mateo, Santa Clara and Stanislaus Counties

Coalition for Women's Economic Development
315 West Ninth Street, Suite 705
Los Angeles, CA 90015
Contact: Margaret Bush-Ware
(213) 489-4995
Service Area: Los Angeles County

Valley Rural Development Corp.
d/b/a Valley Small Business Development Corp.
955 N Street
Fresno, CA 93721
Contact: Michael E. Foley
(209) 268-0166
Service Area: Fresno, Kings, Kern, Stanislaus, Madera, Mariposa, Merced, Tuolumne and Tulare Counties

Colorado

Greater Denver Local Development Corp.
1981 Blake Street, Suite 406
P. O. Box 2135
Denver, CO 80206
Contact: Cecilia H. Prinster
(303) 296-9535
Service Area: City of Denver and Adams, Arapahoe, Boulder, Denver and Jefferson Counties

Region 10 LEAP, Inc.
P. O. Box 849
Montrose, CO 81402
Contact: Stan Broome
(303) 249-2436
Service Area: West Central area including Delta, Gunnison, Hinsdale, Montrose, Ouray and San Miguel Counties

Connecticut

New Haven Community Investment Corp.
809 Chapel Street, 2nd Floor
New Haven, CT 06510
Contact: Salvatore J. Brancati, Jr.
(203) 776-6172
Service Area: Statewide

Delaware

Wilmington Economic Development Corp.
605-A Market Street Mall
Wilmington, DE 19801
Contact: Edwin H. Nutter, Jr.
(302) 571-9088
Service Area: New Castle County and in the cities of Wilmington, Newark, New Castle, Middletown, Odessa and Townsend

District of Columbia

ARCH Development Corp.
1227 Good Hope Road, SE
Washington, DC 20020
Contact: Duane Gautier
(202) 889-5023
Service Area: Portions of the District of Columbia commonly referred to as Adams Morgan, Mount Pleasant and Anacostia, Congress Heights, Columbia Heights and 14th Street Corridor

H Street Development Corp.
611 H Street, NE
Washington, DC 20002
Contact: William J. Barrow
(202) 544-8353
Service Area: Portions of the District of Columbia including specific areas of the Northeast, Southeast and Northwest quadrants

Florida

Community Equity Investments Inc.
302 North Barcelona Street
Pensacola, FL 32501
Contact: Daniel R. Horvath
(904) 433-5619
Service Area: Western Panhandle including Bay, Calhoun, Escambia, Gadsden, Gulf, Jackson, Holmes, Liberty, Leon, Franklin, Wakulla, Walton, Washington, Okaloosa and Santa Rosa Counties

United Gainesville Community Development Corp., Inc.
214 West University Avenue, Suite D
P. O. Box 2518
Gainesville, FL 32602
Contact: Vian M. Cockerham
(904) 376-8891
Service Area: North Central section including Alachua, Bradford, Columbia, Dixie, Gichrist, Hamilton, Jefferson, LaFayette, Levy, Madison, Marion, Putman, Suwanee, Taylor and Union Counties

Georgia

Fulton County Development Corp.
d/b/a Greater Atlanta Small Business Project
10 Park Place South, Suite 305
Atlanta, GA 30303
Contact: Maurice S. Coakley
(404) 659-5955
Service Area: Fulton, Dekalb, Cobb, Gwinnett, Fayette, Clayton, Henry, Douglas and Rockdale Counties

Small Business Assistance Corp.
31 West Congress Street, Suite 100
Savannah, GA 31401
Contact: Tony O'Reily
(912) 232-4700
Service Area: Chatham, Effingham, Bryan, Bulloch and Liberty Counties

Hawaii

The Immigrant Center
720 North King Street
Honolulu, HI 96817
Contact: Patrician Brandt
(808) 845-3918
Service Area: Island of O'ahu within the City and County of Honolulu

Idaho

Panhandle Area Council
11100 Airport Drive
Hayden, ID 83835-9743
Contact: Jim Deffenbaugh
(208) 772-0584
Service Area: Northern Panhandle including Benewah, Bonner, Boundary, Kotenai and Shoshone Counties

Illinois

Greater Sterling Development Corp.
1741 Industrial Drive
Sterling, IL 61081
Contact: Reid Nolte
(815) 625-5255
Service Area: City of Sterling; Whiteside and Lee Counties

Illinois Development Finance Authority
2 North LaSalle Street, Suite 980
Chicago, IL 60602
Contact: Philip S. Howe
(312) 793-5586
Service Area: Statewide with the exceptions of Peoria, Tazwell, Woodford, Whiteside and Lee Counties, the City of Sterling and those portions of Chicago currently served by WSEP.

The Economic Development Council for the Peoria Area
124 SW Adams Street, Suite 300
Peoria, IL 61602
Contact: Michael Kuhns
(309) 676-7500
Service Area: Peoria, Tazwell and Woodford Counties

The Neighborhood Institute and Women's Self Employment Project
166 West Washington Street, Suite 730
Chicago, IL 60602
Contact: Connie Evans
(312) 606-8255
Service Area: Portions of the City of Chicago

Indiana

Eastside Community Investments Inc.
26 North Arsenal Avenue
Indianapolis, IN 46201
Contact: Dennis J. West
(317) 637-7300
Service Area: City of Indianapolis

Metro Small Business Assistance Corp.
1 NW Martin Luther King, Jr. Blvd.
Evansville, IN 47708-1869
Contact: Debra A. Lutz
(812) 426-5857
Service Area: Vanderburgh, Posey, Gibson and Warrick Counties

Iowa	**Siouxland Economic Development Corp.** 400 Orpheum Electric Building P. O. Box 447 Sioux City, IA 51102 Contact: Kenneth A. Beekley (714) 279-6286 **Service Area:** Cherokee, Ida, Monoma, Plymouth, Sioux and Woodbury Counties
Kansas	**South Central Kansas Economic Development District, Inc.** 151 North Volutsia Wichita, KS 67214 Contact: Jack E. Alumbaugh (316) 683-4422 **Service Area:** Butler, Chautaugua, Cowley, Elk, Greenwood, Harper, Harvey, Kingman, Marion, McPherson, Reno, Rice, Sedgwick and Sumner Counties
	Center for Business Innovations, Inc. 4747 Troost Avenue Kansas City, MO 64110 Contact: Robert J. Sherwood (816) 561-8567 **Service Area:** Wyandotte, Johnson, Kansas City and Leavenworth
Kentucky	**Kentucky Highlands Investment Corp.** 362 Old Whitley Road London, KY 40741 Contact: Jerry A. Rickett (606) 864-5175 **Service Area:** Bell Clay, Clinton, Harlan, Jackson, Knox, Laurel, McCreary, Pulaski, Rockcastle, Wayne and Whitley Counties
	Purchase Area Development District 1002 Medical Drive P. O. Box 588 Mayfield, KY 42066 Contact: Henry A. Hodges (502) 247-7171 **Service Area:** Western Kentucky including Ballard, Calloway, Carlisle, Futon, Graves, Hickman, McCracken and Marshall Counties
Louisana	**Greater Jennings Chamber of Commerce** 414 Cary Avenue P. O. Box 1209 Jennings, LA 70546 Contact: Jerry Arceneaux (318) 824-0933 **Service Area:** Jeff Davis Parish

Maine	**Coastal Enterprises, Inc.** Water Street P. O. Box 268 Wiscasset, ME 04578 Contact: Ronald L. Phillips (207) 882-7552 **Service Area:** Statewide excluding Aroostock, Piscataquis, Washington, Oxford, Penobscot and Hancock Counties

Northern Maine Regional Planning Commission
2 South Main Street
P. O. Box 779
Caribou, ME 04736
Contact: Robert P. Clark
(207) 498-8736
Service Area: Aroostock, Piscataquis, Washington, Penobscot and Hancock Counties

Community Concepts, Inc.
35 Market Square
P. O. Box 278
South Parris, ME 04281
Contact: Charleen M. Chase
(207) 743-7716
Service Area: Oxford County

Maryland

Council for Equal Business Opportunity, Inc.
The Park Plaza
800 North Charles Street, Suite 300
Baltimore, MD 21201
Contact: Michael Gaines
(410) 576-2326
Service Area: City of Baltimore and Ann Arundel, Baltimore, Carroll, Harford and Howard Counties

Massachusetts

Economic Development Industrial Corp. of Lynn
37 Central Square, 3rd Floor
Lynn, MA 01901
Contact: Peter M. DeVeau
(617) 592-2361
Service Area: City of Lynn

Jobs for Fall River, Inc.
One Government Center
Fall River, MA 02722
Contact: Paul L. Vigeant
(508) 324-2620
Service Area: City of Fall River

Springfield Business Development Fund
36 Court Street, Room 222
Springfield, MA 01103
Contact: James Asselin
(413) 787-6050
Service Area: City of Springfield

Western Massachusetts Enterprise Fund
324 Wells Street
Greenfield, MA 01301
Contact: Christopher Sikes
(413) 774-7204
Service Area: Bershire, Franklin Counties, the towns of Chester & Chicopes within Hampden County, the towns of Athol, Petersham, Phillipston & Royalston within Worcester County and the following towns within Hampshire County: Amherst, Chesterfield, Cummington, Easthampton, Goshen, Hadley, Huntington, Middlefield, Northhampton, Plainfield, Westhampton, Williamsburg and Worthington

Michigan

Ann Arbor Community Development Corp.
2008 Hogback Road, Suite 2A
Ann Arbor, MI 48105
Contact: Michelle Richards Vasquez
(313) 677-1400
Service Area: Washtenaw County

Detroit Economic Growth Corp.
150 West Jefferson, Suite 1500
Detroit, MI 48226
Contact: Robert W. Spencer
(313) 963-2940
Service Area: City of Detroit

Flint Community Development Corp.
877 East Fifth Avenue, Building C-1
Flint, MI 48503
Contact: Bobby J. Wells
(313) 239-5847
Service Area: Genesee County

Northern Economic Initiatives Corp.
1009 West Ridge Street
Marquette, MI 49855
Contact: Richard Anderson
(906) 228-5571
Service Area: Upper Peninsula including Alger, Baraga, Chippewa, Delta, Dickinson, Gogebic, Houghton, Iron, Keewenaw, Luce, Macinac, Marquette, Menonimee, Ontonagon and Schoolcraft Counties

Minnesota

Northeast Entrepreneur Fund, Inc.
Olcott Plaza, Suite 140
820 Ninth Street North
Virginia, MN 55792
Contact: Mary Mathews
(218) 749-4191
Service Area: Koochiching, Itasca, St. Louis, Aitkin, Carlton, Cook and Lake Counties

Women Venture
2324 University Avenue
St. Paul, MN 55114
Contact: Kay Gudmestad
(612) 646-3808
Service Area: Cities of Minneapolis and St. Paul and, Andra, Carver, Chisago, Dakota, Hennepin, Isanti, Ramsey, Scott, Washington and Wright Counties

Minneapolis Consortium of Community Developers
2600 East Franklin Avenue
Minneapolis, MN 55406
Contact: Karen Reid
(612) 338-8729
Service Area: Portions of the City of Minneapolis

Northwest Minnesota Initiative Fund
722 Paul Bunyan Drive, NW
Bemidji, MN 56601
Contact: Tim Wang
(218) 759-2057
Service Area: Beltrami, Clearwater, Hubbard, Kittsson, Lake of the Woods, Mahnomen, Marshall, Norman, Pennington, Polk, Red Lake and Rousseau Counties

Mississippi

Delta Foundation
819 Main Street
Greenville, MS 38701
Contact: Harry J. Bowie
(601) 335-5291
Service Area: Statewide excluding Issaquena, Sharkey, Humphreys, Madison, Leake, Kemper, Copiah, Hinds, Rankin, Newton, Smith, Jasper, Clarke, Jones, Wayne and Greene Counties

Friends of Children of Mississippi, Inc.
4880 McWillie Circle
Jackson, MS 39206
Contact: Marvin Hogan
(601) 362-1541
Service Area: Issaquena, Sharkey, Humphreys, Madison, Leake, Kemper, Copiah, Hinds, Rankin, Newton, Smith, Jasper, Clarke, Jones, Wayne and Greene Counties

Missouri

Center for Business Innovations, Inc.
4747 Troost Avenue
Kansas City, MO 64110
Contact: Robert J. Sherwood
(816) 561-8567
Service Area: Statewide

Montana

Capital Opportunities/District IX Human Resources Development Council, Inc.
321 East Main Street, Suite 300
Bozeman, MT 59715
Contact: Jeffery Rupp
(406) 587-4486
Service Area: Gallatin, Park and Meagher Counties

Women's Opportunity and Resource Development, Inc.
127 N. Higgins Avenue
Missoula, MT 59802
Contact: Kelly Rosenleaf
(406) 543-3550
Service Area: Lake, Mineral, Missoula, Ravalli and Sanders Counties

Nebraska

Rural Enterprise Assistance Project
P. O. Box 406
Walthill, NE 68067
Contact: Don Ralston
(402) 846-5428
Service Area: Boone, Brown, Burt, Cass, Cherry, Colfax, Custer, Dixon, Gage, Greeley, Jefferson, Johnson, Keya Paha, Knox, Lancaster, McPherson, Nance, Nemaha, Pierce, Rock, Saline, Sauders, Seward, Thurston and Wayne Counties

West Central Nebraska Development District, Inc.
710 North Spruce Street
P. O. Box 599
Ogailala, NE 69153
Contact: Ronald J. Radil
(308) 284-6077
Service Area: Arthur, Chase, Dawson, Dundy, Frontier, Furnas, Gosper, Grant, Hayes, Hitchcock, Hooker, Keith, Lincoln, Logan, Perkins, Red Willow and Thomas Counties

Nevada

Nevada Women's Fund
210 S. Sierra Street, Suite 100
Reno, NV 89501
Contact: Fritsi H. Ericson
(702) 786-2335
Service Area: Statewide

New Hampshire

Institute for Cooperative Community Development, Inc.
2500 North River Road
Manchester, NH 03106
Contact: Don Mason
(603) 644-3103
Service Area: Statewide excluding Grafton, Carol and Coos Counties

Northern Community Investment Corp.
c/o 20 Main Street
St. Johnsbury, VT 05819
Contact: Carl J. Garbelotti
(802) 748-5101
Service Area: Grafton, Carol and Coos Counties

New Jersey

Trenton Business Assistance Corp.
Division of Economic Development
319 East State Street
Trenton, NJ 08608-1866
Contact: James Harveson
(609) 989-3509
Service Area: Portions of the City of Trenton

Greater Newark Business Development Consortium
One Newark Center, 22nd Floor
Newark, NJ 07102-5265
Contact: Henry Hayman
(201) 242-6237
Service Area: Bergen, Essex, Hudson, Middlesex, Monmouth, Morris, Passaic
and Somerset Counties with the exception of the city of Jersey City

Union County Economic Development Corp.
Liberty Hall Corporate Center
1085 Morris Avenue, Suite 531
Union, NJ 07083
Contact: Maureen Tinen
(908) 527-1166
Service Area: Union County

Jersey City Economic Development Corp.
601 Pavonia Avenue
Jersey City, NJ 07306
Contact: Thomas D. Ahearn
(201) 420-7755
Service Area: City of Jersey City

New Mexico

Women's Economic Self Sufficiency Team
414 Silver South West
Albuquerque, NM 87102-3239
Contact: Agnes Noonan
(505) 848-4760
Service Area: Statewide

New York

Adirondack Economic Development Corp.
Trudeau Road
P. O. Box 747
Saranac Lake, NY 12983
Contact: Ernest Hohmeyer
(518) 891-5523
Service Area: Clinton, Essex, Franklin, Fulton, Hamilton, Herkimer, Jefferson, Lewis, Oneida, Oswego, St. Lawrence, Saratoga, Warren and Washington Counties

Hudson Development Corp.
444 Warren Street
Hudson, NY 12534
Contact: Lynda S. Davidson
(518) 828-3373
Service Area: Columbia County

Manhattan Borough Development Corp.
15 Park Row, Suite 510
New York, NY 10038
Contact: Patricia Swann
(212) 791-3660
Service Area: Borough of Manhattan

Rural Opportunities, Inc.
339 East Avenue
Rochester, NY 14604
Contact: W. Lee Beaulac
(716) 546-7180
Service Area: Allegheny, Cattaraugua, Cayuga, Chatauaga, Erie, Genessee, Livingston, Niagara, Ontario, Orleans, Senece, Steuben, Wayne, Wyoming and Yates Counties

North Carolina

Self-Help Ventures Fund
413 East Chapel Hill Street
Durham, NC 27701
Contact: Robert Schall
(919) 956-8526
Service Area: Statewide

North Dakota

Lake Agassiz Regional Council
417 Main Avenue
Fargo, ND 58103
Contact: Irvin D. Rustad
(701) 239-5373
Service Area: Statewide

Ohio

Enterprise Development Corp.
(formerly the Athens Small Business Center, Inc.)
900 East State Street
Athens, OH 45701
Contact: Karen A. Patton
(614) 592-1188
Service Area: Adams, Ashland, Athens, Belmont, Brown, Carrol, Columbiana, Coshocton, Gallia, Guernsey, Harrison, Highland, Holmes, Jackson, Jefferson, Knox, Lawrence, Meigs, Monroe, Morgan, Muskingum, Nocking, Noble, Perry, Pike, Ross, Scioto, Tuscarawas, Vinton and Washington Counties

Columbus Countywide Development Corp.
941 Chatham Lane, Suite 207
Columbus, OH 43221
Contact: Mark Barbash
(614) 645-6171
Service Area: Franklin County and the City of Columbus

Hamilton County Development Co., Inc.
1776 Mentor Avenue
Cincinnati, OH 45212
Contact: David K. Main
(513) 632-8292
Service Area: City of Cincinnati and Adams, Brown, Bugler, Clermont, Clinton, Highland and Warren Counties

Women's Entrepreneurial Growth Organization of NE Ohio
58 West Center Street, Suite 228
Akron, OH 44308
Contact: Barbara R. Honthumb
(216) 535-4523
Service Area: Ashtabula, Cuyahoga, Geauga, Lake, Lorain, Mahoning, Medina, Portage, Stark, Summit, Trumbull and Wayne Counties

Oklahoma

Rural Enterprises, Inc.
422 Cessna Street
Durant, OK 74701
Contact: Sherry Harlin
(405) 924-5094
Service Area: Statewide

Tulsa Economic Development Corp.
130 North Greenwood Avenue, Suite G
Tulsa, OK 74120
Contact: Frank F. McCrady III
(918) 585-8332
Service Area: Northeastern portion of state including Adair, Cherokee, Craig, Creek, Delaware, Hayes, Muskogee, Nowata, Okmulgee, Osage, Ottawa, Pawnee, Rogers, Sequoyah, Tulsa, Wagoner, Washington and Wayne Counties including the City of Tulsa

Oregon

Cascades West Financial Services, Inc.
408 SW Monroe Street
Corvallis, OR 97333
Contact: Deborah L. Wright
(503) 757-6854
Service Area: Benton, Clackamas, Hood River, Jefferson, Lane, Lincoln, Linn, Marion, Multnomah, Polk, Tillamook, Wasco, Washington and Yamhill Counties

Pennsylvania

The Ben Franklin Technology Center of Southeastern Pennsylvania
3624 Market Street
Philadelphia, PA 19104-2615
Contact: Phillip A. Singerman
(215) 382-0380
Service Area: Bucks, Chester, Delaware, Montgomery and Philadelphia Counties

The Washington County Council on Economic Development
703 Courthouse Square
Washington, PA 15301
Contact: Malcolm L. Morgan
(412) 228-6816
Service Area: Southwestern area of Pennsylvania including Greene, Fayette and Washington Counties, as well as Monogalia and Preston Counties of West Virginia

York County Industrial Development Corp.
One Market Way East
York, PA 17401
Contact: David B. Carver
(717) 846-8879
Service Area: York County

Puerto Rico

Corporation for the Economic Development of the City of San Juan
Avenue Munos Rivera, #1127
Rio Piedras, PR 00926
Contact: Jesus M. Rivera Viera
(809) 756-5080
Service Area: Specified communities within the City of San Juan

South Carolina

Charleston Citywide Local Development Corp.
496 King Street
Charleston, SC 29403
Contact: Sharon Brennan
(803) 724-3796
Service Area: City of Charleston

Santee Lynches Regional Development Corp.
115 North Harvin Street, 4th Floor
Sumter, SC 29151-1837
Contact: James T. Darby, Jr.
(803) 775-7381
Service Area: Clarendon, Kershaw, Lee and Sumter Counties

South Dakota

Northeast South Dakota Energy Conservation Corp.
414 Third Avenue, East
Sisseton, SD 57262
Contact: Arnold Petersen
(605) 698-7654
Service Area: Beadle, Brown, Buffalo, Campbell, Clark, Codington, Day, Edmunds, Faulk, Grant, Hand, Hyde, Jerauld, Kingsbury, McPherson, Marshall, Miner, Potter, Roberts, Sanborn, Spink and Walworth Counties

Tennessee

South Central Tennessee Development District
815 South Main Street
P. O. Box 1346
Columbia, TN 38402
Contact: Joe Max Williams
(615) 318-2040
Service Area: Bedford, Coffee, Franklin, Giles, Hickman, Lawrence, Lewis, Lincoln, Marshall, Maury, Moore, Perry and Wayne Counties

Texas

Business Resource Center Incubator
4601 N. 19th Street
Waco, TX 76708
Contact: Curtis Cleveland
(817) 754-8898
Service Area: Bell, Bosque, Coryell, Falls, Hill and McLennan Counties

San Antonio Local Development Corp.
100 Military Plaza, 4th Floor City Hall
San Antonio, TX 78205
Contact: Robert Nance
(210) 299-8080
Service Area: Atascosa, Bandera, Bexar, Comal, Frio, Gillespie, Guadalupe, Karnes, Kendall, Kerr, Medina and Wilson Counties

Southern Dallas Development Corp.
1201 Griffin Street West
Dallas, TX 75215
Contact: Jim Reid
(214) 428-7332
Service Area: Portions of the City of Dallas

Utah

Utah Technology Finance Corp.
185 South State Street, Suite 208
Salt Lake City, UT 84111
Contact: Todd Clark
(801) 364-4346
Service Area: Carbon, Emery, Grand, Iron, Juab, Milard, Salt Lake County,
San Juan, Sanpete, Sevier, Tooele, Washington and parts of Utah and Weber
Counties

Vermont

Economic Development Council of Northern Vermont, Inc.
155 Lake Street
St. Albans, VT 05478
Contact: Connie Stanley-Little
(802) 524-4546
Service Area: Franklin, Grand Isle and Lamoille Counties

Northern Community Investments Corp.
20 Main Street
St. Johnsbury, VT 05819
Contact: Carl J. Garbelotti
(802) 748-5101
Service Area: Caledonia, Essex and Orleans Counties

Virginia

Ethiopian Community Development Council, Inc.
1038 S. Highland Street
Arlington, VA 22204
Contact: Tsehaye Teferra
(703) 685-0510
Service Area: Prince William, Arlington and Fairfax Counties and the cities
of Alexandria and Falls Church

Lynchburg Regional Small Business Partnership, Inc.
147 Mill Ridge Road
Lynchburg, VA 24502
Contact: Karen Mauch
(804) 582-6100
Service Area: Amherst, Appomattox, Bedford, Campbell Counties, and cities
of Lynchburg, Bedford and the town of Amherst

People, Incorporated of Southwest Virginia
988 West Main Street
Abingdon, VA 24210
Contact: Robert G. Goldsmith
(703) 628-9188
Service Area: Buchanan, Dickerson, Lee, Russell, Scott, Washington and
Wise Counties, and the cities of Bristol and Norton

Washington

Snohomish County Private Industry Council
917 134th Street, SW, Suite A-10
Everett, WA 98204
Contact: Emily Duncan
(206) 743-9669
Service Area: Adams, Chelan, Douglas, Grant, King, Kittitas, Klickitat,
Okanogan, Pierce, Skagit, Snohomish, Whatcom and Yakima Counties

Tri-Cities Enterprise Association
2000 Logston Blvd.,
Richland, WA 99352
Contact: Dallas E. Breamer
(509) 375-3268
Service Area: Benton and Franklin Counties

West Virginia

Ohio Valley Industrial and Business Development Corp.
12th and Chapline Streets
Wheeling, WV 26003
Contact: Terry Burkhart
(304) 232-7722
Service Area: Marshall, Ohio and Wetzel Counties

Wisconsin

Advocap, Inc.
19 West First Street
P. O. Box 1108
Fond du Lac, WI 54936
Contact: Richard Schlimm
(414) 922-7760
Service Area: Fond du Lac and Winnebago Counties

Impact Seven, Inc.
100 Digital Drive
Clear Lake, WI 54005
Contact: William Bay
(715) 263-2532
Service Area: Statewide with the exceptions of Fond du Lac, Kenosha,
Milwaukee, Oasukee, Racine, Walworth, Waukesha, Washington and
Winnebago Counties, and the inner city of Milwaukee

Northwest Side Community Development Corp.
5174 North Hopkins Avenue
Milwaukee, WI 53209
Contact: Howard Snyder
(414) 462-5509
Service Area: Inner City of Milwaukee

Women's Business Initiative Corp.
3112 West Highland Blvd.,
Milwaukee, WI 53208
Contact: Becky Pileggi
(414) 933-3231
Service Area: Kenosha, Milwaukee, Oazukee, Racine, Walworth, Washington
and Waukesha Counties

Appendix H
SBA Small Business Development Centers (SBDCs)

REGION I

Charles Davis, State Director
Small Business Development Center
University of Southern Maine
96 Falmouth Street
Portland, ME 04103
(207) 780-4420
FAX: (207) 780-4810

John Ciccarelli, State Director
Small Business Development Center
University of Massachusetts
School of Management, Room 205
Amherst, MA 01003-4935
(413) 545-6301
FAX: (413) 545-1273

John P. O'Connor, State Director
Small Business Development Center
University of Connecticut
Box U-41, Room 422
368 Fairfield Road
Storrs, CT 06269-2041
(203) 486-4135
FAX: (203) 486-1576

Douglas Jobling, State Director
Small Business Development Center
Bryant College
1150 Douglas Pike
Smithfield, RI 02917
(401) 232-6111
FAX: (401) 232-6416

Donald L. Kelpinski, State Director
Small Business Development Center
Vermont Technical College
P. O. Box 422
Randolph Center, VT 05060
(802) 728-9101
FAX: (802) 728-3026

Helen Goodman, State Director
Small Business Development Center
University of New Hampshire
108 McConnell Hall
Durham, NH 03824
(603) 862-2200
FAX: (603) 862-4876

REGION II

Brenda B. Hopper, State Director
Small Business Development Center
Rutgers University
Ackerson Hall, Third Floor
180 University Street
Newark, NJ 07102
(201) 648-5950
FAX: (201) 648-1110

James L. King, State Director
Small Business Development Center
State University of New York
SUNY UPSTATE
SUNY Plaza, S-523
Albany, NY 12246
(518) 443-5398
FAX: (518) 465-4992

REGION II (continued)

James L. King, State Director
Small Business Development Center
State University of New York
SUNY DOWNSTATE
SUNY Plaza, S-523
Albany, NY 12246
(518) 443-5398
FAX: (518) 465-4992

Chester Williams, Director
Small Business Development Center
University of the Virgin Islands
8000 Nisky Center, Suite 202
Charlotte Amalie
St. Thomas, Virgin Islands 00802-5804
(809) 776-3206
FAX: (809) 775-3756

Jose Romaguera, Director
Small Business Development Center
University of Puerto Rico
Building B
Box 5253 - College Station
Mayaguez, PR 00681
(809) 834-3590
FAX: (809) 834-3790

REGION III

Gregory L. Higgins, State Director
Small Business Development Center
University of Pennsylvania
The Warton School
444 Vance Hall
Philadelphia, PA 19104
(215) 898-1219
FAX: (215) 573-2135

Levi Lipscomb, Acting Director
Small Business Development Center
Howard University
2600 6th Street, N. W., Room 128
Washington, DC 20059
(202) 806-1550
FAX: (202) 806-1777

Clinton Tymes, State Director
Small Business Development Center
University of Delaware
Purnell Hall, Suite 005
Newark, DE 19711
(302) 831-2747
FAX: (302) 831-1323

Hazel Kroesser, State Director
Small Business Development Center
Governor's Office of Community
and Industrial Development
1115 Virginia Street, East
Charleston, WV 25301
(304) 558-2960
FAX: (304) 558-0127

Woodrow McCutchen, State Director
Small Business Development Center
Department of Economic and
Employment Development
217 East Redwood Street, Ninth Floor
Baltimore, MD 21202
(410) 333-6995
FAX: (410) 333-4460

Dr. Robert Smith, State Director
Small Business Development Center
Dept. of Economic Development
1021 East Cary Street
Richmond, VA 23206
(804) 371-8258
FAX: (804) 371-8185

REGION IV

John Lenti, State Director
Small Business Development Center
University of South Carolina
College of Business Administration
1710 College Street
Columbia, SC 29208
(803) 777-4907
FAX: (803) 777-4403

Jerry Cartwright, State Director
Small Business Development Center
University of West Florida
19 West Garden Street, Third Floor
Pensacola, FL 32501
(904) 444-2060
FAX: (904) 444-2070

John Sandefur, State Director
Small Business Development Center
University of Alabama
1717 11th Avenue South, Suite 419
Birmingham, AL 35294
(205) 934-7260
FAX: (205) 934-7645

Hank Logan, State Director
Small Business Development Center
University of Georgia
Chicopee Complex
1180 East Broad Street
Athens, GA 30602
(706) 542-6762
FAX: (706) 542-6776

Janet Holloway, State Director
Small Business Development Center
University of Kentucky
College of Business and Economics
225 Business & Economics Building
Lexington, KY 40506-0034
(606) 257-7668
FAX: (606) 258-1907

Raleigh Byars, State Director
Small Business Development Center
University of Mississippi
Old Chemistry Bldg., Suite 216
University, MS 38677
(601) 232-5001
FAX: (601) 232-5650

Dr. Kenneth J. Burns, State Director
Small Business Development Center
University of Memphis
South Campus
Getwell Road, Bldg. #1
Memphis, TN 38152
(901) 678-2500
FAX: (901) 678-4072

Scott Daugherty, State Director
Small Business Development Center
University of North Carolina
4509 Creedmoor Road, Suite 201
Raleigh, NC 27612
(919) 571-4154
FAX: (919) 571-4161

REGION V

William H. Pinkovitz, State Director
Small Business Development Center
University of Wisconsin
432 North Lake Street, Room 423
Madison, WI 53706
(608) 263-7794
FAX: (608) 262-3878

Mary J. Krueger, State Director
Small Business Development Center
Dept. of Trade And Economic Dev.
500 Metro Square
121 Seventh Place East
St. Paul, MN 55101-2146
(612) 297-5770
FAX: (612) 296-1290

REGION V(continued)

Robert Stevens, Acting State Director
Small Business Development Center
Wayne State University
2727 Second Avenue
Detroit, MI 48201
(313) 964-1798
FAX: (313) 964-3648

Jeffrey J. Mitchell, State Director
Small Business Development Center
Dept. of Commerce and
Community Affairs
620 East Adams Street
Springfield, IL 62701
(217) 524-5856
FAX: (217) 785-6328

Steve Thrash, State Director
Small Business Development Center
Economic Development Council
One North Capitol, Suite 420
Indianapolis, IN 46204
(317) 264-6871
FAX: (317) 264-3102

Holly Schick, State Director
Small Business Development Center
Department of Development
77 South High Street
Columbus, OH 43226-1001
(614) 466-2711
FAX: (614) 466-0829

REGION VI

Janet Nye, State Director
Small Business Development Center
University of Arkansas
Little Rock Technology Center Bldg.,
100 South Main, Suite 401
Little Rock, AR 72201
(501) 324-9043
FAX: (501) 324-9049

Dr. John Baker, State Director
Small Business Development Center
Northeast Louisiana University
College of Business Administration
700 University Avenue
Monroe, LA 71209
(318) 342-5506
FAX: (318) 342-5510

Dr. Grady Pennington, State Director
Small Business Development Center
SE Oklahoma State University
517 West University
Station A, Box 2584
Durant, OK 74701
(405) 924-0277
FAX: (405) 920-7471

Dr. Elizabeth Gatewood, Region Dir.
Small Business Development Center
University of Houston
1100 Louisiana, Suite 500
Houston, TX 77002
(713) 752-8444
FAX: (713) 756-1500

Robert M. McKinley, Region Dir.
South Texas Border
Small Business Development Center
University of Texas at San Antonio
Cypress Tower, Suite 410
1222 North Main Street
San Antonio, TX 78212
(210) 558-2450
FAX: (210) 558-2464

Craig Bean, Region Dir., NW Texas
Small Business Development Center
Texas Tech University
2579 South Loop 289, Suite 114
Lubbock, TX 79423-1637
(806) 745-3973
FAX: (806) 745-6207

REGION VI (continued)

Liz Kimback, Region Director
North Texas
Small Business Development Center
Dallas County Community College
1402 Corinth Street
Dallas, TX 75215
(214) 565-5833
FAX: (214) 565-5815

Lily Tercero, Acting State Director
Small Business Development Center
Santa Fe Community College
P. O. Box 4187
Santa Fe, NM 87502-4187
(505) 438-1362
FAX: (505) 438-1237

REGION VII

Robert Bernier, State Director
Small Business Development Center
University of Nebraska at Omaha
60th & Dodge Streets, CBA Room 407
Omaha, NE 68182
(402) 554-2521
FAX: (402) 554-3747

Ronald Manning, State Director
Small Business Development Center
Iowa State University
137 Lynn Avenue
Ames, IA 50010
(515) 292-6351
FAX: (515) 292-0020

Max Summers, State Director
Small Business Development Center
University of Missouri
University Place, Suite 300
Columbia, MO 65211
(314) 882-0344
FAX: (314) 884-4297

Tom Hull, State Director
Small Business Development Center
Wichita State University
1845 Fairmount
Wichita, KS 67260-0148
(316) 689-3193
FAX: (316) 689-3647

REGION VIII

David Nimkin, State Director
Small Business Development Center
University of Utah
102 West 500 South
Salt Lake City, UT 84101
(801) 581-7905
FAX: (801) 581-7814

Robert Ashely, State Director
Small Business Development Center
University of South Dakota
School of Business
414 East Clark
Vermillion, SD 57069
(605) 677-5498
FAX: (605) 677-5272

Wally Kearns, State Director
Small Business Development Center
University of North Dakota
Gamble Hall, University Station
Grand Forks, ND 58202-7308
(701) 777-3700
FAX: (701) 777-3225

Gene Marcille, State Director
Small Business Development Center
Department of Commerce
1424 Ninth Avenue
Helena, MT 59620
(406) 444-4780
FAX: (406) 444-2808

REGION VIII (continued)

Rick Garcia, State Director
Small Business Development Center
Office of Business Development
1625 Broadway, Suite 1710
Denver, CO 80202
(303) 892-3809
FAX: (303) 892-3848

David Mosley, State Director
Small Business Development Center
University of Wyoming
College of Business
Laramie, WY 82071-3275
(307) 766-3505
FAX: (None)

REGION IX

Samuel Males, State Director
Small Business Development Center
University of Nevada in Reno
College of Business Admin., Room 411
Reno, NV 89557-0100
(702) 784-1717
FAX: (702) 784-4337

Michael York, State Director
Small Business Development Center
Maricopa County Community College
2411 West 14th Street
Tempe, AZ 85281-6941
(602) 731-8720
FAX: (602) 731-8729

Darryl Mleynek, Acting State Director
Small Business Development Center
University of Hawaii at Hilo
200 West Kawili Street
Hilo, HI 96720-4091
(808) 933-3515
FAX: (808) 933-3683

Maria Morris, State Director
Small Business Development Center
Calif. Trade and Commerce Agency
801 K Street, Suite 1700
Sacramento, CA 95814
(916) 324-5068
FAX: (916) 322-5084

REGION X

Lyle M. Anderson, State Director
Small Business Development Center
Washington State University
College of Business & Economics
245 Todd Hall
Pullman, WA 99264-4727
(509) 335-1576
FAX: (509) 335-0949

Mr. Sandy Cutler, State Director
Small Business Development Center
Lane Community College
44 West Broadway, Suite 501
Eugene, OR 97401-3021
(503) 726-2250
FAX: (503) 345-6006

Ronald R. Hall, State Director
Small Business Development Center
Boise State University
1910 University Drive
Boise, ID 83725
(208) 385-1640
FAX: (208) 385-3877

Jan Fredericks, State Director
Small Business Development Center
University of Alaska at Anchorage
430 West 7th Avenue, Suite 110
Anchorage, AK 99501
(907) 274-7232
FAX: (907) 274-9524

Appendix I
Commonly Used Financial Terminology

Amortize: To put money aside for gradual payment of a debt at or before maturity.

Applicant: A person, group or firm applying for a loan or investment.

Appraisal: A professional estimate as to the value of certain assets.

Balance Sheet: A financial statement summarizing the assets, liabilities and net worth of a firm or individual on a given date.

Bottom Line: The actual profit of a firm after all operating expenses have been deducted from sales or revenues.

Capital: Wealth in any form that can be used to produce more wealth.

Capital Asset: Any asset, tangible or intangible, that is held for a long-term investment.

Capital Gain: A profit realized from the sale of an investment. Selling price less cost equals a capital gain.

Cash Flow: A monthly forecast of expected cash receipts less the known expenditures of a firm. Cash flow demonstrates the availability or non-availability of cash for each month into the future. Forecasts are generally made for 12-month periods and revised frequently.

Cheap Stock Formula: A formula established by each state's securities code to determine the percentage of ownership that can be retained by the founders and promoters of a company should they elect to raise additional funds through a public offering. Generally, this formula is based on the current value of the shares outstanding verses the number of shares to be sold and the amount of money to be raised. It also takes into consideration the intangible contribution the founders and promoters have made to establish or develop the company.

Client: A person or firm receiving goods or services.

Commercial Loan: Loans made to commercial businesses, firms or enterprises engaged in selling goods or services.

Co-signer: A person willing to assume liability for a loan if the borrower should default.

Debenture: An interest-bearing bond issued by a corporation or other entity to raise funds, often with no specific pledge of assets.

Dividend: Generally, a portion of the after-tax profits of a corporation which is distributed to its shareholders at certain intervals.

Equity: The cash value of a property or business after all debts and other liabilities have been deducted.

Equity Capital: Funds contributed by investors and/or founders of a firm.

Factors: Institutional lenders and finance companies that loan money to firms who pledge or sell their accounts receivable to them as collateral.

Financial Statement: A statement showing all assets and liabilities on a given date with the difference being the net worth of a person or firm.

First Mortgage: The first or senior mortgage where property is pledged as loan collateral.

Foreclosure: The forced sale of property or a business to satisfy the defaulted payment of a mortgage or other loan.

Forecast: In business terms, a projection of sales, inventory costs, production, overhead, cash flow and debt servicing expenses for a given period of time.

Industrial Loans: Loans made to industries such as manufacturing or mining.

Institutional Loans: Loans made to hospitals, schools, etc.

Liabilities: Debts or other obligations of a person or firm which must be paid at some future date.

Loan Closing: The final meeting to sign a loan agreement and the disbursement of the proceeds to the borrower.

Loan/Investment Commitment: A written promise or pledge from a lender or investor to provide funds to a borrower, person or firm on a specified date based on certain conditions.

Loan Package: Complete information requested by a lender to make a lending decision.

Mortgagee: The firm or person holding the mortgage as security for a loan.

Mortgagor: A person or company who pledges the mortgage as collateral to secure a loan.

Net Profit: The difference after subtracting expenses from sales or revenues — before or after taxes have been applied.

O-P-M: Commonly referred to as "Other Peoples' Money".

P & L Statement: A "profit and loss statement" showing the income and expenses for a specific period of time with the difference being a profit or loss.

Payables: Referred to as "accounts payable". Money that is owed by a firm for goods and services received.

Points: The percentage of interest is frequently called "points" instead of "percent".

Private Offering: The sale of a company's stock to private individuals or firms to raise funds.

Proforma Statements: Generally, a group of financial statements predicting or forecasting the performance of a business such as sales, expenses, cash flow, etc., for a specific period of time.

Public Offering: The sale of a company's stock to the general public to raise funds.

Receivables: Referred to as "accounts receivable". Invoices, notes or bills due from others by a certain date for goods and services rendered.

Refinance: The act of paying off one loan with the proceeds of another.

Second Mortgage: The second or junior mortgage. Used to secure a portion of the equity buildup in a mortgaged property.

Securities: Could be the stock in a company, interest in a partnership, bonds, debentures, certificates of deposit, etc.

Specs: Specifications required for loans to finance certain projects such as blueprints and a description of materials, labor and other associated costs.

Trade Credit: Buying raw materials, merchandise, equipment or services on credit extended by a supplier.

Index

THE OASIS PRESS® ORDER FORM

Call, Mail, or Fax Your Order to: PSI Research, 300 North Valley Drive, Grants Pass, OR 97526 USA

Order Phone USA & Canada: **+1 800 228-2275**   Inquiries & International Orders: **+1 541 479-9464** Fax: **+1 541 476-1479**

TITLE	✔ BINDER	✔ PAPERBACK	QUANTITY	COST
Bottom Line Basics	☐ $39.95	☐ $19.95		
The Business Environmental Handbook	☐ $39.95	☐ $19.95		
Business Owner's Guide to Accounting & Bookkeeping		☐ $19.95		
Buyer's Guide to Business Insurance	☐ $39.95	☐ $19.95		
Collection Techniques for a Small Business	☐ $39.95	☐ $19.95		
A Company Policy and Personnel Workbook	☐ $49.95	☐ $29.95		
Company Relocation Handbook	☐ $39.95	☐ $19.95		
CompControl: The Secrets of Reducing Worker's Compensation Costs	☐ $39.95	☐ $19.95		
Complete Book of Business Forms	☐ $39.95	☐ $19.95		
Customer Engineering: Cutting Edge Selling Strategies	☐ $39.95	☐ $19.95		
Develop & Market Your Creative Ideas		☐ $15.95		
Doing Business in Russia		☐ $19.95		
Draw The Line: A Sexual Harassment Free Workplace		☐ $17.95		
The Essential Corporation Handbook		☐ $19.95		
The Essential Limited Liability Company Handbook	☐ $39.95	☐ $19.95		
Export Now: A Guide for Small Business	☐ $39.95	☐ $19.95		
Financial Management Techniques for Small Business	☐ $39.95	☐ $19.95		
Financing Your Small Business		☐ $19.95		
Franchise Bible: How to Buy a Franchise or Franchise Your Own Business	☐ $39.95	☐ $19.95		
Friendship Marketing *Availble in Spring 1997!*		☐ $18.95		
Home Business Made Easy		☐ $19.95		
Incorporating Without A Lawyer *(Available for 32 states)* SPECIFY STATE:		☐ $24.95		
Joysticks, Blinking Lights and Thrills *Availble in Spring 1997!*		☐ $18.95		
The Insider's Guide to Small Business Loans	☐ $29.95	☐ $19.95		
InstaCorp – Incorporate In Any State (Book & Software) *New for 1997!*		☐ $29.95		
Keeping Score: An Insider Look at Sports Marketing		☐ $18.95		
Know Your Market: How to Do Low-Cost Market Research	☐ $39.95	☐ $19.95		
Legal Expense Defense: How to Control Your Business' Legal Costs and Problems	☐ $39.95	☐ $19.95		
Location, Location, Location: How To Select The Best Site For Your Business		☐ $19.95		
Mail Order Legal Guide	☐ $45.00	☐ $29.95		
Managing People: A Practical Guide	☐ $39.95	☐ $19.95		
Marketing Mastery: Your Seven Step Guide to Success	☐ $39.95	☐ $19.95		
The Money Connection: Where and How to Apply for Business Loans and Venture Capital	☐ $39.95	☐ $19.95		
People Investment	☐ $39.95	☐ $19.95		
Power Marketing for Small Business	☐ $39.95	☐ $19.95		
Profit Power: 101 Pointers ro Give Your Small Business A Competitive Edge	☐ $39.95	☐ $19.95		
Proposal Development: How to Respond and Win the Bid	☐ $39.95	☐ $19.95		
Raising Capital	☐ $39.95	☐ $19.95		
Retail in Detail: How to Start and Manage a Small Retail Business		☐ $14.95		
Secrets to Buying and Selling a Business *New for 1997!*		☐ $19.95		
Secure Your Future: Financial Planning at Any Age	☐ $39.95	☐ $19.95		
The Small Business Insider's Guide to Bankers *Availble in Spring 1997!*		☐ $18.95		
Start Your Business *(Available as a book and disk package – see back)*		☐ $ 9.95 (without disk)		
Starting and Operating a Business in... book INCLUDES FEDERAL section PLUS ONE STATE section	☐ $29.95	☐ $24.95		
PLEASE SPECIFY WHICH STATE(S) YOU WANT:				
STATE SECTION ONLY (BINDER NOT INCLUDED) SPECIFY STATE(S):	☐ $8.95			
FEDERAL SECTION ONLY (BINDER NOT INCLUDED)	☐ $12.95			
U.S. EDITION (FEDERAL SECTION – 50 STATES AND WASHINGTON DC IN 11-BINDER SET)	☐ $295.95			
Successful Business Plan: Secrets & Strategies	☐ $49.95	☐ $24.95		
Successful Network Marketing for The 21st Century		☐ $14.95		
Surviving and Prospering in a Business Partnership	☐ $39.95	☐ $19.95		
TargetSmart! Database Marketing for the Small Business		☐ $19.95		
Top Tax Saving Ideas for Today's Small Business		☐ $15.95		
Which Business? Help in Selecting Your New Venture		☐ $18.95		
Write Your Own Business Contracts	☐ $39.95	☐ $19.95		

BOOK SUB-TOTAL (FIGURE YOUR TOTAL AMOUNT ON THE OTHER SIDE)

OASIS SOFTWARE   Please check Macintosh or 3-1/2" Disk for IBM-PC & Compatibles

TITLE	3-1/2" IBM Disk	Mac-OS	Price	QUANTITY	COST
California Corporation Formation Package ASCII Software	☐	☐	$ 39.95		
Company Policy & Personnel Software Text Files	☐	☐	$ 49.95		
Financial Management Techniques (Full Standalone)	☐		$ 99.95		
Financial Templates	☐	☐	$ 69.95		
The Insurance Assistant Software (Full Standalone)	☐		$ 29.95		
Start A Business (Full Standalone)	☐		$ 49.95		
Start Your Business (Software for Windows™)	☐		$ 19.95		
Successful Business Plan (Software for Windows™)	☐		$ 99.95		
Successful Business Plan Templates	☐	☐	$ 69.95		
The Survey Genie - Customer Edition (Full Standalone)	☐		$149.95		
The Survey Genie - Employee Edition (Full Standalone)	☐		$149.95		

SOFTWARE SUB-TOTAL

BOOK & DISK PACKAGES   Please check whether you use Macintosh or 3-1/2" Disk for IBM-PC & Compatibles

TITLE	IBM-PC	Mac-OS	BINDER	PAPERBACK	QUANTITY	COST
The Buyer's Guide to Business Insurance w/ Insurance Assistant	☐		☐ $ 59.95	☐ $ 39.95		
California Corporation Formation Binder Book & ASCII Software	☐	☐	☐ $ 69.95	☐ $ 59.95		
Company Policy & Personnel Book & Software Text Files	☐	☐	☐ $ 89.95	☐ $ 69.95		
Financial Management Techniques Book & Software	☐		☐ $129.95	☐ $ 119.95		
Start Your Business Paperback & Software (Software for Windows™)	☐			☐ $ 24.95		
Successful Business Plan Book & Software for Windows™	☐		☐ $125.95	☐ $109.95		
Successful Business Plan Book & Software Templates	☐	☐	☐ $109.95	☐ $ 89.95		

BOOK & DISK PACKAGE TOTAL

AUDIO CASSETTES

TITLE	Price	QUANTITY	COST
Power Marketing Tools For Small Business	☐ $ 49.95		
The Secrets To Buying & Selling A Business	☐ $ 49.95		

AUDIO CASSETTE SUB-TOTAL

OASIS SUCCESS KITS   Call for more information about these products

TITLE	Price	QUANTITY	COST
Start-Up Success Kit	☐ $ 39.95		
Business At Home Success Kit	☐ $ 39.95		
Financial Management Success Kit	☐ $ 44.95		
Personnel Success Kit	☐ $ 44.95		
Marketing Success Kit	☐ $ 44.95		

OASIS SUCCESS KITS TOTAL

COMBINED SUB-TOTAL (FROM THIS SIDE)

SOLD TO: *Please give street address*

NAME:

Title:

Company:

Street Address:

City/State/Zip:

Daytime Phone: Email:

SHIP TO: *If different than above give street address*

NAME:

Title:

Company:

Street Address:

City/State/Zip:

Daytime Phone:

YOUR GRAND TOTAL

SUB-TOTALS (from other side) $

SUB-TOTALS (from this side) $

SHIPPING (see chart below) $

TOTAL ORDER $

If your purchase is:	Shipping costs within the USA:
$0 - $25	$5.00
$25.01 - $50	$6.00
$50.01 - $100	$7.00
$100.01 - $175	$9.00
$175.01 - $250	$13.00
$250.01 - $500	$18.00
$500.01+	4% of total merchandise

PAYMENT INFORMATION: *Rush service is available, call for details.*
International and Canadian Orders: Please call for quote on shipping.

☐ CHECK Enclosed payable to PSI Research   Charge: ☐ VISA   ☐ MASTERCARD   ☐ AMEX   ☐ DISCOVER

Card Number: Expires:

Signature: Name On Card:

catalog winter 97

Call toll free to order 1-800-228-2275 PSI Research 300 North Valley Drive, Grants Pass, OR 97526 FAX 541-476-1479

Use this form to register for advance notification of updates, new books and software releases, plus special customer discounts!

Please answer these questions to let us know how our products are working for you, and what we could do to serve you better.

Title of book or software purchased from us:_____

It is a:
- ☐ Binder book
- ☐ Paperback book
- ☐ Book/software combination
- ☐ Software only

Rate this product's overall quality of information:
- ☐ Excellent
- ☐ Good
- ☐ Fair
- ☐ Poor

Rate the quality of printed materials:
- ☐ Excellent
- ☐ Good
- ☐ Fair
- ☐ Poor

Rate the format:
- ☐ Excellent
- ☐ Good
- ☐ Fair
- ☐ Poor

Did the product provide what you needed?
- ☐ Yes ☐ No

If not, what should be added?_____
_____
_____
_____
_____

This product is:
- ☐ Clear and easy to follow
- ☐ Too complicated
- ☐ Too elementary

Were the worksheets (if any) easy to use?
- ☐ Yes ☐ No ☐ N/A

Should we include:
- ☐ More worksheets
- ☐ Fewer worksheets
- ☐ No worksheets

How do you feel about the price?
- ☐ Lower than expected
- ☐ About right
- ☐ Too expensive

How many employees are in your company?
- ☐ Under 10 employees
- ☐ 10 – 50 employees
- ☐ 51 – 99 employees
- ☐ 100 – 250 employees
- ☐ Over 250 employees

How many people in the city your company is in?
- ☐ 50,000 – 100,000
- ☐ 100,000 – 500,000
- ☐ 500,000 – 1,000,000
- ☐ Over 1,000,000
- ☐ Rural (under 50,000)

What is your type of business?
- ☐ Retail
- ☐ Service
- ☐ Government
- ☐ Manufacturing
- ☐ Distributor
- ☐ Education

What types of products or services do you sell?
_____
_____
_____
_____

What is your position in the company?
(please check one)
- ☐ Owner
- ☐ Administration
- ☐ Sales/marketing
- ☐ Finance
- ☐ Human resources
- ☐ Production
- ☐ Operations
- ☐ Computer/MIS

How did you learn about this product?
- ☐ Recommended by a friend
- ☐ Used in a seminar or class
- ☐ Have used other PSI products
- ☐ Received a mailing
- ☐ Saw in bookstore
- ☐ Saw in library
- ☐ Saw review in:
  - ☐ Newspaper
  - ☐ Magazine
  - ☐ TV/Radio

Where did you buy this product?
- ☐ Catalog
- ☐ Bookstore
- ☐ Office supply
- ☐ Consultant
- ☐ Other_____

Would you purchase other business tools from us?
- ☐ Yes ☐ No

If so, which products interest you?
- ☐ EXECARDS® Communication Tools
- ☐ Books for business
- ☐ Software

Would you recommend this product to a friend?
- ☐ Yes ☐ No

If you'd like us to send associates or friends a catalog, just list names and addresses on back.

Do you use a personal computer for business?
- ☐ Yes ☐ No

If yes, which?
- ☐ IBM/compatible
- ☐ Macintosh

Check all the ways you use computers:
- ☐ Word processing
- ☐ Accounting
- ☐ Spreadsheet
- ☐ Inventory
- ☐ Order processing
- ☐ Design/graphics
- ☐ General data base
- ☐ Customer information
- ☐ Scheduling

May we call you to follow up on your comments?
- ☐ Yes ☐ No

May we add your name to our mailing list?
- ☐ Yes ☐ No

If there is anything you think we should do to improve this product, please describe:_____
_____
_____
_____

Thank you for your patience in answering the above questions. Just fill in your name and address here, fold (see back) and mail.

Name_____
Title_____
Company_____
Phone_____
Address_____
City/State/Zip_____

If you have friends or associates who might appreciate receiving our catalogs, please list here. Thanks!

Name_____   Name_____

Title_____   Title_____

Company_____   Company_____

Phone_____   Phone_____

Address_____   Address_____

City/State/Zip_____   City/State/Zip_____

FOLD HERE FIRST

||||

NO POSTAGE
NECESSARY
IF MAILED
IN THE
UNITED STATES

BUSINESS REPLY MAIL
FIRST CLASS MAIL PERMIT NO. 002 MERLIN, OREGON

POSTAGE WILL BE PAID BY ADDRESSEE

PSI Research
PO BOX 1414
Merlin OR 97532-9900

IIıIıIııIıIıIııIIııIıIIIıIıIıIııIIııIIııIIıI

FOLD HERE SECOND, THEN TAPE TOGETHER

✁
**Please cut
along this
vertical line,
fold twice,
tape together
and mail.
Thanks!**